Brisbane:
Relaxation, Recreation and Rock'n'Roll
Popular Culture 1890-1990

Edited by Barry Shaw

Brisbane History Group
Papers No.17
2001

First published by Brisbane History Group (Incorporated)

National Library of Australia
Cataloguing-in-Publication data

Brisbane: relaxation, recreation and rock'n'roll:
popular culture 1890-1990

Bibliography
Includes index

ISBN 0 9586255 2 2 ISSN 1035-1040

1. Recreation - Queensland - Brisbane. 2. Leisure - Queensland - Brisbane. 3. Brisbane (Qld) - History. 4. Popular culture - Queensland - Brisbane. I. Shaw, Barry, 1947-. II. Brisbane History Group.

306.09943

Edited by Barry Shaw

Designed and produced by Church Archivists Press, Brisbane

Printed by Toowoomba Education Centre

Published by Brisbane History Group
PO Box 12, Kelvin Grove DC
Qld 4059 Australia

Contents

Pubs, publicans and the law: 'A square meal sixpence. A perfect gorge one and sixpence'.

Illustrations

Contributors

Pam Barnett, a graduate in fine arts from UQ, is archivist at Brisbane Grammar School.

Raymond Evans, a reader in history at UQ, has written extensively on society, race relations and social conflict in Queensland.

Jennifer Harrison, a past president of BHG, is Queensland researcher for the *Australian dictionary of biography.*

Ian Jobling, a senior lecturer in human movement studies at UQ, has written about sport in Queensland.

Patricia Joynes, a volunteer at John Oxley Library, is interested in family history.

John Kerr, a professional historian, has written about the mining and sugar industries and railways in Queensland

David Larkin, a family historian and research consultant, publishes widely on the Irish in Queensland.

Maureen Lillie, former listings officer for NTQ, is researching Queensland governors, and works at the Environment Protection Agency.

Robert Longhurst, a former librarian at John Oxley Library, is a history consultant and has published on the history of the Gold Coast.

Margaret Maynard, a lecturer in art history at UQ, has written widely on nineteenth century dress.

Shirley McCorkindale, a former librarian at State Library and longstanding member of BHG., is currently studying theology

Tim Moroney, a librarian in the Queensland Parliamentary Library, is a graduate from UQ.

Judy Rechner, a masters graduate from UQ, is a professional historical researcher, specialising in Queensland house styles.

Barry Shaw, publications coordinator of the BHG, is an honorary research adviser at UQ.

Sue Ward, a doctoral graduate from Griffith University, is currently on the editorial committee of the magazine *QPIX.*

Preface

There are two major problems in producing thematic volumes. First, there is the inevitable delay in obtaining sufficient papers to form a volume. Secondly, as in this case, recent functions produced a surfeit of papers. As this volume began to assume gargantuan proportions, it was decided to place a section on parks and the University of Queensland in a forthcoming publication. The result is a somewhat slimmer but still highly entertaining and informative collection of papers.

In April 1993 the Brisbane History Group embarked on a series of seminars examining popular culture from the 1890s to the present. The first in the series, entitled 'Brisbane at leisure in the 1890s', comprised a number of short, often humorous, vignettes together with several lengthier papers. There are glimpses into the active recreational pursuits on offer: cycling, cricket, enjoying the bathing facilities in the Brisbane River and patronising the seaside resorts of Sandgate and Southport. The problems and benefits of 1890s train travel to such destinations are also considered. More passive activities included sampling the literature of the period and the growing interest in art. The section concludes with an examination of the type and style of leisurewear on offer to Brisbanites in the 1890s.

A subsequent seminar in October 1993 on popular culture in the 1940s and 1950s was appropriately entitled 'As time goes by', replete with a screening of *Casablanca*. The scene was set with a glimpse into outdoor entertainment, especially open-air cinema in Brisbane at the beginning of the twentieth century. The impact of radio and television, particularly during the 1950s, was carefully considered with special reference to programming, advertising and censorship. Of course Brisbane's most popular programs and presenters earned a mention, which brought memories flooding back. The teeny-boppers among the audience were then treated to a paper about the arrival of rock'n'roll in Brisbane. Even conservative members were jolted to attention when they heard the memorable question asked of disc jockey, Bob Rogers: 'Is you is or is you ain't a square?' Echoing the crowds who saw kiss-curled Bill Haley and his Comets perform at the Brisbane Stadium, the BHG audience was also suitably restrained, if not by the presence of police!

The BHG 'Bush Christmas', held at the rural setting of Pullenvale Hall in November 1993, included bush ballads and a paper about visitors to Brisbane. Beginning with the often perceptive observations of novelist Anthony Trollope and concluding with the caustic comments of that irascible conductor of the London Philarmonic, Thomas Beecham, the paper provided a more or less chronological overview of those who entertained us before the Second World War.

The idea for the third section of this volume arose after a successful BHG pub tour. A subsequent seminar day entitled, 'Time gentlemen please', was held at the Irish Club in August 1997. Various aspects of the hotel industry were explored including the changing role of hotels, legislation, and the Irish founders of Queensland's brewing and cordial manufacturing industries.

Several of the seminars, as befitted the subject matter, incorporated slide displays, posters, early film of Brisbane and, on one memorable occasion, live operatic interludes. Our day at the Irish Club allowed participants the opportunity to sample Irish fare, beverages and live music.

The production of this volume involved many people who unstintingly gave of their time. Shirley McCorkindale proofread the volume several times, Rod Fisher read and commented on the volume overall and Barry Shaw edited and indexed the text. Leo Ansell of Church Archivists Press expedited production. The illustrations in this volume have come from several sources, the authors, the John Oxley Library, Queensland Newspapers, the Applied History Centre at UQ and the Royal Historical Society of Queensland.

As ever, the Brisbane History Group is indebted to the authors and others who have contributed in some way to this book. The papers contained in this volume are, to say the least, wide-ranging. They cover a multiplicity of subjects from the early days of cycling to open-air cinema, from radio to rock'n'roll. Within these pages there is surely something to attract and entertain every reader who has an interest in Brisbane's past.

Brisbane at leisure in the 1890s

'Mixed bathing ... not allowed here'

Chapter 1

The Brisbane River: A source of recreation 1890-1900

Patricia Joynes

'It is the river for which Brisbane most is memorable'. These words were written by Geoffrey Tebbutt, an Australian, working at the *Courier-mail* from 1936-38. On leaving Brisbane to describe the Australian XI tour of England, he wrote a farewell to good-natured Brisbane. This was published in the *Courier-mail* on 12 February 1938. Some of his impressions of the Brisbane River were:

> early mornings when the river is very blue ... the thrash of propellers as the ships nose up to their berths ... about the waterfront there is an aura of adventure ... the siren of a freighter rounding Kangaroo Point at midnight blasts echoes from the cliffs. Its noblest view ... is through the masts of Circular Quay across the bend of the river to the yellow glare of that cliff pile, especially when the grey, gracefully-ageing Canberra is berthed at its foot.

These images and even the very plop of ripened mangoes falling to the grass in the quiet night of early-to-bed Brisbane have left their mark on the sound track of recollection.[1]

The Brisbane River in the 1890s

This paper focuses on the locations and the official openings of facilities where weekend activities for leisure were held during 1890-1900.

Floods in Brisbane in 1890, 1893, 1896 and 1898 curtailed activities planned to be held on the Brisbane River. The floods, especially that of 1893, caused severe destruction, loss of life, personal loss of homes and income, and generally resulted in extreme hardship for the population of the city.

To their credit the citizens of Brisbane looked ahead to the future. Plans for the city included some facilities which contributed to enjoyment of the river.

People who used the river for leisure mainly enjoyed swimming, fishing, aquatic events, sailing, rowing and boat-trips. Their destinations on these occasions were the popular picnic spots at Queensport Aquarium and Zoological Gardens, and the sandy beaches along the banks of the Brisbane River.

Public swimming baths

Early swimming baths on land or in the river were introduced, not for pleasure but more for health reasons, due to the lack of bathrooms in houses. Swimming in the Brisbane River was made safer by some form of swimming enclosure, for example, floating baths.

1.0 Metropolitan Baths, Petrie Bight, 1867-68 (JOL)

The first floating baths for public use in Brisbane were ready for patrons by the 18 April 1857.[2] By the early 1890s, Brisbane had two baths on land supplied with water from the Brisbane River: the Corporation Salt-Water Baths in Arthur Street, Spring Hill, and the Imperial Swimming, Bathing and Skating Rink Co., at the corner of Stanley and Ernest streets, South Brisbane.[3]

The floating baths were: the Metropolitan Bathing Co. Ltd, Alice Street, the Victoria Swimming Baths, Stanley Street, South Brisbane, the New Farm Swimming Baths, Merthyr Street, New Farm.[4]

New baths 1890-1900

During the decade, two new public baths were built in Brisbane. After the Metropolitan Baths were swept down the river in the 1893 flood,[5] the new Metropolitan Baths were moored at the same location at the end of Alice Street.[6] The Booroodabin Baths in Wickham Street, Fortitude Valley, were opened for public use on Saturday 19 September 1896.[7]

Imperial Swimming Baths

On the night of 30 January 1889 the Imperial Swimming Baths and Skating Rink in South Brisbane were officially opened. The following day the *Evening observer* reported on the opening by Mr W. Stephens, mayor of South Brisbane, in the presence of a large number of spectators:

> The opening dive was taken by Mr W. Morris, followed by Madame Saigemann, who has been engaged as the ladies' instructress, after which swimming became general, a large proportion of those present having evidently come prepared to put the new baths to a practical test. The building was tastefully decorated with small flags and Chinese lanterns. ... During the evening, proceedings were enlivened with music. Swimming was indulged in until 10 pm when the baths were closed.[8]

The baths were specially reserved for ladies from 10am to 1pm. Admission on opening night was 1s, and after that 6d, including towel and bathing dress.[9] The architect under whose supervision the work was carried out was H.G.O. Thomas, and the cost of the baths was £3000. All the necessary machinery was supplied by Messrs Smellie & Co.[10]

New Farm Swimming Baths, 1889

On 26 April 1889 the Booroodabin Divisional Board recommended that permission be granted to B. Campbell to erect floating baths at the south end of Merthyr Street, New Farm.[11] In June 1889 architect John Jacob Cohen advertised for tenders for the floating baths.[12] On Saturday 5 October 1889 the *Brisbane courier* reported the following:

> Mr Burns Campbell, lessee of the New Farm ferry, has been engaged for three months in the erection of a floating bath moored close to the New Farm side of his ferry crossing at the end of old Racecourse Road and overlapping Sir Samuel Griffiths ground. The structure is to be opened at noon today by Sir Samuel's son, Llewellyn. Externally the bath house measures 81 ft by 41 ft. The well or swimming basin is 70 ft by 29 ft beginning at the entrance side with a depth of 3 ft 3 ins and deepening to 7 ft 3 ins on the further side. It is surrounded by a platform of 2 ft and between this and the exterior wall are thirty-eight dressing rooms, 5 ft x 4 ft with other conveniences. The structure rests on ten strongly built pontoons, sheathed with Muntz metal, six of which are 27 ft long and four 16 ft. The entire cost will be about £1,200. Mr. Campbell hopes to make arrangements for ladies on two days a week, and to be able before long to add a fresh water shower.[13]

An entry in the 1891 directory for the New Farm Swimming Baths records: W. Rowe. caretaker, Merthyr St, New Farm.[14] The baths are not listed after 1891. The 1892 directory lists E.W. Rowe as proprietor of the Victoria Baths, Stanley St, South Brisbane.[15] Did Mr Rowe purchase the New Farm Baths, re-locate and re-name them?

Metropolitan Baths, 1894

The Metropolitan Baths which some of our present-day senior citizens swam in or at least remember, were, according to council records, built in 1894.[16] These baths were a most popular swimming venue. In the 1920s they were used by artist and sculptor Wilson Cooper who later recalled that 'it was quite fun to try and catch the Johnny Dorys which swam through the slatted timber sides and flooring of the pool, the water was so clear one had no trouble following the darting fish'.[17] No doubt swimmers in the 1890s could have told the same story. The Metropolitan Baths were destroyed by flood in the early hours of the morning of 21 April 1928.[18]

Booroodabin Baths, 1896

The Booroodabin Divisional Board adhered to strict swimming regulations. Complaints about unacceptable bathing behaviour in the vicinity of Breakfast Creek and the drowning of nine children one holiday season in and around the creek, directed attention to the need for a safe swimming enclosure in the Booroodabin Division.[19] The Baths Committee decided on a reserve in Wickham Street, Fortitude Valley.[20] Tenders were called by architect John James Clarke.[21] Quotations ranged from £2120 to £1555. The latter tender, from W. Taylor, Norman Park, was accepted.[22]

A report on the Booroodabin Baths was published on Saturday 19 September 1896 in the *Brisbane courier*:

> Everything is now completed and the baths will be open to the public today. ... The baths were thrown open for inspection yesterday, and were visited by a large number

> of people who expressed pleasure at the general appearance of the building and the excellence of the accommodation. ... Special attention has been given to its ventilation. ... The large bath is 90 ft long by 30 ft wide, and the depth of the water varies from 3 ft to 6 ft 8 ins. The water is pumped from Breakfast Creek and while the bath is being used a continual flowing in and flowing out is arranged for. ... Mr Albert Butterfield and Mrs Butterfield have been appointed caretakers. Today there will be no opening ceremony, but arrangements are being made for holding aquatic sports at no distant date, and several of the local clubs have promised their co-operation.[23]

Planning for these baths commenced in 1894, but one of the committee members was sure that if the baths were erected they would prove to be a white elephant.[24] Time has proved otherwise. Swimming traditions, which began in 1896, continued when a new pool was built alongside. This new pool at Wickham Street was opened on 27 February 1926.[25]

Queensport Aquarium and Zoological Gardens

If swimming was not the chosen outing for a family, they could enjoy the river from one of the paddle-steamers which transported them to the new and popular attraction at Queensport. Paddle steamers left Campbells Wharf at the end of Creek Street. Fare and admission was 2s for an adult and 1s for a child. Another means of arriving at Queensport Aquarium was by train and a five minute walk from Hemmant railway station.[26]

The formal opening of Queensport Aquarium took place on Wednesday 7 August 1889. The following day an account of the opening was published in the *Evening observer*:

> Mr J.F. Buckland member for the district occupied the chair, and Mr J.D. Campbell the Vice-chair. ... The Aquarium grounds cover 11 acres and are situated about two miles beyond the meat works at the back of Gibson Island. In the centre is the Aquarium consisting of a two story building, fernery, seal pond etc. ... In the Aquarium itself there are six fish tanks each 13 ft long 5 ft deep and 4 ft wide, some 3 tons of plate-glass having been used in their construction. Around the supports of the building,

1.1 Queensport Aquarium and Zoological Gardens (RHSQ)

> grottos have been arranged and in the centre is a large (salt-water) fountain. One end has been reserved for refreshment booths.
>
> Immediately opposite the outlet from the fernery is the seal's tank and basking grounds enclosed with iron railings. Over the aquarium is the Concert Hall, 100 ft by 50 ft surrounded by a 12 ft promenade. The stage is 14 ft by 36 ft with two dressing rooms. ... At one side is fixed the electric organ – the only one in the Colony we believe and at the other a piano. ... It is estimated that the hall will seat 1,400 people. At intervals around the grounds are placed small houses, and seats for the use of picnickers, or visitors, together with swings etc. [27]

Fauna attractions included fish, animals and reptiles, penguins and sea lions. There were also black bears. 'Flying Machines', a switch-back railway, and later a cricket pitch and a bicycle track were added for the patrons to enjoy. The floods of 1893 put an end to the aquarium. All the animals, except the bears, were saved and later sold to a circus.[28]

Picnics continued to be held there after the 1893 flood. The *Brisbane courier* on 18 September 1895 described the Graziers' Butchering Picnic which attracted 1300, who were transported there by three steamers and two doubledecker omnibuses.[29] Special holiday attractions continued to be advertised, for example, Boxing Day 1895.[30]

The aquarium building was also used as a dance hall, and as a venue to welcome local men returning from the Boer War. After demolition, material from the hall was used in the construction of three houses at Wynnum North.[31]

1.2 River picnic of the Queensland Press Club on board the Natone, Chelmer Reach, 12 Nov. 1892 (JOL)

Conclusion

The happy crowd on board the steamer Natone on 12 November 1892, attending the Queensland Press Club picnic in honour of Miss Shaw, the special commissioner of the *Times*, highlighted some of the pleasures to be enjoyed on a Brisbane River cruise. On 19 November 1892 the *Queenslander* reported the event:

> The journey was continued as far as Chelmer. ... [Aborigines] gave a capital exhibition of boomerang and spear throwing. ... The guest of the occasion took great interest in the flight of the boomerangs and spears, and indeed, all onboard were much pleased with the exhibition. ... the homeward journey was commenced. The time was spent in pleasant converse, and admiring the beauty of the scenery, and in listening to the numerous selections of Benvenuti's excellent string band.[32]

On 13 September 1897 the *Brisbane courier* carried a Palings advertisement listing new songs. One of the songs was titled 'Brisbane River'.[33] Perhaps this song was included in the musical selections of the paddle-steamer bands during the remaining years of the decade.

The citizens of Brisbane in the 1890s had a variety of recreational activities available to them, either on or along the river. Such exposure to the river may indeed have given them the same impression as Geoffrey Tebbutt: 'It is the river for which Brisbane most is memorable'.[34]

Chapter 2

Cricket and cycling in the 1890s

Ian Jobling

A survey of the variety of sports available to Brisbanites in 1888 has already received some attention.[1] However during the 1890s, two of these sports, cricket and cycling, can be used to provide some insight into the role and place of sport in the lifestyle of Brisbane. The city, which had grown from a population of approximately 95,000 to almost 120,000 in the decade from 1891–1901, reflected the impact of technology on society, which was not only apparent in urban, commercial, and industrial development, but also in the lifestyle and leisure patterns of its inhabitants.[2]

Cricket - The Brisbane Cricket Ground

On 11 April 1993 the Australian Football League teams, Brisbane and Melbourne, played at a renovated, some might say rejuvenated, sports venue at Woolloongabba. Although this venue has hosted many different sports, its most notable function has been for cricket. It was less than a century ago, in 1895, that an area of a little over 12 acres was dedicated as the Brisbane Cricket Ground. Prior to that it had been a reserve for the supply of water and was also used by some people as a place to live, much to the annoyance of residents in the area.

The venue was close to a busy shopping centre, with major stores such as Sinclairs, and Allan & Stark in Stanley Street, but the popularity of the area for shopping declined due to extensive flooding in the early 1890s. There were also many hotels in this Stanley Street area at the beginning of that decade: Victoria Bridge Hotel, Royal Mail Hotel, Grahams Hotel, Ship Inn, Brown's Plough and the Bowen Hotel, the oldest hotel in the street – named after Queensland's first governor.[3]

The Queensland Cricket Association (QCA), established in 1876,[4] and its rival, the Southern Queensland Cricket Union, amalgamated in 1891 'in the interests of cricket'.[5] The QCA had been reliant upon other agencies for the provision of appropriate venues and playing surfaces. Usage of the Albert sports ground and the Exhibition Grounds, which belonged to the National Association, meant that the QCA could not generate revenue when teams visited Brisbane from other colonies. At a monthly meeting of the QCA in September 1893, it was stated that the QCA was contracted to the Northern Rugby Union (NRU) to pay 15.5 per cent of the takings to that organisation regardless of whether matches were played on their venues. It was clear that the QCA was keen to obtain a cricket ground over which it had full control.[6]

The QCA sought support from the South Brisbane Council in 1893, but it was not until January 1895 that approval for that council to allocate the Woolloongabba reserve to the QCA was authorised by the under-secretary of lands of the Queensland government.[7]

Meanwhile, £120 was allocated by the QCA towards the new ground, and additional support was sought from the cricketers of Brisbane. The annual report of the QCA for 1895 included details as to how the ground was to be managed: 'a committee of eight gentlemen were [sic] appointed by the Trustees, four being nominated by the Association and four by the Trustees, to take over the management of the above ground for a term of two years from the 1st October next'.[8]

'Observer', writing in the *Brisbane courier* of 14 March 1895, extolled the work of those gentlemen associated with the procuring of the Woolloongabba Reserve as a cricket ground:

Cricket in Brisbane

> Sir, Having resided in Brisbane for the past six months, and being fond of our great British game of cricket which has so many votaries in the colonies, I cannot in common with other visitors, help noticing how very far behind the other colonies we are in the manner of turning out good cricketers .... Undoubtedly if we want our Queensland children to be a credit to the land of their birth, they must have physical and healthy education.
>
> J.V. Francis ... has done more good for cricket than any other man in Brisbane. Besides there are many other gentlemen I could mention who would gladly assist us in providing for our rising generation suitable grounds and the necessary apparatus to give our youngsters the physical education they require; and if this is done with the assistance of say a couple of good professionals, Queenslanders will in a short time be amongst the front rank of first class cricketers, etc., and we shall have cricket contests worthy of our colony.[9]

This is a most interesting statement but not particularly prophetic; however, Queensland did eventually win the Sheffield Shield but only just before the centennial of acquiring the Brisbane Cricket Ground!

Approximately 60,000 tons of landfill was used to level the playing surface in readiness for the first match, which was between a Parliament XI and a Press XI on 19 December 1896. The *Brisbane courier* reported the event: 'The game on Saturday was historic in its way, since it opened the Woolloongabba Sports Ground, on which in the near future international and intercolonial athletes will try for championship honours'.[10]

During this opening match, a drainage problem in the outfield became obvious; this took many years to alleviate. In 1897 £800 was spent on a drain across the ground. An additional improvement in that year was the erection of a fence at a sum of £400. Plans for a grandstand were approved in 1897 and the building was erected at a cost of £2000 – it was completed just before the touring team from England played later that year.

Preparations were proceeding to secure the visit of A.E. Stoddart's English XI but problems arose within the ranks of the QCA when it became known that the organisation would receive none of the gate receipts. Not surprisingly, this issue was raised at the QCA's annual general meeting held in September 1897. The *Brisbane courier* covered the heated discussion in detail:

> Mr Halstead said he understood the proposal was that the management of the English team should receive 60 per cent of the takings and that 40 per cent should go to the Brisbane Cricket Ground. The committee, however, were to spend 100 pounds in fetching five players from the Southern colonies. The proposal had emanated from the business men, and was purely a business proposal. The Ground Committee had nothing to do with the suggestion that men should be imported to take part in the

match. The managers contended that it was no use playing a team of fifteen or eighteen Queenslanders.

Mr Bale: An insult to Queensland cricketers ....

Dr Macdonald said the only enemies the Brisbane Cricket Ground had were a few members of the Queensland Cricket Association. The public could not appreciate the work that had been carried on in construction with that ground. The construction of the fence alone cost 400 pounds, the drain across the ground 800 pounds, beside which 60,000 tons of filling up had to be done. Of course there was not much to show for the outlay yet. Still he thought what had been done reflected great credit upon the committee. It would be a pity to disturb the friendly relations between the two bodies, and he thought it should be their aim to work together. The plans of the grandstand were already out, and the building would be erected at a cost of 200 pounds. The ground was essentially for cricket.

Voices: No, no; it is not.

Dr Macdonald: What is it for?

Voices: Skittles, -Athletics, Horse racing, A sports ground.

Dr Macdonald said the purpose for which it was originally granted was cricket, and he thought as the trustees were honourable men, they would see that cricket had first claim. 'Football to a great extent had been shut off during the last few weeks in order to allow of the preparation of the pitch'. It was most unjust to oppose what had been done in connection with the ground.[11]

Despite these misgivings, preparations for the match proceeded in haste, even to the extent of ensuring the traffic arrangements around the ground were well publicised:

The cab and omnibus stands are appointed in Main-street, near Stanley-street, whilst the engaged cabs and private vehicles are to be permitted to stand in Stanley-street,

2.0 The grandstand at the Brisbane Cricket Ground, Dec. 1897 (JOL)

2.1. The international cricket match – watching the play, Q 4 Dec 1897 (JOL)

> near Logan Road, and extending in the direction of Wellington Road; also in Vulture-street, near the entrance to the grandstand enclosure. Between the hours of 10.30 a.m. and 3 p.m. each day, cyclists, horsemen, and vehicular traffic returning from the Cricket Ground, on arriving at Vulture-street, will be diverted into Grey-street to Melbourne-street, for the purpose of relieving a portion of Stanley-street of unnecessary traffic.[12]

The improvements which had been made to the BCG were highlighted in a description of the new grandstand featured in an article published in the *Brisbane courier* of 26 November 1897 – the morning of the first day of play:

> The preparation at the Brisbane Cricket Ground in connection with the international cricket match, Queensland and New South Wales (combined) v. Stoddart's English team, which commences today had yesterday been completed, and will come almost as a revelation to those of the public who have not visited them during the past two or three months. The place will scarcely be recognised, for what was once the old-time reserve has now been transformed into an athletic ground which promises to equal anything of its kind in the colonies.
>
> Since the time when the bicycle track was opened, two fine stands, capable of accommodating 1400 persons have been erected. The grandstand is a fine building, and will seat 1000 persons comfortably, while the smokers' stand will provide seating accommodation for about 400 persons. The stands are not quite complete, but only the finishing touches are required, so that the spectators will suffer no inconvenience in this respect.[13]

The architects of the new grandstand were J. Hall and Robin S. Dods.[14]

On the opening day, declared a public holiday in Brisbane, there were more than 11,000 spectators. A similar number was estimated on the second day. Clearly, this international match was an auspicious occasion. Moreover the hosts (Queensland and NSW) had two more players than the England team.

The Brisbane Cricket Ground Act of 1897 was assented to on 15 December. The act named Messrs T.J. Byrnes, George Down and Ernest J. Stevens as trustees and gave them power to mortgage the land for £4000, for the purpose of ground improvements. Further acts were assented to in 1906 and 1958. The invasion of the Brisbane Bears, now the Lions, and AFL football to what has become known as 'The Gabba' is the beginning of a new era for what became in the 1890s, and what is still regarded officially, as the Brisbane Cricket Ground.

Cycling

The first 'bicycle', defined as being a 'two-wheeled velocipede that could be ridden with the feet entirely off the ground' was introduced to the world in 1839.[15] The development of the two-wheelers led to machines variously known as the 'High-Wheeler', 'Spider', 'Ordinary' and 'Penny Farthing', all of which were much faster than the boneshakers. A major problem was their lack of stability caused by the rider being elevated in such a position to exert force on the large front wheel. The skills necessary for riding these contraptions were such that women, because of their cumbersome clothing and other social restrictions, were discouraged from becoming cyclists. But women were most active in cycling throughout the 1890s following the advent of a more suitable bicycle.

In the mid 1880s, J.K. Starkley, an English inventor and manufacturer, devised what became known as the 'safety' bicycle – a machine that has become the prototype of our current bicycle.[16] It was not until the 1890s though, that the 'safety', with its chain-driven rear wheel and pneumatic tyres out-performed the 'ordinary' in sales for leisure and sport.

The safety bicycle was probably first imported into Australia in 1887; the pneumatic tyre arrived approximately two years later. One of these new 'machines' was introduced at the Australasian championships of 1890, and a member of the Brisbane Safety Bicycle Club, formed in 1891, stated that a 'new influence' was at work and it was intended 'to knock out the prejudice against the dainty little safety wheels'.[17] Although treated with scepticism initially, by the mid 1890s there was a bicycle boom throughout Australia.[18] A report in the *Brisbane courier* of 28 October 1892 provided evidence of the technological improvements in the machine and its effect on the popularity of cycling:

> Perhaps no form of sport ever increased the circle of its patrons as rapidly as cycling has done of late years, and this for two good reasons. In the first place the sense of mastery over time and distance, the wild rush through the atmosphere, the exhilaration of spirit natural when man is employing his limbs in pleasant and graceful fashion, have combined to multiply wheelmen in every civilised quarter of the globe. In the second place the wonderful improvements effected in the construction of cycles within the last decade have contrived to make the sport fit, not only for adventurous youth, but for staid maturity and green old age.
>
> The earlier promise of the modern 'safety' was despised by the more daring young man some years back as a reversion to the antiquated 'bone-shaker' type. But improvement quickly followed improvement until it had to be recognised that almost perfect security from accident could not be considered a drawback, when combined with durability and speed equal or superior to that of the once fashionable and elegant 'spider' bicycles.[19]

James Smith's cycling business in Brisbane became a substantial commercial enterprise throughout this decade. The following paragraph from the *Queenslander* of 6 April 1893 reflects the nature of the cycling business:

> Mr James Smith, of Petrie's Bight, landed another large shipment of the well-known James bicycles last week .... I noticed several little improvements. In the oil-containing hubs on the back wheel for instance, the oil cups screw into the flanges on either side of the hub not on the axle as formerly, which now insures oil going at once into the ball races. The chain wheel on the hub is detachable. A number of the machines are fitted with large chain wheels – ten teeth on the hub wheel, with twenty-one and twenty-two on the bracket axle ... Dunlop tires, plain and Welch, as well as clinchers are fitted. The new Dunlop pump is novel, the rubber connection disappearing inside the pump when not in use. Mr Smith has now on his premises over 100 machines, comprising high and low frames besides sufficient parts to make thirty more.[20]

Initially, bicycles were not cheap – some models cost the equivalent of several months income. Efficiency in manufacturing, associated with large–volume production, saw prices drop considerably by the end of the decade.[21] Saturday continued to be the main day for cycling excursions or carnivals although this did preclude some shop assistants and many unskilled workers from participating in organised cycling.[22]

In the early 1890s racing tracks for bicycles were marked at numerous locations, especially cricket and football ovals.[23] The demand for 'specific tracks' is reflected in this extract from the *Queenslander* of 1 June 1895:

> The bicycle track at the Exhibition Grounds, Brisbane, is undergoing a vast improvement. I visited the grounds the other afternoon and found that the track had been resurveyed, and, to judge from present appearances, we should have one of the best bicycle tracks in the colonies, and no more complaints from the Southern competitors on 'bringing us up to ride on goat tracks, all corners, and with a probability of having to be dug out of a cutting', should be heard. With this track and the one at Breakfast Creek – which is also I believe undergoing extensive repairs, – we shall have two of the fastest and safest circles to race on – fit for a Zimmerman, a Megson or a Kerr.[24]

The three persons named in the above quotation were renowned track cyclists who attracted many spectators. As Ronald Lawson has stated, the emergence of such professional sportsmen was a result of 'the growth of official organisations controlling sporting activities, which are a necessary prerequisite for regular large–scale competition and for commercialisation of sport'.[25] Cycling was one of the sports in which the concepts of amateurism and professionalism caused divisions and arguments. In 1887 the Brisbane Bicycle Club had offered to meet with cyclists from Gympie 'to absolve them from the sin of professionalism'.[26] Even by 1900 the *Brisbane courier* reported the contrasts between professionalism and amateurism in cycling: '[In professionalism] the individual element should be magnified and self interest find full scope, while with the amateur, or certainly with the best school of amateur, and one that is not insignificant in numbers and esprit de corps, a determination to achieve not so much success as success through the avenue of chivalrous respect for the rules and ethics of the contest is the predominant impulse'.[27]

The term cash 'amateur' also appeared in this period of the 1890s and applied to cyclists who accepted their prizes in cash.[28] It was suggested that cash amateur riders were 'men who could not afford to be "gentlemen" as the term understood by the cash men'.[29] A contemporary writer, Fletcher Brunsdon, noted that the 'cash' system had interfered with club membership in Queensland and 'at present amateur and professional cyclists are like the Guelfs and Ghibellines of the Middle Ages in their love of one another'.[30]

The League of Queensland Wheelmen, which comprised 'professionals/cash amateurs', began in November 1894 with a membership of 35; by April of the next year it was reported that its membership included more active cyclists than any two of the amateur clubs.[31] The cycling track at the Woolloongabba Cricket Ground was opened in mid 1897; more than 8000 spectators attended the Wheelmen's winter carnival which was held there.[32] The money available to them in prizes was such that it attracted North American, European and other international riders, along with those from other Australian colonies. The American A. Zimmerman competed at several Queensland race-meetings for which he was paid £150.[33]

Amateur cycling continued to flourish throughout the 1890s. In 1893 a controlling amateur cycling body, the Queensland Cycling Union (later changed to the Queensland Amateur Cyclists Union) was formed. It was through this association that the Australian Track Cycling Championships were organised.

Clearly, the introduction of the safety bicycle made cycling the boom sport of the 1890s. Significantly, as cycling as a competitive sport developed, recreational cycling and touring, by both sexes, became extremely popular.[34]

Chapter 3

Train excursions for the masses in the 1890s

John Kerr

The rot started with the railways. Sandgate used to be a quiet little bayside community. And then they built the railway. Soon hundreds and thousands of people descended on it each public holiday. By steam train, Sandgate was less than an hour's travel and there were several trains each day, even on Sundays. Some people built a second house there, others came to live and commute. Another spot ruined. The problem has now migrated to the motor car, the bus and the jumbo jet, but in the 1890s the train was the only menace on the horizon.

We could trace the beginnings back to Britain and the dire and timely warnings of those opposing railway construction. Apart from the pollution, the disruption caused by railway construction and the danger of travelling at speeds for which mankind was never intended, there was the hidden risk. The railway would enable the masses to use their idle time to travel for pleasure.

3.0 One of the first locomotives in Queensland (JOL)

In Queensland our first railway started from Ipswich and went west to the Darling Downs. It was meant to serve commerce and the squatters who controlled both the colony's economy and its parliament. River steamers could trade to Ipswich so the railway started there. Brisbane was spared the evils of mass transport. But in August 1865, only a few weeks after the first section of Queensland Railways opened, the commissioner began running Sunday trains. The residents of Ipswich with a few shillings to spare could travel by train to that centre for sin and scandal, Grandchester. Next year when the line was extended, they could enter the world of darkness by plunging into the confines of the Victoria Tunnel under the Little Liverpool Range and frolic for the day in the Lockyer Valley. Concerned citizens led by presbyterian minister Charles Ogg protested.[1] A year and a month later Commissioner Herbert sought permission from his minister to cease this demoralising practice.[2] The novelty was wearing off and it was no longer profitable. One Sunday spent in Grandchester or Laidley was sufficient for most residents. Without some attraction like the seaside, or the power to order a special train at no cost to themselves, as enjoyed by Macalister and other ministers of the crown, there was little incentive to repeat the experience.

Among the first to provide some incentive were, of course, the real estate agents. The first privately organised special train on the railway was from Ipswich to Walloon. The tickets were free as was the lunch, and by the end of the day all the land was sold. The lucky purchasers who held on might be delighted to find their blocks served by electric train, over a century later.[3]

Building the railway from Ipswich to Brisbane brought new possibilities. The first excursion was nearly a riot with the Orange and the Green confronting each other in Berry's Paddock at Oxley Point, opposite the river from Indooroopilly in November 1874. The preliminary skirmishes were held in the Ipswich School of Arts. To ensure there were no dastardly acts, a pilot engine went first, then a special train with police and finally the excursion train carrying the picnickers under the auspices of the Orange Association. Nearly 2000 people assembled by train, steamer and by road. Bishop James Quinn, who had earlier admonished the faithful at mass to non-violence and non-interference, joined the excursion and addressed the gathering. There was not a murmur and the day passed peacefully.[4]

The railway opened to Brisbane in June 1875. To cross the river meant a ferry ride, with an engine and carriages running a shuttle service four times a day between Brisbane and Indooroopilly. Sunday trains were inaugurated in August. Three return trips began running to Indooroopilly each Sunday, the first time that Brisbane people could take a train excursion on a Sunday.[5] Within a few months Sunday trains were cancelled and not reintroduced until 5 October 1879 when they ran all the way from Brisbane to Ipswich.

The opening of the railway from Brisbane to Sandgate on 10 May 1882 meant trains to the seaside and the real start of regular leisure travel. At the same time, a branch line was built to Racecourse, now Ascot, solely to enable racegoers to reach the course in comfort. Regular trains ran – until 1993 – but only as an afterthought.

Ipswich churchgoers signed a protest petition against Sunday trains on moral grounds, adding that, judging by patronage, there was little demand for Sunday trains.[6] Brisbane was barely large enough to support suburban trains. Unlike Melbourne, Sydney, Adelaide and Perth, Brisbane did not have regular interval suburban trains until 1978 and even now there are stations only two kilometres from the city with only a train each half hour and hourly at weekends.

Rather than cancel Sunday trains, economies were effected by not bringing the overworked station staff on duty, and relying on enginemen and guards keeping strictly to the timetable. Remembering that the entire system was single line, this was very important. The system came unstuck on Sunday 15 April 1883. The 8.50am Sunday morning train from Sandgate was due to meet the 9.20am train to Racecourse or Hamilton, today's Ascot, at Mayne. The crew of whichever train arrived first at Mayne was to operate the points and let their train into the loop and then signal the other train past. Driver Peter Jackson had just steamed the Racecourse train through Bowen Park, now Exhibition. He went slowly but did not stop, as there were no passengers on the platform and none to set down. George Ferguson, driver of the train from Sandgate, had not left Mayne and passed the original Bowen Hills station, then just on the northern side of today's Campbell Street level crossing, when he saw the Racecourse train. He blew his whistle furiously. This was not only to alert Driver Jackson. It was also to alert the guard of the Sandgate train to apply the brake in the guard's van. Trains had little braking power, and although the driver was able to put his engine into reverse gear to provide the maximum stopping force, the two engines collided on a bridge over a swampy area, now part of the Exhibition Grounds. Both locomotives were derailed but the damage was slight.[7] This little experiment in ignoring the strict procedures for safe-working had proved unsafe. Although safe practices were adopted for Sundays, it took another year and another accident on a weekday for the lesson to be properly learned.[8]

The Sunday trains continued. In 1889 Central railway station was opened, and on 1 November 1890 the line through the Valley was completed. Brisbane had railways on the southside, opening from Stanley Street, South Brisbane, near the Dry Dock to Corinda on 2 June 1884. Even though this was really built to bring coal for bunkering steamers in the river, Stanley Street became the terminus for lines to the south coast and to Cleveland. From January 1889 the intrepid Brisbane resident could spend Sunday on the glistening beach at Southport.[9] The same year, just before the summer season, the railway opened to Cleveland, bringing Wynnum, Manly and Raby Bay within the reach of the daytripper. The new South Brisbane station, often known as Melbourne Street, was opened four days before Christmas 1891.[10]

3.1 Brisbane Central Railway Station, 1895 (JOL)

By this time, the railway to the north coast had been completed through to Gympie, linking Brisbane with Maryborough and Bundaberg. This was no terrain for Sunday trips but it did give Brisbane people scope for travel, especially as there were also branches to Beaudesert, Boonah and Esk, besides the line to the Darling Downs, now linked west to Charleville and south to Wallangarra and Sydney.

Most excursion travel was short distance to the beaches or to special events. The National Association held a summer show for two days in January 1883, soon after the Sandgate Railway opened, and six special trains each way made it easy to travel out to the Exhibition Grounds.[11] Next year Queensland Railways put on special trains to the ball at the Bowen Park grounds. The return trains to Ipswich and Sandgate at 2am allowed time for enjoyment of the evening to the full.[12] On 28 June 1884 there was the then major Hanlan Regatta on the river at Indooroopilly and special trains ran to the Albert Bridge, passengers detraining right beside the river for the day's entertainment.[13] The Shorncliffe extension was opened in May 1897, another bonus for the 1890s traveller. The branch line to Enoggera opened in February 1899.[14]

Travel was still leisurely by today's standards: the first Sunday trains took double the time to Ipswich of today's electric trains and between 40 and 50 minutes to reach Sandgate, despite having many fewer stops.

Imagine making your way to the railway station, basket and hamper in hand and children dressed up fit for the day's outing. If travelling on days when excursion tickets were on sale – a return journey for the price of a single ticket – there was sure to be a queue.[15] Walking onto the platform at Roma Street, there was perhaps an American engine, a Baldwin A12, with its driving wheels, large by Queensland standards, coupled to half a dozen carriages of different shapes and sizes. At first carriages were imported, but soon they were being built by local manufacturers, the design altering from year to year as the standards improved. Second-class seats were usually padded but not sprung.

The guard in charge of the train, but under the direction of the stationmaster, blew his whistle once all the passengers were aboard. The engine driver gave an acknowledging whistle and eased open the regulator. Steam expanding in the cylinders steadily but slowly moved the train forward. The large driving wheels on the A12 meant a slower start than with the British built B13 class engine with its six-coupled driving wheels, but on the long run between Nudgee and Cabbage Tree – now known as North Boondall – the A12 could reach nearly 40 miles per hour. If the starts were slow, so too were the stops. The adoption of continuous brakes in the 1880s, first the vacuum brake as used in Britain and then the Westinghouse brake, made for much smarter stops, as every carriage had its own brake operating automatically, instead of relying on the guard winding the windlass to apply the brake on his van and, where it was linked up by chains, the brake in the adjoining carriage.

Christmas and New Year were not a time of fun and frolic for railway employees. There was no time off and no holidays for them. It was the busiest time of the year. Band concerts and moonlight entertainments and picnics all brought crowds in their thousands.[16]

Brisbane was not alone in this push for pleasure. Lots of country centres had their railways by the 1890s, and excursions were held from Warwick in the south to Cooktown and Croydon in the north. In the country there was often a full turnout, far exceeding the capacity of the available carriages. The better class of wagons was utilised, which sometimes meant the bogie cattle wagon, cleaned out, with seats fitted and even sometimes an oil light hung uselessly above to provide a suggestion of illumination for the dark part of the return journey. Brisbane people usually fared better, but all the old carriages, many better retired, were pressed into service. Brisbane excursionists often had to travel in goods wagons during holiday periods. To save having carriages idle most of the year, the railways built a number of convertible carriages, covered wagons with a strong wooden floor and several doors each side augmented by wooden shutters which could be let down to allow the light in when seats were fitted.[17] During the last war, meat workers in Townsville travelled in such splendour to work.

Regular departmental excursions, which were to become a weekly event with diverse destinations in the twentieth century, offered Saturday and Sunday travel to all points of the compass around Brisbane then accessible by rail. Mass transit by rail brought the beaches and the delights of the city within the reach of the working man. A century later the trains carry few excursions while the masses are poisoned by pollution in the comfort of their own cars.

Chapter 4

Southport in the 1890s: Decline and temporary fall from favour

Robert Longhurst

For most of the 1890s, Southport could only reflect with regret upon the passing of those great vice-regal days of the previous decade when much of Queensland society followed Sir Anthony and Lady Lucinda Musgrave to the southern seaside resort town. Musgrave's West Indian origins meant that he delighted in Queensland's climate, unlike his predecessors and most of his successors who fled to the hills as the summer months appeared. Government House or 'Summer Place' (later the nucleus of The Southport School) was Southport's claim to fame in the years 1884-88, but Musgrave's sudden death came as a body blow to the flourishing township's estate developers and businessmen. Shops such as George Andrews' Southport Store had flourished upon the custom of the colony's 'worthies', who would spend many months each year in their own or rented houses, and few country stores in the nation would have traded so many bottles of French champagne, cognac and tins of pate de foie gras.

Brisbane's main resort of Sandgate had suffered accordingly. Those with the means to enjoy longer holidays left Sandgate to the shop assistants and hands who could seldom afford the time, let alone the fare, to take one of the splendid paddle steamers which plied the Southport route before 1889. The passage, aboard such steamers as the Natone or the President, took some six hours through usually smooth and charming waters, the only inconvenience being occasional stranding upon mosquito-infested sand bars. One writer reflected in 1905 that the President would literally '"rub along" for something like half the journey, till the passengers were not quite sure whether they were out for a sail on the ocean or engaged in a sort of marine steeplechase'.[1] But the trip by steamer was part of Southport's charm and would be much regretted in the years to come, even if it generally meant two days travelling. It was certainly far preferable to the long and tiresome coach trips of the early 1880s, or the 'alternative' route after 1885 – catching the train to Beenleigh and then coaching it through mud to Southport. The coach fares were far beyond the pockets of holiday excursionists; the trip was somewhat bone-rattling and still took most of one day.

Isolation reinforced Southport's exclusiveness. Brisbane's elite felt comfortable there, rubbing shoulders with the families of the Downs squattocracy and relishing the chance to throw their daughters at an eligible ADC or two. The beach was better and there was very little chance of meeting persons of lower degree as one might at Sandgate. There was also the Southport Easter Regatta, a major social event since 1879, the numerous balls, soirees and theatricals at the School of Arts, the Southport Volunteers, and the exhilarating buggy trips along the main ocean beach to Burleigh or boat trips to Stradbroke. And then there were the less environmentally friendly pursuits of pelican and parrot shooting, or staghorn collecting on Stradbroke Island. Perhaps no structure so epitomised Southport's aspirations in those years as the Grand Hotel, a massive 'American' type building which was constructed overlooking the Broadwater at Deepwater Point.

Southport's resident population at the time of the 1886 census was 750. Its state school in 1889 had an attendance of 145, and it could boast a healthy trading community: builders, bakers, painters, glaziers and several storekeepers; a weekly paper, the *Southern Queensland bulletin* established in 1885; two sawmills, a chemist, some five boarding houses and four hotels. Miss Davenport's School for young ladies, Goy-te-Lea, was acclaimed among the colony's finest.

Such a booming resort naturally welcomed the extension of the railway line from Brisbane, which officially opened on Thursday 24 January 1889 with much local pomp and ceremony. Henceforth Southport could be reached in three hours by rail, hardly a fast service, yet sufficiently quicker to allow many who had previously found it impossible to reach Southport to arrive en masse. The local *Bulletin* especially welcomed the announcement that a new Melbourne Street extension line to the southern end of the Victoria Bridge was to be constructed, on the grounds that it would attract more persons to Southport who until then found it inconvenient and expensive to catch public transport or a 'cab to the existing Stanley Street Station'. [2]

Initially fares at 8s 5d first class and 5s 9d second class for a single journey were found to be too high, indeed more expensive than the steamers. In March 1889 Executive Council approved new rates of 6s and 4s respectively and introduced excursion fares, issued on Saturdays and Sundays and available for return on either Saturday, Sunday or Monday. These cost 7s 6d first class and 5s second, the same fares as those to Sandgate and from Rockhampton to its seaside resort at Emu Park.[3] Southport benefited to an extent. Within days Lewis Thomas' mine employees and their families from the Aberdare Colliery at Ipswich, numbering some 400, arrived by train. Southport's publicans provided 'traps' to carry what was described as 'a new class of visitor' to the watering holes. The town's prices had, however, been adjusted in past years to a freer-spending clientele, and complaints were soon heard from the less affluent that food, drink and board in Southport – in spite of its attractions – were overpriced.[4] Some 9845 tickets, exclusive of season tickets, were purchased from Brisbane to Southport in 1889-90, hardly a flood of visitors. Only privileged workers knew anything of the five day or forty-hour week in 1890 and most shop assistants worked at least 70 hours and late into Saturday nights as well, whilst religious observance occupied the Sundays of many.[5] Six hours in a train to and from Southport was therefore a luxury affordable only by a few, often at the grace and favour of an employer.

Musgrave's successor, Sir Henry Norman, was in residence at Government House, Southport, in the summer of 1889. However, an inspection of Harlaxton House, Toowoomba, had been made in August of that year. Norman was an old India hand and by dint of that experience looked for a summer hill station. Southport awaited his decision with bated anticipation, only to suffer decreasing and sporadic vice-regal patronage. In 1891 the Normans decided upon Toowoomba for their summer residence.[6] 'Summer Place' was to be virtually deserted until its final sale in 1898. By 1891, the town's reputation had suffered severely from the effect of the new class of excursionist.

To old hands the sight of too many 'faultlessly dressed young Queen Street gentlemen' was too much, too 'swell' and they passed on to the wilder delights of Burleigh or Coolangatta.[7] To others, the language now heard in Southport on weekends was far too coarse and common. Some families, like the Palmers, stayed loyal to the town, but others followed the Normans to Toowoomba, or took advantage of the new rail connections via Wallangarra to Sydney and on to the south during summer. Even the once picturesque country folk of Nerang were dangerously affected by the new spirit of Southport, with one report deploring the new *fin de siecle* tendency for young men to 'lean languidly against doorposts for longer than is good for them'.[8]

Southport's Regatta also sank into decline, as did the once highly successful School of Arts as the 'quality' packed up and left. Nature then determined to wreak its own particular vengeance. A succession of cyclonic storms battered the shoreline. In 1890 the swimming baths attached to the pier were destroyed, and for almost two years Sandgate enjoyed a considerable advantage over her competition. In March 1891 another storm destroyed numerous bathing houses and damaged some of the divisional board's concrete sea wall. Whilst much of this was repaired and extended, January and February 1893 saw Brisbane devastated by its worst flood on record, and much of Southport's sea wall was again destroyed, as were new baths.[9] A year later, with no substantial repairs undertaken owing to the financial situation, a further storm accompanied by a high tide again attacked the foreshore to such an extent that much of the Esplanade was threatened. Only with the return of better times in 1896 was work recommenced.

In late 1891 the first admissions appear in the local *Bulletin* that Southport was definitely in decline. Separation Day, 10 December, passed quietly with hardly any visitors 'and every other day, too, for that matter'.[10] The council attempted to counter the decline in visitor numbers by purchasing the Southport Pier, removing the toll, and re-erecting baths, but storms, unemployment and bank failures were to have the stronger hand. By 1893 Southport's ratepayers could scarcely pay their due rates. Even the local branch of the Queensland National Bank closed its premises, and in 1894 a special approach to the chief secretary to try to obtain a special loan to repair the foreshore was dismissed.[11] With deteriorating facilities, Southport was hardly likely to attract visitors. Even the pier required re-decking and new piles by March 1894. Railway figures from Brisbane to Southport declined by 30% between 1889-90 and 1894-95, when they plummeted to 6581.

The renewal of the Southport Regatta at Easter 1894 was therefore a bold venture. The program was hardly a patch upon the grand days of a decade earlier, with a tub race, walking a wet pole, swimming races and a 'dinghy race for boys'; but the affair was generally regarded as a great success, reviving a degree of confidence. Amongst the committeemen was one Cyril Lambart, grandson of the Marquess of Conyngham and son of the state steward to the lord lieutenant of Ireland. Aged twenty-seven, upon a visit to Queensland in 1893 as a member of the Dunville Whisky Company, he took a great interest in the town and district, commissioning a set of photographs of members of local Aboriginal tribes and generally dispensing his favour to hard-strapped local merchants. His lavish hospitality, especially his generosity with French champagne, even led to a local request for him to stand as parliamentary candidate for Albert, an offer he declined.[12] The Gold Coast has always attracted remarkable visitors, Lambart not least amongst them.

Gradually the names of prominent visitors, the Drurys, the Hunter-Browns, the Misses Griffith, returned to the social pages, and an increasing number of lady-bathers –

described ungallantly by one visitor as so many 'derelict buoys bobbing violently'.[13] Children in bright 'Kate Greenaway' costumes, armed with spade and bucket could also be seen in numbers on the beach. Southport, however, 'closed' as soon as the cooler autumn winds arrived. 'It remains in a semi-comatose state for more than half the year until the wealthier Queensland residents are again ready to exchange the enervating inland summer heat for the cool breezes of the seaboard'.[14] Nor did the dreaded onslaught by rail of shop girls and factory hands eventuate. They were the chief victims of the depression and bank crashes, and trips to the distant seaside became increasingly impossible. Sunday trains ceased running for almost eighteen months, owing to lack of traffic.

Nevertheless the 'quality', or what was left of it, gradually returned in 1895 and 1896, at much the same time as the general economy began slowly to revive. By 1896 the Easter Regatta was fully revived. Good Friday saw the southern end of Stradbroke alive with tents and camp fires and some sixty-seven boats arrived from Brisbane.[15] The autumn Southport races were also well attended and the divisional board commenced work upon the long-awaited sea wall restoration in April. The 1896-97 summer season saw a return to full hotels and boarding houses and a scarcity of good houses to lease. Rail figures prove the gradual return of holiday makers: 1894-95, 6581; 1895-96, 7768; 1896-97, 8539; 1897-98, 8404; 1898-99, 9114.

On 12 April 1897 some 1000 rail excursionists took advantage of a special excursion fare to visit the town,[16] bringing a much needed boost to local traders, who were also enjoying the benefits of a revived local sugar industry with the construction of the Nerang Central Mill. Even in July 1897, hotels which had been virtually empty for some eight winters, could boast a 'goodly number of visitors'. The *Brisbane courier*'s

4.0 A hotel buggy moves up Scarborough Street, having collected travellers from Southport Station. The errant cow speaks volumes about the coast's pace of life, 1898 (JOL)

Southport correspondent could boast that 'the youthful heir of the House of Lamington with his nurse, is staying at the Southport Hotel'.[17]

Fishing excursion parties became very much the thing in the late nineties, with the 'smart little steamer' Mystery available to those wishing to try their hand at deep sea fishing. By September 1897 the owners were railing some 250 to 350 schnapper to Brisbane each trip and taking holiday makers on Sunday bay trips, accompanied on occasion by the newly-formed Southport Band. Fishing from the Southport Pier was then little short of an angler's dream, with virtually weekly reports of jewfish and rock cod up to 58 pounds in weight being caught. At night the pier was often bedecked with fishermen's lanterns.

Easter of 1898 saw the commissioner of railways provide two trains leaving Brisbane on Thursday evening, quite packed full. The winter seasons of 1898 and 1899 found Southport full of visitors, with many cottages rented and even a revival in the property market. An increasing number of special excursion trains arrived bringing, for example, PMG and Colonial Sugar Refinery employees, while the first references to southern visitors staying in private homes or hotels appeared in the social columns. Increasingly after 1897 Southport gained a reputation as a winter as well as a summer resort, with obvious benefit to local tradespeople.

This revival had much to do with the strengthening economy, the gradual improvement in working hours and conditions, and the rise of a more tolerant, democratic social order in the late nineties. It also had its origins in a remarkable ecological transformation, which increasingly protected the town from erosion from the open sea after 1896. Indeed by 1899 the Southport Esplanade was more at danger from encroaching sand than waves.

4.1 The oft-repaired Southport Jetty with Stradbroke Island in the background, 1900 (JOL)

In 1895 reports first appeared of a major change in the ocean beach at Jumpinpin on Stradbroke Island close to the site of the wreck of the Cambus Wallace a year earlier. Storms in 1894 and 1895 had so seriously demolished the sea beach that pandanus were strewn along the coast, even exposing the remains of mangrove roots, proof that what was then the sea front had once been the shore of the inner bay.[18] By 1897 a break had virtually occurred, with ocean water washing into the southern reaches of the bay, and in early 1898 a storm caused a 700 yard wide break, washing away the Cambus Wallace graves.[19] The flow of water not only devastated much of the oyster beds near Southport, but also changed the shape and direction of what then was known as Main Beach Point, edging it across the mouth of the Nerang towards the small pier near the Southport Hotel.[20] Sand began to accumulate in banks to the north of the point – the origin of today's Spit – and in the Broadwater itself. Sand dunes began to float onto and over the Southport seawall, whilst the privately-owned secondary jetty was, by May 1897, standing several yards from the eroded foreshore. It was standing mid-stream by September 1898. Queens Park was awash and honeysuckles growing on the western mouth of the Nerang were washed away.[21]

Southport's foreshore, however, became more attractive as a peaceful swimming place, while the quality of the fishing improved by leaps and bounds. Easter of 1898, for example, saw anglers filling their baskets full of bream from the Southport Pier as well as making good catches of tailor and flathead. The days, however, of large boats of the likes of the SS Tweed entering over the Southport Bar had passed. By July 1898 a writer could state that 'sandbanks in the lower portion of the Broadwater spread at the present time from Porpoise Point (then the southern end of Stradbroke Island) almost across to the Southport jetty in a series of shallows and low bars'.[22] Thus began that gradual development of today's Spit and, eventually by 1916, the erosion of South Stradbroke Island.

The contrast between the placid Broadwater and the open Main Beach would become increasingly pronounced. In the late 1890s this worked to the town's advantage, and in 1905 it could once again be confidently stated that 'Southport easily holds sway among metropolitans as the queen of our southern watering-places ... an ideal seaside resort, affording safe and convenient boating on its land-locked waters and surf-bathing on its open beaches'.[23]

Chapter 5

Sandgate in the 1890s: Attractions and minor irritations

Barry Shaw

In the 1890s Sandgate finally came of age as crowds flocked to this bayside resort on each holiday occasion. True, the *Brisbane courier* had commented on Sandgate's popularity as early as Christmas Eve 1873: 'This favorite watering place was, as is usual on holidays, very largely frequented by Brisbaneites ... fully 300 visitors being present'.[1] But this was small fare compared with the estimated 8000 people who journeyed by train to Sandgate on New Year's Day 1899.[2] Clearly the former backwater and preserve of Brisbane's elite had been transformed into the 'Brighton of the Brisbanites'.[3]

Ease of access, due primarily to the opening of the railway in May 1882, allowed increasing numbers of visitors to sample Sandgate's charms. In 1887 *Cassell's picturesque Australasia* listed these as 'a pier of no mean pretensions for the accommodation of visitors from the capital ... facilities for bathing ... several public bathing houses and shelter sheds. With these and other attractions it is not so surprising that the place should be so largely resorted to by the citizens of Brisbane, pining for breezes that are the breath of life to lungs which, in the heated air of the capital, have almost forgotten their office'.[4]

The beneficial effects of the sea air would certainly not have been lost on the resort's visitors during the 1890s. Indeed the construction of the Lady Musgrave Sanatorium in 1884 testified to the early recognition of one of Sandgate's most important natural assets.

Built at a cost of £400, the sanatorium was officially opened three years later by the governor's wife, Lady Musgrave, who had personally provided funds for the furnishing of a ward. In the yearly report for 1896-97 it was noted that the convalescent home catered for 87 patients.[5] Most of these were children, but a number of weary nurses also benefited from the healthful effects of Sandgate.

In most respects the sanatorium was ideally located for recuperative purposes, but during inclement weather it was perilously close to Cabbage Tree Creek. One reporter, describing the near isolation of the sanatorium by flood water, a not uncommon occurrence in the 1890s, commented, 'It indeed seems at the present time a most insanitary and uncomfortable refuge for either adults or children, be they sick or ill'.[6]

Of course, weather permitting, the hale and hearty could always partake of the invigorating sea air with a stroll along the pier. Sandgate's attempt to emulate the fashionable resorts on the south and east coasts of Victorian England, where possession of a pier symbolised prosperity, was not entirely successful.

The Sandgate Pier Company had been formed on 16 February 1882 'to acquire freehold or leasehold property in the municipality of Sandgate on which to erect a Pier, bathing houses, hotel, pavilions etc. for the purpose of business and amusement ...'. Unfortunately the pier did not get off to an auspicious beginning. As first constructed, it was 18 feet 9 inches wide and 850 feet long, but due to a miscalculation of the water depth, an extra 300 feet had to be added in 1883-84 to enable passenger vessels to dock at the end.

Baths and dressing rooms were constructed on both sides of the pier extending to the 300 foot mark and were enclosed by wire netting secured on ti-tree saplings and swamp mahogany piles. The male baths, measuring 90 feet by 40 feet, and the male dressing rooms were on the southern side, while the smaller female baths, 68 feet by 40 feet and dressing rooms, were on the northern side. The latter were protected from prying eyes by a tin fence. The men's bathing enclosure was subsequently shark proofed by iron railway battens.[7] This was just as well, considering a newspaper report of December 1894:

> Those who indulged in fishing from the pier at Sandgate yesterday morning were treated to a bit of excitement consequent on the hooking of a shark by Mr Brosnan ... he was rewarded by the hooking of the brute about 7 feet in length ... . But at an inopportune moment the line became caught on the pier and with a terrific jerk something gave way and the big fish made off.

The writer then offered a few salutary words of caution: 'Bathers especially at high tide should be careful, and not venture out too far'.[8]

Despite the people who came to fish, bathe in the segregated areas and promenade, the pier was bedevilled with financial problems. In 1888 it went into voluntary receivership, and when Sandgate Municipal Council took control in 1901 extensive repairs were necessary.

For those who did not wish to avail themselves of the pier's bathing facilities, public decency was still scrupulously maintained by the provision of private and public bathing

5.0 Sandgate Pier in turbulent times, after the 1893 cyclone (JOL)

5.1 Sandgate Pier in tranquil times, 1895 (JOL)

boxes. Scattered along the beachfront in pairs, one for men, one for women, the private bathing boxes were wheeled to the water's edge so that bathers could enter the water with the utmost dignity and discretion.[9] Even so, the bathing boxes quickly became a source of controversy. In 1905 when Sandgate's mayor proposed a tax on private boxes, a letter to the *Brisbane courier* complained vehemently about the 'obnoxious bathing-box tax' claiming that 'when the first big storm washes them away they will not be re-erected as hitherto, thus ruining one of the main attractions to Sandgate as a watering place'.[10] For some the removal of the bathing boxes presented not such a disagreeable prospect. Comparing Sandgate with Lady Macquarie's Chair at Sydney, one correspondent asked, and with some justification, 'Would that be as beautiful if the view were interrupted by backyard boxes?'[11]

While bathing boxes preserved modesty, the construction of groynes encouraged segregated swimming areas. This practice was rigidly enforced at Sandgate throughout the 1890s, and remained a particularly long-lived feature of the resort. A letter from 'Shocked' in 1909 noted that at

> our premier watering place ... the latest fad ... is to have a police constable parading up and down Flinders Parade with the ostensible object of checking 'mixed bathing'. Last Sunday the cry was raised, 'Hi, there, do you know that mixed bathing is not allowed here?' 'No,' said the startled delinquent. 'Well it isn't; and so stop it,' said the bobby. In a short while instead of having fathers and mothers and families bringing their little ones down on Sundays and holidays to enjoy a swim at the seaside, and thus invigorate and recuperate them from the effects of the sweltering heat in the city, we will find them going to Wynnum and Manly, where the officious policeman won't interfere.[12]

If bathing was too energetic, and liable to arouse the ire of the law, the visitor could always watch the annual Sandgate regatta – weather permitting! Inaugurated in 1889, the regatta of 1895 was memorable for all the wrong reasons. First there was a problem with the crowded early morning trains. To alleviate the congestion, it was decided that the 9.10am would run express from Central, but as the *Brisbane courier* gloomily reported, it 'stopped at almost every station to pick-up passengers and so limited was the accommodation that women and children who held second-class tickets had to travel by the first-class carriages set aside for smokers'. This inconvenience to smokers paled to insignificance as spectators and yachtsmen alike realized that the weather was hardly conducive to sailing. 'Up to noon', the *Courier* continued, 'there was not a breath of wind, and this combined with the continuous rain, considerably marred the day's enjoyment'.

The lack of a breeze induced many competitors to remain at their moorings in Cabbage Tree Creek, but others, 'more keen on the races got out of the creek ... under difficulties'. Within half an hour of the start the wind 'was blowing with considerable force' with the result that three boats collided while rounding the marked boat off Woody Point and one, the Plover, capsized. Fortunately the crew were quickly rescued from their upturned vessel, and later the water police from Lytton towed the Plover to Woody Point jetty.[13]

Not all Sandgate's attractions offered quite as much excitement. For music lovers there were regular performances by the town band at the end of the pier or in Moora Park with its graceful palms and substantial fig trees and its commanding views of the bay. Sandgate was also keen to utilise the park's potential. In November 1897 a bandstand, complete with gaslight and surrounding seats was erected. A kiosk, which was to have been built beneath the bandstand, was not proceeded with, as the mayor was uncertain as to his position in charging for its use.

The *Courier* described the preparations for the official opening: 'The Town Band, which had been practising hard for some time, will open the stand on Friday of this week, and intends to give public performances every Friday through the summer'.[14] Perhaps the band needed to practise hard, for only the year before a correspondent had noted the reaction to a performance at the pier: 'Surprise was expressed at the great improvement the band had made in its playing during the past few months, and although possessing only thirteen instruments the programme was very creditably got through'.[15]

5.2 The bandstand, Moora Park, Sandgate, late 1890s (JOL)

By Christmas 1900, however, the Town Band had improved. It was not only musically proficient but apparently also capable of remarkable feats of endurance. At 9pm on Christmas Eve the band commenced playing carols at Moora Park, and afterwards was invited into Howrah for 'refreshments'.[16] Not to be outdone, three prominent Sandgate citizens decided to do likewise and 'would not be denied, so the band had to again partake'. The band 'then went the round of some twenty-eight places partaking of refreshments at Messrs. A. H. Hill, George Agnew, H. J. Brown, George Cowlishaw, having to refuse the kind offers of Messrs. F. Matthews, F.W.B. Mann, E. Phelan, W. Barrett, L. Browne, George Staheli, and others'. Their final performance at 2.15am on Christmas morning was sensibly followed by coffee.[17]

Sandgate also offered other forms of entertainment. In July 1890 a brass band heralded the first public appearance of the Sandgate Minstrels by parading through the streets of the town. The troupe, under the direction of Constable McCarthy, performed at Sandgate's Victoria Skating Rink, which had been specially decorated with 'flags, Chinese lanterns and coloured oil lamps'. The audience, 'the largest ever seen at a concert in Sandgate', was entertained by Tommy Morris, a South Sea Islander who performed the best song in the first part of the program. Despite some local talent, the reporter for the *Courier* ominously singled out only one other performer for praise: 'One of the tambourine players was exceptionally good'. The paper concluded that, 'The entertainment was full of fun, and highly appreciated', although probably not quite up to the demanding standards of the reporter: 'No doubt at the next concert, which is said will take place soon, a great improvement will be observable'.[18]

Possibly the lecture offered by the Reverend G.D. Buchanan on 'Naples and Pompeii' was more to the taste of the refined members of Sandgate society. Even so, prospective patrons were warned that the lecture would be punctuated 'at intervals' by musical selections performed by local amateurs.[19] Clearly there was no escaping the attentions of Sandgate's welter of musical talent.

For gourmets a highlight of the trip to Sandgate was the opportunity to sample the seafood on offer at Baxter's Oyster Saloon. John Thomas Baxter, a fisherman, had been among the first land purchasers at Sandgate. In 1862 he opened his famous saloon opposite the jetty which still until recently bore his name.[20]

Baxter specialized in crab and oyster suppers claiming that 'the oysters are always kept in the water and taken out as required'.[21] This was no less than the truth, for he stored his catch in fish traps and oyster sheds in Cabbage Tree Creek.

While patrons enjoyed fresh seafood throughout the 1890s, there were difficulties. On 23 January 1893 the *Brisbane courier* reported that during 'a storm of terrific force ... one of Mr Baxter's fishing-boats, with net ... dragged her moorings and was swamped; the net and other gear were washed out of her'.[22] More seriously, in March 1897 Baxter drowned after his foot became entangled in the steps of his jetty. His widow, however, continued to operate the saloon for some years after her husband's death.

During the 1890s Sandgate boasted a variety of attractions, and whether the visitor came for the invigorating sea air, the stroll along the pier, the regatta, fishing, seafood, bathing or the concerts in Moora Park, there was something for everyone. Even the budding beetle and butterfly collector, Millais Culpin, found the trip to Sandgate rewarding, if not a little irritating:

> On Sunday I footed it to Sandgate, a watering place on Moreton Bay. Took another new species, & made my acquaintance with real live mosquitoes at Cabbage Tree Creek, West Sandgate. (I've not done itching yet).[23]

Chapter 6

Painters and patrons: Art in Brisbane 1890-1906

Pam Barnett

After the marine painter Isaac Walter Jenner arrived to settle in Queensland in 1883, he stated that one of the first things he noticed was the 'absence of such a fruitful educational institution as an Art Gallery'.[1] Although he set about stimulating public support to establish such an institution, it was years before the Queensland National Art Gallery was finally opened to the public, and then without Jenner in its principal guiding role as curator.

6.0 Isaac Walter Jenner (JOL)

Not only was there no gallery at this time, but opportunities for exhibiting any fine arts in Brisbane were extremely limited. The only venue in which a practising artist could regularly show works to the general public was at the annual Queensland National Association Exhibition, where the first separate fine arts section was catalogued in 1884, including eight pictures by Jenner. The other two local Brisbane painters, who were to join him in forming the Queensland Art Society in 1887, Oscar Fristrom and Karl Wirth, also entered pictures in this exhibition.

This formation of an artists' association, with the express purpose of providing a specific environment in which to exhibit fine arts, augmented the annual QNA exhibition, and began to accustom potential patrons to the leisurely pleasures of picture galleries. Although Jenner stated that he was, 'obliged to hang some of the most abominable stuff imaginable at first', he went on to say: 'it will I am afraid be yet many years before the people here see clearly the civilizing influence that art exercises on a country'.[2]

Jenner appreciated that cultivating a taste for the viewing and collecting of works of art required a community of some maturity, one which had advanced beyond many of the elemental rigours of pioneering life, and had achieved a standard of security where leisure hours could extend beyond mere respite from labour, and, in their highest form, provide morally uplifting experiences. In nineteenth century theory, art was the ideal vehicle to provide these pleasures, and the cultivation of taste for such experiences was well within Jenner's perception of his capacity both as a painter and an art educator. He outlined his educational program thus:

> One of my schemes is to hold occasional Art Unions of my works so as to try and increase and improve the public taste for art in an inexpensive way. Next to inform my patrons (few of whom have been to England and still fewer who have ever thought of studying the usages of a civilized country) how and where to hang their oil and water colours in their houses giving them hints as to what are good or bad qualities in pictures, where to stand and look at them and how to focus a picture and how to treat works of art generally.[3]

Jenner, like most other artists working in Brisbane at that time, gave lessons in painting, albeit mostly private lessons. Those artists lucky enough to obtain teaching positions at the Technical College (School of Arts), where the art lessons had become a recreational activity mainly for ladies of the middle classes, and at the more prestigious schools, were assured of a small income of patronage and the opportunity to espouse their theories on art.[4]

The education for cultivated leisure was undoubtedly an important part of secondary schooling, particularly for girls. Mrs O'Connor's school, Duporth, at Oxley, utilised the services of local artist Robert Rayment as a teacher, until his death in 1892, as well as her own considerable talent. Janet O'Connor and her girls are recorded as having exhibited in the 'fine arts' section at the National Agricultural and Industrial Exhibition in 1887.

The students at Brisbane Girls Grammar School had received some instruction in watercolour painting since 1878, when Miss Mary MacKinlay, the 'Lady Principal', engaged through the assistance of Girton College, Cambridge, insisted that a 'gentleman be engaged' to instruct the girls.[5] By 1885, these lessons (and it is not known who gave them) had ceased, and the girls were only receiving lessons in drawing from the boys' teacher, Thomas MacLeod, who (probably resuming the same services he had performed for Mrs O'Connor when she was principal of the school in the 1870s) crossed the no-man's land between the schools for their lessons until his death in August 1886.[6] His place was then taken for drawing at the girls' school by Joseph Augustus Clarke, who had organised the drawing curriculum for the Normal School.[7] The headmistress, by now Miss Pells, stated in her annual report, 'The drawing classes are making good progress and in several instances I have found not only much skill and accuracy but evidences of considerable artistic taste'.[8]

When Clarke died in 1890, the school quickly found a replacement. Godfrey Rivers, engaged to follow Clarke at the Technical College in Brisbane, was employed as a visiting master to teach drawing at the Girls Grammar School at the end of 1890. Described in the annual report as 'a gentleman from Sydney', he arrived in 1891 to find J. Findlay McFadyen already employed as a visiting member of staff to teach painting.[9] A large collection of McFadyen's works was owned and loaned to the Society of Artists' exhibitions by Henry J. Oxley, a member of the school's board. However, Rivers assumed the teaching of both subjects the following year.

To the new headmistress, Miss Eliza Fewings, who felt that 'the love of order, neatness and beauty should, I think, be fostered at school', it was a matter of some pride that works done in the girls' leisure hours 'at short notice' should attract special prizes at the QNA in 1896. Her satisfaction at the 'high character of the work being done' had been noted in the previous year's annual report. Her satisfaction is demonstrated in the fact that Rivers added the Brisbane High School for Girls, later Somerville House, to his teaching commitments when Miss Fewings left BGGS and opened her own school on Wickham Terrace in 1900.

The purpose of this 'art' teaching was definitely not intended to encourage female students to embrace the life of an artist. Its purpose was to nurture an artistic sensibility, to foster a love of art, and to provide for future recreational pleasure in drawing, watercolour painting and other activities allied to the 'fine arts'.

There is no doubt that schools played an important role in the patronage of local artists. The presence of Sir Samuel Griffith, Edwin Lilley, Henry J. Oxley and Sir Arthur Palmer, at various times members of the grammar schools' board of trustees and also that of the National Art Gallery when established, meant that an artist employed at the grammar schools was selected by powerful men who were in a position to promote the artist and were also eager collectors of art themselves. The collections of loaned art works hung at the Queensland National Association and Queensland Art Society exhibitions show that all these men owned works by Jenner, McFadyen and other prominent local artists as well as minor international ones. It is known that Rivers painted a portrait of Griffith, but little research has been done on local portraiture.

The most notable international works owned and shown locally before the opening of the gallery were a suite of engravings of religious subjects by Gustave Doré. These had been purchased by E.T.B. Hutchinson of the Elite Photographic Studio, who hoped to profit from his entrepreneurial venture, and were offered for sale to the public at 15 guineas a piece at the QNA exhibition in 1887.

Jenner was not alone in his desire to procure that 'indispensable ornament' of a gallery for Brisbane.[10] Philanthropic parties had presented works to the government for the express purpose of establishing a public art collection, and the general public, by now aware of the leisure delight of visiting local, inter-colonial and international expositions, which had become popular over the last half of the nineteenth century, were receptive to the extension of this type of spectacle as a leisure activity.

One of Jenner's schemes to raise money for an art gallery, as well as a means of cultivating local 'artistic taste', was to hold occasional art unions of his works. This means of selling paintings had arrived in Australia from England about 1840 and became immensely popular.[11] For the first of these ventures in 1887 he offered 400 tickets at one guinea each in a drawing of 58 works of art. He obtained the 'distinguished patronage' of, among others, Griffith and Sir Arthur Palmer, and the services, as referees, of Reginald Heber Roe, S.W. Brooks and E. MacDonnell, all of whom were connected with the grammar schools at various times.[12] Apparently another art union drawn in 1890, offered 76 works and utilised the services of Henry Oxley, another BGS trustee, as one of the three referees.[13]

All the well known collectors of Brisbane secured works in the drawing of this art union: Griffith, T.J. Byrnes, Roe, Oxley and D.T. Thistlethwaite, who was the secretary of the Queensland Artists' Association. The possession of fine original works of art was supposed to greatly enhance the hours spent privately at leisure in one's home. Despite the 1890s being years of floods, financial crises and anxiety, collectors were able to, and desirous of, acquiring fine works.

Many fine painters visited Queensland and exhibited in Brisbane in the 1890s. These included Henri Tebbitt and Henry Reilly, but it was the arrival of Rivers to work in Brisbane which added the greatest stimulus to the local art scene. His recent overseas

6.1 Queensland Art Gallery, 1895 (JOL)

experience and his more modern approach to art was to gain him personal support, and his three page manifesto presented to the government for the establishment of an art gallery was finally to gain the support of Sir Hugh Nelson.

On the 25 March 1895 a gallery, to be known as the Queensland National Gallery, was finally opened on the upper floor of Brisbane Town Hall in Queen Street. Griffith, Horace Tozer, Boyd Morehead, William Townley and Alderman Robert Fraser were named as trustees. Griffith was elected president. Rivers acted as inaugural secretary and, in practical terms, the director.

The opening exhibition of the Queensland National Gallery was a mix of minor old master works, copies of old masters, prints and works by local artists, many of which were lent.[14] Since that time – in fact quite recently – conservation work has been carried out on the works bequeathed by Thomas Lodge Murray-Prior, which were the nucleus of the collection. Many of them have now been securely attributed to more distinguished painters than was originally thought. The collection included works by David Teniers, Willem van der Velde, Peter Breughel the younger, Alexander Coosemans and Gerard Seghers.

It is well to examine some of the first works exhibited more closely, as the selection gave not only an overview of local painters and patrons, but was also to be important in the formation of local taste. Even a gallery with such a 'modest' beginning could, and did, present a didactic journey through the history of art, echoing that presented by the great 'survey' museums of Europe. The copies of antique statuary, which were added to the collection in the late 1890s, made a logical beginning with Greek purity, and recalled the lofty antecedents of current sculpture, and indeed all art in the 'western tradition'. A mini renaissance was then evoked with Bartolozzi's engravings after Michelangelo and Raphael's *Madonna della sedia,* in copy of course, which is so clearly visible in the centre of the photograph showing the hanging in the first display, and illustrating the next great phase of western art.

The copy after Titian's *Danae,* also clearly visible in the photograph, was one of a group of such copies, painted and donated by pastoralist and amateur painter William George Wilson. They linked nicely with the series of engravings purchased in London specifically for the gallery by Griffith. This brought the collection through the logical progression of the baroque to the development of the English schools, climaxing with Turner and sublime landscape, and then on to the embryonic Australian school.

The opening exhibition was enlarged by loans from the private collections of notable local patrons such as James Dickson, Griffith and Oxley. Although many had been shown before, the 'gallery' context added lustre to their works, as did their own names to the gallery.

The etchings by Gustave Doré, mentioned before and still unsold, were presented to the gallery by Hutchinson, and local artist Oscar Fristrom gave a small portrait of a local man, James Davis, known as *Duramboi.* It was one of only a handful of works which would have had a contemporary Queensland reference.

It is here that two major works given by local artists present strongly contrasting approaches to what constituted a 'gallery piece'.

Jenner's *Cape Chiddley, Coast of Labrador* was his special and carefully considered gift to the new gallery. Shown at the Queensland Art Society's exhibition in 1893, he altered it somewhat for presentation. His letter of gift to the trustees said:

> I am desirous as the parent of the Art Society of Queensland to offer one of my works ... through and by favour of you to the people of Queensland to be their property forever. This new picture has historical interest as having been somewhat connected with an expedition sent in search of Sir John Franklin and on account of the singular manner of return to England of one ship of the squadron after having been abandoned 16 months earlier by Sir E. Belcher.[15]

The picture is a summation of all the elements needed for an uplifting experience for the viewer. Jenner called it 'a tragic romance of the North West Passage'.[16] Its message is, that despite the heroic and epic endeavours of man, his achievements are insignificant

6.2 Queensland National Art Gallery (JOL)

in the face of the forces of nature and the might of God. Its connection with Australia is tenuous, but it speaks of Jenner's knowledge, as an ex-sailor, of the sea. It makes an interesting comparison with his *Sunrise, Sandgate Beach,* now in the Queensland Art Gallery's collection, a picture which he would have considered purely domestic.

In one of his writings, Jenner listed the qualities which he felt the 'genuine artist' must have. The list illustrates clearly his commitment to the English landscape tradition which had produced painters like Thomas Girton and J.M.W. Turner. The artist 'must possess judgement to select a picturesque subject, ability to sketch the same correctly, talent to compose grandly, an active faculty for invention, a fine sense of feeling for light, space, and atmosphere, a thorough appreciation of tone in colour, and power to combine them into a harmonious whole'.[17]

Rivers also presented a painting to the gallery: *Woolshed, New South Wales*. It presages the direction which gallery purchases took in the ensuing years under his curatorship. It has no elevated theme, but portrays men at work, albeit shearing by hand – a type of work strongly under pressure from steam shears in 1890 – and makes naturalism, not nature, its subject. It takes its inspiration from the works of the French Barbizon school and the Newlyn Group in Britain, and it is the works of these schools which featured in the first purchases made by the new gallery, expressly on Rivers' recommendation.

One of the most distinguished pictures in the inaugural exhibition was the one loaned by James Dickson. In 1881 Miss Mary MacKinlay had resigned her position as lady principal of the Girls Grammar School to marry Dickson. The following year the couple must have bought a fine painting by Angelica Kauffmann, *The Deserted Costanza,* whilst travelling in Europe. Dickson eventually bequeathed this work to the Queensland National Gallery in 1900. The literary subject, the elevated theme of wrongful abandonment, its high tragedy and its Roman setting, made this picture the type of work Jenner would have considered highly appropriate for a gallery picture.

The main problem for the new gallery was to sustain attendances after the initial enthusiasm. In excess of 20,000 people visited the gallery in the first twelve months. The ability to lure patrons resided not in a constant and unchanging display, but in the opportunity to see new work or works. This depended upon the purchasing power of the meagre funding allowed by the governments of the day. Even before the first month of viewing was completed, a letter to the *Brisbane courier* called for exchange programs of works of art with the southern colonies.

Several purchases were made in the first years, but they were not sufficient in number to change the static nature of the collection. Difficult access to the rooms, with the climb up flights of stairs, discouraged the general public. This was not made easier when the gallery moved to a 'permanent home' in the specially constructed space at the top of the newly completed Executive Building in George Street in 1905.

In that year the southern states of Australia witnessed the triumphant tour of Holman Hunt's re-creation of his celebrated painting *The Light of the World.* The first version of this was painted in 1851, the second in 1881, and the third of 1904 was purchased by Charles Booth and sent on a triumphal tour of the empire. Crowds flocked to see it. It was exhibited everywhere free of charge, and it was estimated that in Sydney 8.39 persons per minute passed in front of it. Norman Lindsay irreverently said, 'that in Australia people were naturally keen to see a picture of Jesus going out late at night to the dunny at the back of the house'.[18] 60,000 people saw it in Brisbane while it was on show, and on the last Sunday more than 60 persons per minute were admitted to the gallery.[19]

Isaac Walter Jenner had died in 1901. He had seen the fruition of his dream and a gallery established in Brisbane. His own representation to the government for a gallery had borne no fruit, and he sustained a querulous relationship with the Art Society he helped form. His gift to the gallery was its sole representation of his work, for none was purchased from him. He must have felt his efforts to promote art in Brisbane had gone largely unnoticed and wrote his own vindication of his efforts which is now in the Art Gallery files. He did not live to see the triumph of the exhibition of Holman Hunt's work, nor the acclaim his own work was to later achieve. Of course, as he said, 'I, as the founder and I hope the benefactor of art in this colony ... was marked out for martyrdom and have been figuratively hung, drawn and quartered'.

Chapter 7

Books and reading in the 1890s

Shirley McCorkindale

In a paper presented to the conference of the Library Association of Australasia in 1896, A.G. Melville, discussing the Australian appetite for books, said: 'Since 1860 existing public libraries and literary institutions have expanded, new ones have been opened, and all round the literary and intellectual life of the Australian people has been kept alive, and also quickened'.[1] If this were applied to the literary and intellectual life of Brisbane in the 1890s, we would find a decided imbalance in favour of the middle class who were offered much more in the way of intellectual and literary stimulation than members of the working class.

Brisbane was not lacking in libraries in this period. *Pugh's almanac* lists several clubs and associations with libraries, for example the Johnsonian Club, Brisbane Liedertafel, Brisbane Musical Union, Queensland Amateur Photographic Society, Royal Society of Queensland and Royal Geographical Society (Queensland).[2] Some of these libraries even had a designated librarian. The Temperance Hall and the Oddfellows Hall offered free public libraries. While the various municipalities throughout the city boasted government subsidised schools of arts, the only such institution of real significance was the (North) Brisbane School of Arts which claimed the majority of subscribers throughout the Brisbane area, and which had by far the biggest collection.[3] However, the most significant and prestigious library in Brisbane was the library of the parliament, although it had (and still has) a very restricted circle of users. The quality and size of its

7.0 Denis O' Donovan CMG (JOL)

collection was outstanding, and it maintained its ascendancy as the state's most impressive library until well into the twentieth century.

Just a week after the first sitting of parliament in May 1860, the Legislative Assembly set in train moves for the establishment of a library. Library committees of the Legislative Council and Legislative Assembly proposed the establishment of a joint library with an annual budget of £300.

The first full-time librarian, Reverend James R. Moffatt, was appointed on 1 August 1861. When Moffatt retired, he was succeeded by Denis O'Donovan, who served from 1874 to 1901. Before coming to Australia, O'Donovan worked in France as a professor of modern languages and literature.[4] During his incumbency he compiled the three volume, *Analytical and classified catalogue of the Library of the Parliament of Queensland.* Apart from the social sciences, the major emphases of the collection were biography and foreign travel. Evidence of O'Donovan's scholarship and industry is provided by the catalogue which featured indexing of periodicals and also of selected monographs. Entries for persons included brief biographical details. Today O'Donovan's catalogue still has significance as a major bibliography; it is interesting to note some of the rare and more valuable works listed, works more suited to the library of a bibliophile rather than to a reference library for parliamentarians.

The Brisbane School of Arts, established in 1849, did not aim at an exclusive clientele. On 15 June 1866 Governor George Bowen, speaking at the opening of a new hall and shops for the School of Arts, said, 'In such associations all classes of the community can have their moral tone elevated, their intellectual faculties sharpened, their industry excited and their exertions stimulated by friendly emulation and combined study'.[5] Bowen was merely echoing in part the philosophy behind the establishment of mechanics' institutes (or schools of arts as they were called in New South Wales and Queensland), the improvement of the minds and the moral tone of the working class.[6]

However, poorly paid workers would have had little incentive to join the School of Arts, paying an annual subscription of £1, 5s a quarter or 7s 6d for a quarterly family subscription. While the Brisbane School of Arts had the largest subscriber base of any school of arts in the Brisbane area, the actual number of subscribers was a tiny proportion of the total Brisbane population; in the reports of the general committee subscriber statistics for the decade hovered around 1600. In 1892, as a special project, government offices and businesses were canvassed for new subscribers – just five new subscriptions were obtained.[7]

Nevertheless non-subscribers were not welcome to use the library facilities; at one meeting of the general committee a complaint was made about the large number of visitors and non-members using the library.[8] The general committee relented slightly during Exhibition week of that year and advertised, inviting visitors to the reading room and the chess club.[9] Students of the Brisbane Technical College were offered special terms but could not borrow fiction.[10]

The general committee and its library sub-committee, consisting of many of Brisbane's prominent citizens, approached its duties with missionary zeal. Materials from the collection were purchased from overseas booksellers, for example Mudie's, and from local and interstate booksellers. Subscribers' suggestions for purchases were regularly voted upon and donations were solicited; local authors donated their works. An impressive range of newspapers and journals was held; in late 1890 it was agreed that a subscription to the *Bulletin* be taken out specifically for the ladies' reading room.[11] The titles purchased were indicative of the wide-ranging and often fairly sophisticated interests of some subscribers. However, even with government subsidy, budgetary constraints ensured that purchases were carefully monitored.

At one library sub-committee meeting, a member, noting that fiction represented 77 percent of loans, suggested that a much larger quantity of fiction be purchased. 'Mr Brooks and Dr Lyons objected to the idea of purchasing novels to such an extent and thought it unnecessary to pander to such a taste for novel reading'.[12] Sometimes the committee was not able to maintain this high moral tone. 'In consequence of the demand for the *Sorrows of Satan*, by Marie Corelli, it was agreed that 6 more copies be procured'. Nine copies in all were purchased.[13] Nevertheless, at the end of the decade the general committee could say that: 'Although in view of the large demand for works of fiction the preponderance was necessarily given to that section, the sub-committee was still adhering to their determination to improve all departments of general literature by the gradual addition of the best and most notable works, and they had no hesitation in spending from £1 to £1 10s, or even more, on a single work if its importance warrants such an expenditure'.[14]

The age-old problems of theft and mutilation in libraries seem to have come as a complete surprise to committee members who waxed indignant over the anti-social behaviour of some subscribers. After one serious bout of mutilations, the library sub-committee, reporting on the trial of the man arrested for the charge, stated that 'the culprit had been sentenced to 18 months imprisonment with hard labour but that the sentence had been suspended under the First Offenders Act'.[15] Just four months later, after a member had confessed to the 'serious irregularity' of hiding a book thus 'depriving other members of its use for a time', it was agreed that, in the future, such offence would result in the cancellation of membership.[16]

The minutes of the general committee meeting of 19 February 1890 recorded approval for the Brisbane Literary Circle to meet in the library. The Circle was championed by Reginald Heber Roe, principal of Boys Grammar School. In an address entitled, 'A plea for a reading society', Roe, speaking at a meeting sponsored by the School of Arts, proposed a literary circle using reading courses and based on the American literary society, the Chatauqua Literary & Scientific Circle.[17] The Brisbane Literary Circle was established in August 1888; in December 1892 the journal, *The AHR*, published by the Australasian Home Reading Union, announced:

> The Brisbane Literary Circle the pioneer of the Home Reading Movement in Australia has, after a distinguished career of four years, sworn allegiance to the younger and more national association, and is henceforth a part of the Australasian Home Reading Union. This will probably mean in the near future an accession of several hundred members, without taking into account the influence of its example, and of the active proselytism throughout the colony of Queensland.[18]

The first issue announced the purpose of the Australasian Home Reading Union, founded in January 1892 under the auspices of the Literature Section of the Australasian Association for the Advancement of Science. The Union was to draw up and publish reading courses to meet the tastes and needs of all classes of reader, publish a journal supporting the reading courses, and promote the organisation of groups in various centres.[19] Annual membership was 2s 6d, which included a subscription to *The AHR*. Meetings could include papers and discussions on selected readings, musical items and recitations. The Brisbane circles included in their program river excursions and picnics.

In August 1894 there was discussion within the Union on the desirability of aligning Union reading courses with university extension courses. In the same issue the Toowoomba Circle reported:

> Courses of lectures are being delivered by the doctors of the town who have already volunteered their services. Dr Faulkner gave the last, a very interesting and lucid lecture on 'Respiration'. He illustrated with the organs of a sheep specially prepared for the purpose of the lecture. This course is really in the nature of university extension work, and is of a strictly educational nature.[20]

In 1894 there were reports of three circles in Brisbane – Brisbane Literary Circle, Highgate Hill Circle, St Andrews Circle.[21] Ipswich, Toowoomba and Rockhampton also had circles, but in the following year it was noted that membership was decreasing: 'Members who join for custom's sake, or to wile away an idle hour, gradually drop off, and those who really desire companionship instead of reading, join quiet groups'.[22] The most popular reading circles were in English literature.

At the annual assembly of the Union in 1895 the comment was made that, 'so far the working classes had fought somewhat shy of them'; nevertheless the hope was expressed, 'in circles where some members had a little time to spare an evening during the month would yet be devoted to small circles of men and women belonging to the working classes. Amongst those who came to their doors with goods or waited at their tables there were many well able to appreciate high thinking'. Members should try to establish new circles to encourage those 'who would otherwise read unwisely or not at all'.[23] If members of the working class could tolerate such patronising, how relevant would they have found a group in which headmaster Roe had pressed for the retention of Greek literature in the readings because of the 'similarity of many salient phases of modern life with those of ancient Greece'?[24]

The Brisbane School of Arts and the literary circles had an obvious middle-class bias, but there were some resources, admittedly few in number, designed specifically for the working class. On 10 August 1894 the general committee of the School of Arts reported on a request for books by a representative of the Trades Hall. The committee offered 100 unwanted books at a nominal price and a further 100 gratis. The offer was accepted. The minutes give no indication as to the quality or condition of the works offered.

Moreover, by 1890 the working class had its own paper, the *Worker*. As Joy Guyatt has observed:

> From the 1880s, leaders of the labour movement consistently believed that only by educating the rank and file would the wage earners achieve the organized solidarity necessary to obtain justice from the employing class. A labour paper was to be the

7.1 Library, Brisbane School of Arts, 1908 (JOL)

means to this end for experience had shown that the capitalistic press was on the side of the employers'.[25]

On 1 March 1890 volunteers handed out the first issue of the *Worker* along the route of the Eight Hour Day procession.[26] The subtitle of the first issue read: 'monthly journal of the associated workers of Queensland'.

The first editor of the *Worker* was the utopian, William Lane, who had previously worked as a journalist on the *Courier*, *Queensland figaro* and the *Evening observer*. In November 1887 Lane established the *Boomerang* with J.G. Drake and Alfred Walker. The initial editorial stated:

> We are for this Australia, for the nationality that is creeping to the verge of being, for the progressive people that is just plucking aside the curtain that veils fate. Behind us lies the Past with its smashing empires, its falling thrones, its dotard races, before us lies the Future into which Australia is plunging, this Australia of ours that burns with the feverish energy of youth and that is wise with the wisdom for which ten thousand generations have suffered and toiled.[27]

Despite this fairly meaningless bombast the *Boomerang*, during its brief life, was a vehicle for vigorous discussion on social and industrial issues.

The editorial for the first issue of the *Worker* stated: 'The political attention of the WORKER will be limited to those questions which closely affect the welfare of the wage-earning masses ...'.[28] The paper covered labour and socialist news and educational articles on economics, history and Marxist philosophy. It also featured extracts from writers such as Macaulay, Locke and Southey, and published poems by Henry Lawson, William Kidston, Francis Adams and Charles Mackay.[29]

Lane was extremely interested in a work by American novelist Edward Bellamy, *Looking backward 2000-1887*. Bellamy's theory was that the solution to American society's ills was adherence to the principle of absolute economic equality. His novel tells the story of a young man who, like Rip Van Winkle, fell asleep and woke up into a different society, in this case a utopian, egalitarian society.[30] Lane started the serialisation of *Looking backward* in the first issue of the *Worker*.

Soon he was promoting the *Worker* Book Fund, the purpose of which was to raise funds to establish a cooperative book exchange to obtain copies of socialist books such as: Bellamy's *Looking backward*; Morrison Davidson, *The old order and the new*; H.M. Hyndman, *Historical basis of socialism*; Henry George, *Social problems*; H.V. Mills *Poverty and the state*; members of the Fabian Society, *Essays on socialism*; George Bernard Shaw, *An unsocial socialist*.[31] 'A sailor, a bushman, an artisan, a farmer or a labourer' could acquire such books cheaply. Shearing sheds could build up libraries cheaply, but this project could also be useful for the townsman: 'How hard it is to get progressive books even in Brisbane! How they are jumped and begged for, almost stolen, by hundreds who have heard of them and ache to read them when they see them!'[32]

In August 1890 the *Worker* advised of the opening of a reading room within the paper's office where Queensland, interstate and overseas papers were available.[33]

By the end of the decade, provision of library facilities was still substandard; Brisbane lagged behind the rest of Australia in establishing a free public library. There was, however, considerable agitation for the establishment of such a facility. As early as 1871 during a period of financial difficulty for the Brisbane School of Arts, when membership had fallen to 350, Samuel Griffith suggested that the government be requested to establish a free public library and that the School of Arts should hand over the property to the government as the basis for such a library. This proposal was rejected, the committee decided on a membership drive.[34] On 2 October 1895 a meeting was convened at the Town Hall to discuss the establishment of a free public library. It was proposed that, as the nucleus of such a library, the library of the late Justice Thomas Harding be purchased. In the opinion of Arthur Rutledge, who attended the meeting,

> As to the School of Arts he did not think much of the books there, or the condition in which they were kept. With the late Justice Harding's library it was different and they ought to make some effort to acquire it.

Another attendee even suggested that the parliamentary library be opened to the public.[35]

The government did purchase Harding's library and on 18 January 1896 announced the establishment of the Brisbane Public Library. In 1898 the name was changed to the Public Library of Queensland, but the library, complete with a board of trustees, remained closed to the public for lack of a suitable building. The library finally opened on 29 April 1902 in the Old Museum building, a building never designed for a library, and just too late for Brisbane's reading public of the 1890s.

Chapter 8

Proliferating habits: Leisure and clothing in the 1890s

Margaret Maynard

We all like to take our annual holiday entitlements, regarding these relaxing periods almost as a sacred right. We are bombarded with offers of possible travel destinations and ways to fill our recreation hours with entertainment and activities. The range of clothing we can purchase for these particular periods and events is almost limitless. On the other hand we worry about excess leisure time and unpaid leave, for these resemble too closely the feared state of unemployment. Today free time can be a mixed blessing.

The concept of regularised, non-productive free time was enshrined in the modern city of the nineteenth century. Compared to today, fixed periods of leisure were not a certain part of work practices but, as the century progressed, the acquisition of rights to guaranteed leisure periods occupied many unions and working groups. By the end of the century, substantial gains had been made in Australia as in Britain although still, as a rule, the higher the status of worker the greater the time of available leisure. Thus for some classes of worker the struggle for the eight-hour day continued through the 1890s.

As designated leisure time was gradually acquired, in conjunction with improved economic and working conditions, it became more specifically and symbolically categorised as different from the workday hours. A proliferation of many new forms of social activities, amusements and pastimes occurred to fill these hours, which were deemed invigorating, healthy and of sound moral benefit to workers. One could say that the later nineteenth century was a time of substantial and accelerating changes to the way leisure time was consumed. In Brisbane these changes were especially marked in the 1890s.[1]

Jean Baudrillard has suggested that, despite the middle-class valorisation of labour, and the association of idleness with moral reprobation, leisure is not simply an aspect of the need to enjoy free unworking time or a form of functional repose. The consumption of empty time is an index of social status, and becomes trademarked time. Because it is an obligatory social phenomenon, with class specific structures and changing social rules, free time thus assumes symbolic value.[2] Its uselessness can readily be exploited by capitalism for its own ends.

One of the ways in which this happened at the end of the nineteenth century was through expanding the possible needs of leisure consumers, and investing these needs with associations and social values. The creation of completely new kinds of clothing, readily disseminated to the public through the mechanism of department stores, was part of this commercial exploitation. The other important factor which contributed to capitalist investment in leisure dress was the changing position of women. New activities, which were becoming socially acceptable for more emancipated women, especially those connected with sport and exercise, opened up an extended and extremely viable aspect of the clothing market.

The new leisure market was crucial to the expanding commercialisation of fashion at the time. Similarly, it was one facet of the increasing categorisation and subdivision of bourgeois wardrobes into specialised garments for all kinds of activities.[3] This matched other aspects of middle-class lives that were simultaneously being structured and regulated. The times of the day and the activities were so fractured that, in place of a more general categorisation into formal and informal clothing as before, manufacturers and garment producers began to create specialised travel, sport, nightwear, morning, dinner, tea and recreational clothes. For the upper and middle classes the choice of available types of garment could be extensive. *Australian etiquette*, published in 1885, described twenty-two different categories of women's garments, not counting wedding and mourning dress. These included dress for carriages, for promenading, riding, walking, theatre, lectures and concerts, bathing costumes, travelling dress, clothing for morning calls, morning street dress and visiting costumes.[4]

Of course, not all the new categories of dress can be described as leisure outfits. In fact defining the term leisure clothing is by no means straightforward, and there are significant implications with regard to class and gender. For the purposes of this paper the term leisure will be deemed to be recreation. The dress for certain leisured activities such as calling, shopping, dining and evening balls will not be included. In the nineteenth century some social rituals such as dinner parties, calling on neighbours, weddings etc., organised by bourgeois women and apparently leisurely and non-productive, were in fact active ways of supporting the class order and thus undertakings of crucial social value.[5] In this regard women's clothes for these occasions cannot be classed as recreational. Neither will uniforms for sports such as rowing or athletics be discussed. Whilst recreational and sporting activities often coincided, the formalisation and professionalisation of sport and the codification of rules that was occurring at this time also extended to the development of sports uniforms. As with dress in many of the professions like nursing and with school uniforms, these regularised garments were increasingly common in Queensland during the 1880s, but they should be regarded in a somewhat different light.

Men and women of all classes in Australia began to distinguish between their occupational and recreational clothing during the 1870s. This separation occurred at much the same time as the working week was restructured.[6] With additional time to spend on pastimes including sporting activities, adults wanted to relax in clothing that was different from their formal or occupational city wear. For instance, James Inglis described the leisure garments worn by men on an outing to Botany in 1880, clothes which could equally well have been worn in Brisbane at the same date. He writes of moth-eaten fur caps, slouching sombreros, dilapidated wideawakes, cricket caps, red night caps, jumpers, guernseys and tatterdemalion jackets, instead of the 'natty habiliments' and 'shining beavers' of city life.[7] In a certain sense his description matches with the kinds of clothing used even today by spectators at cricket or football matches.

The emergence of recreational dress, as described by Inglis, was not simply the use of old clothes or a straightforward informal alternative to occupational city clothing. There were many additional complexities. In Brisbane, for instance, the climatic conditions effectively encouraged men to use cool khaki or white, loose fitting tropical gear (often imported readymade from India) with straw boaters, white hats or sun helmets even for formal occasions.[8] They continued this habit long after men abandoned it for black suits and top hats elsewhere in Australian cities. Yet tropical clothing worn by Brisbane men was very similar to sporting and leisurewear used throughout Australia for boating, beach holidays, picnicking and sports like tennis and cricket. These informal outfits consisted of white tropical trousers and shirts, occasionally white or striped jackets, straw boaters and sometimes coloured cummerbunds.[9] Thus in Queensland during the 1890s, white trousers and jackets were acceptable for formal city wear, as well as for tennis, cricket, golf and other leisure activities.

There are further important factors with gendered implications that need to be acknowledged. Leisure clothing must also be seen in context of the radical changes taking place in women's roles and occupations, and the gains being made in their social and legal positions. Although specialised leisurewear remained largely the prerogative of bourgeois women at the end of the nineteenth century, the general implications for all classes of new and more practical garments for sporting and casual wear was especially far reaching. Indeed by the latter part of the century the range of recreational activities deemed appropriate for women and girls was expanding dramatically.[10] With women pursuing more active lifestyles from the 1870s onward, garments suitable for sports such as calisthenics, gymnastics, swimming and tennis were being marketed.[11] In Brisbane, as elsewhere, many of these new categories of outfit were commonly to be seen.

As part of these changes for women, the wearing of practical so called 'reformed' or 'rational' dress became an important issue. Although discussion about sensible clothing for women in Australia lagged behind America and Britain, it was certainly being fairly

8.0 Riding outfits, 1890s (JOL)

widely discussed in the popular press by the 1890s. At this time, calls became quite numerous for a new and sensible kind of dress for more 'advanced thinking' women that was light, warm, healthy and unrestrictive, compared to the tyranically tight corsetry, cumbersome long skirts, high heels and tight sleeves of the 1870s and 1880s.[12] A good deal of the media publicity about rational dress was merely polemical. It is debatable how many radical loose fitting garments were actually worn in Australia. In any case, simpler, functional styles of clothing were becoming quite general for women's streetwear in colonial towns by the late 1870s, as a female equivalent of the male suit, obviating somewhat the need for radical styles.

Yet there remained a tension between the acknowledged need for women to wear special clothes for participation in sport and the conservative requirements of traditional femininity.[13] The relationship between the new practical garment styles and recreational clothing for women was equally complex. For instance, innovations in streetwear for women had much in common with traditional tailored clothing worn for riding. It was a long-held custom in Britain for well-to-do women to wear riding dress made by tailors (not dressmakers), featuring masculine details, trims and accessories. This convention was taken over by women in Australia quite early in the colonial period and continued throughout the century. A photograph of young women in the 1890s shows the tradition being maintained in Brisbane. The women are wearing specialised and well-tailored riding outfits (two double-breasted), as well as a man's bow tie, stiff collar, gloves and a straw boater.

Although this dress was, strictly speaking, for leisured pastimes, by the 1890s much fashionable formal wear for women was itself playing quite self-consciously with masculinised features such as ties, jackets, collars and shirts, formerly common to riding dress. These were a further kind of rationalisation of women's attire and suited younger women increasingly taking up positions in the paid workforce. They also suited those able to indulge in freer kinds of activities such as walking, cycling and country picnicking. Yet it was a kind of flirtation with the masculine only, whereby cross gender features of masculine attire were used for tantalising and erotic purposes. Such dress continued, as it had in the past, to sexualise features like a small waist and a well endowed bosom. For instance, readymade walking costumes were advertised by Chapman & Co. in 1898, showing the new masculinised style of double-breasted jacket, deep collar revers and cuffs. But these were still essentially feminine styles, although clearly designed for tropical summer weather in cool, washable fawn drill.[14]

Costumes like this could also be worn for cycling, although with a different style of hat. Cycling was a sport and leisure obsession of the mid-nineties in Brisbane, as elsewhere. The town had both professional and amateur cycling clubs in the 1890s and a number of new clubs were formed including the Brisbane Safety Bicycle Club in 1892 and the Queensland Amateur Cyclists Union in 1893, in addition to the original Brisbane Bicycle Club founded in the early 1880s.[15] Several specialist magazines were published like the *Brisbane cyclist* in 1890 and the *Queensland wheel* which came out in 1896.[16] Yet there were recognised drawbacks to cycling in Brisbane. The roads were bumpy and were often either dusty or muddy. The road to Oxley was considered to be quite atrocious and only good for shaking up a sluggish liver.[17]

Women took eagerly to the new activity in Brisbane and were encouraged to cycle as an aid to physical and mental fitness.[18] By 1896 there were lady members of the Amateur Cyclists Union and in July 1897 the inauguration of the Brisbane Ladies Bicycle Club took place, celebrated with a processional ride down Queen Street.[19] Cycling, as a mixed

8.1 Cycling costume, 1890s (JOL)

and democratic recreation, was something that had the capacity to change orthodox social relations and offered a serious challenge to traditional structures of class and gender. In many ways women on cycles challenged prevailing notions of femininity, for the machines offered a new kind of mobility and independence, and greater freedom for sexual encounters.

The practice was also at the centre of important changes in the conventions governing dress, for cycling dress was often quite masculinised.[20] It consisted of skirts and blouses or bloused jackets, often with stiff masculine collars. The skirt and blouse outfits were called costumes if the blouse and skirt were made of the same fabric. These outfits were frequently worn with masculinised neckwear and straw boaters. Mountcastle & Sons and Pike Brothers were both distributors of ladies' cycling dress in Brisbane, the latter advertising imported Cawnpore Khaki serge in fawn and navy blue for such garments in 1896.[21]

Some attempts were made to encourage women into wearing bifurcated garments for cycling, like divided skirts, bloomers or knickerbockers. In 1894 the Australia-wide pattern service run by Madame Weigel provided a paper pattern for a cycling costume of knickerbockers and Eton jacket.[22] Yet such garments were controversial and it is unclear if the really radical bifurcated styles were ever worn in Brisbane. Even in the more worldly Melbourne, the Cycling Tourists Club prohibited lady members from joining club rides in rational dress, presumably knickerbockers. An article in the *Australian storekeeper's journal* describing the banning suggests long frock coats to the knees and knee breeches would be a more modest alternative to the sight of divided legs.[23]

Men wore quite varied garments for cycling including knickerbockers, skin-tight undervests like skivvies, laced boots and small caps or boaters, somewhat similar to the three-quarter length trousers, sleeveless shirts and small peaked caps worn by amateur rowers. Nevertheless some signs of uniforms or uniform sashes and details were emerging in Brisbane men's cycling dress in the 1890s.[24]

As with cycling, women wore somewhat masculinised dress for physical education classes. For instance such garments were worn by ladies at segregated classes at the Brisbane Gymnasium where they worked with dumbbells, the 'horse', the horizontal bar and swings. Their clothes consisted of a navy blue skirt reaching slightly below the knee, short trousers, a sailor bodice and sandshoes, much along the lines of a bloomer costume of the 1850s. According to an enthusiastic journalist, this dress was neat, unobtrusive and thoroughly becoming, as well as 'a costume which allowed every muscle to have freedom of action'.[25] Bifurcated garments such as these were acceptable within the privacy of the gymnasium but certainly not on the open road.

Apart from cycling, other sporting pastimes in which women participated were tennis, croquet, golf, swimming and shooting. Tennis was an activity that was one of the few organised sports deemed appropriate for women. Primarily social rather than physical, it was not considered to be too exhausting, trained women in graceful movement, and allowed their believed charms to be shown to advantage.[26] It was first played in Brisbane by the wealthy, but soon became a middle class, though still 'polite', activity. Although from 1892 women's events were featured in the Queensland tennis titles, it was not really a serious sport for women and was played at a very leisurely pace.

In the 1880s women played in quite formal clothing, retaining the bustle, ankle length skirts and well-fitted bodices of fashionable dress. Contemporaries readily acknowledged the hampering effects of women's clothing on their strokes.[27] The solution seemed to lie in learning to volley and taking as few balls as possible on the bounce, so as to minimise the dress problems. The restrictive dress of the 1880s was replaced in the 1890s by a much more practical blouse and shorter skirt formula, or a plain gown, without a bustle, and a straw hat. This kind of outfit was commonly seen in Queensland, although the hats were by no means always so practical. In fact headwear could sometimes be quite large with decorative trims, and would have been very restrictive to the players.

8.2. Tennis dress, 1890s (JOL)

Tennis was one of the first sports to have specialised costume for women.[28] Some women's tennis garments, hats and aprons (to hold back the skirt and with pockets to hold balls), were beginning to be advertised in Brisbane in the late 1880s, and women's tennis dresses of plain and fancy flannel could be purchased as well.[29] For men, there were also specific lawn-tennis shirts, jackets and also ventilating shoes available through mail order.

In 1887 the *Queenslander* illustrated a women's tennis blouse of flannel or soft washing silk with 'sailor revers' and a masculinised collar, which could be made by the home dressmaker. In 1890 full details were published for making a tennis blouse, skirt and jockey cap in various shades of blue.[30] This cap was also recommended for travelling, as the rear peak could be turned up to rest the head in a railway carriage. The *Queenslander* also advised lightweight corsets for tennis players and for rowing in the summer, as they were cool and comfortable although still 'splendidly boned'.[31] The long waisted S and S ventilating corset, for instance, doubled for tennis wear, as manufacturers claimed it was 'always porous and cool'.

Much active recreation in Brisbane centred on outdoor or waterside activities as it does today. From Brisbane's earliest years, swimming was a popular pastime, especially in the hot summer months. Some floating river and tidal baths in the Brisbane River still existed in the early 1890s and there was one at the end of Edward Street.[32] Seaside bathing, or more popularly, wading, was undertaken at Sandgate and Wynnum, and all bathing was normally segregated. The construction of the Spring Hill Municipal Baths in 1886 led to the increased popularity of swimming, and by the end of the 1890s a number of swimming clubs were formed.[33]

Specialised readymade and modestly capacious woollen 'seaside costumes' for swimming were readily available for women, or could be made up from paper patterns. *Australian etiquette* advised women to use grey flannel for their bathing costumes and that they be worn with oil skin caps and merino socks.[34] A photograph of four young women bathers on Magnetic Island about 1890 shows the capacious nature of these outfits, some with skirts or else completely bifurcated.

The Botanic Gardens were a favourite leisure spot in the 1890s, where sport and other amusements were undertaken. The public took great interest in the ferneries, the bush houses, the flowers and plants and the tea kiosk with its charming turrets. On holidays hundreds of children (many boys dressed in sailor suits and girls in pinafores) and their parents picknicked under the trees or near the fountains, whilst cricketers and football players had their own areas in adjacent Queens Park. Cyclists claimed the greater part of the walks. According to J.J. Knight in 1897, 'The rustic seats and tables, the out of door tete-a-tetes, social croquet and tennis, with the accompaniment of clatter from cups and saucers, ice glasses and the likes, smacks strikingly of the continental'.[35] A photograph of 'Afternoon Tea in the Botanic Gardens' published in the *Queenslander* in 1898 shows a group of ladies quite formally dressed in voluminous long skirts and large hats taking tea. Some are playing croquet in front of the garden kiosk designed by the German architect Edward Kretschmer.[36]

Increasingly Australia's urban-based population of the 1880s and 1890s sought their outdoor pleasures further afield than botanical and acclimatisation gardens. As cities grew larger and busier, citizens began to invest the countryside with idealised notions of peace and rural tranquillity. Visits to the country and picnics had become popular summer holiday outings even in the 1870s, and longer stays at beach resorts were increasingly common. Specific yet still elegant clothing for some country visits was advised for women, although by the 1890s, for walking and picnics, masculinised rational dress with tailored jackets and bloomers was sometimes worn.

More usual were sunbonnets with wide side flaps or frills worn to shade the face from the detrimental effects of the heat. Broad felt hats were frequently used as an alternative to straw hats. A photograph of a group of picknickers in the bush in the 1890s shows a range of quite informal outfits. The men are without jackets and several women are in blouses and skirts. One of the women and a child wear large frilled sunbonnets for protection, while several men have tropical helmets. Fly veils are worn by both sexes. Women wore bonnets at the seaside and men often used wide brimmed hats for protection. Southport was a vacation venue largely for the wealthy at this time and only for those who could afford to stay overnight. A photograph taken outside the Grand Hotel, Deep Water Point, Southport in 1889 shows a wide variety of headwear being worn by the male guests, including deerstalkers and one very large hat which looks like a sombrero.

Toward the end of the nineteenth century the scientific community became increasingly preoccupied with the belief that tropical climates were unfit for civilised peoples. It was felt that long exposure to the sun would be detrimental to the European physique and cause moral and physical degradation.[37] This led inevitably to some awareness of the dangers of wearing inappropriate clothing. In 1896 Mountcastle & Sons, a Brisbane firm, were pressing customers to buy new 'Tropo' shaped sunhats and patented air-chamber helmets medically recommended for wear in the tropics.[38] Teleaven & Begg, also of Brisbane, sold practical folding 'Land and Water Hats' for outdoor activities and travelling, assuring readers that 'Men in these hats are irresistible'.[39]

In Australia during the 1890s leisurewear for men and women was an increasingly important aspect of the fashion market. Brisbane was no exception. Yet the tropical climate, and generally more relaxed lifestyle and manners, meant that some categories of leisurewear intersected with the styles worn for formal, everyday activities. This overlap gave a specific, regional character to Brisbane dress which, it can be argued, still exists in some respects even today.

Brisbane at leisure in the twentieth century

'Is you is or is you ain't a square?'

Chapter 9

Brisbane by night: Al fresco 1900-1914

Sue Ward

During this period of transition a new technological phenomenon, 'living pictures', rose to the fore as the most popular form of entertainment. Although this paper is about the earliest form of cinematic exhibition, the social context is broadened a little. Its purpose is to recreate from newspaper reviews and advertisements, a window, if you like, that looks out onto the urban landscape of Brisbane before the First World War and in particular the popular open-air entertainment forms patronised by the average family.

Brisbane by night at the turn of the century had many open-air amusements on offer. For more masculine tastes there were sports meetings where one could view horse or foot racing by gaslight; or for the more refined or romantic, musical concerts in the Gardens or a moonlight river excursion to the Pile Light on Moreton Bay.

Brisbane's balmy summer evenings were recognised as a feature of difference that set a Queensland lifestyle apart from the southern states. Taking part in evening entertainments in the open-air became a positive assertion of local identity. 'What can be pleasanter than to lie at ease, the sultry summer evening air tempered by the cool river breeze, and drink in the entrancing beauty of the scene?'[1] The early exhibition of 'Living pictures' took its place in a long established tradition of evening entertainments in parks, sporting fields and exhibition grounds, in a roll up of vaudeville entertainment, musical recitals and brass band overtures.

For some, the pick of outdoor summer entertainment was Earl's Court Pleasure Resort, at the corner of Kent and Brunswick streets, New Farm. It had 'many novel forms of healthy amusements' including a Canadian water chute, a camel-backed toboggan slide, an ocean wave (like rocking on imaginary billows) and an electric fish pond. To round off the evening, there was always a 'first-class concert' with such notables as 'Dr Carr the eminent mesmerist demonstrating his power of human magnetism'. One reviewer in the *Daily mail* on 9 October 1906 wrote:

> Large attendances are being nightly attracted to Earl's Court Pleasure Resort, where Prof. Davey's bioscope and moving pictures are watched with interest and admiration. Prof. Adriano is at present performing the remarkable feat of riding down the water chute on a bicycle, and every night he is warmly applauded. The water chute has now become a popular form of amusement, and is always well patronised. The many other novelties and sensations provided help to make Earl's Court a place where a pleasant evening's entertainment may be obtained at a very cheap rate. To-night Prof. Adriano will shoot the chute while enveloped in flames of fire.

> Refreshments are procurable at a kiosk within the grounds, and everything is al fresco, which in view of the sultry atmospheric conditions now ruling, may prove an incentive to the amusement loving public.[2]

Miss Bella Sutherland and company was one of many itinerant troupes of entertainers who travelled the state hiring halls, or set up their tents wherever they found a large enough audience. In 1904 Miss Bella's company passed through Brisbane equipped with 10,000 feet of Pathé's patent films and Edison's latest electric duo kinetoscope and stereopticon.[3] This was an early attempt to synchronize the image of the cinematograph with the sound of the phonograph. The two machines worked in tandem, though never very effectively, while the film subject was usually a famous singer or actor performing before the camera.

On one of her many sojourns in the district in 1907, Miss Bella and her company of 20 artists set up their 'Theatre Under Canvas' in the Tivoli Gardens on Hamilton Road opposite Toombul Wharf. Part of the dramatic entertainment was the 'latest Kinetoscope and up to date animated Pictures' accompanied by a brass band that played on the lawn.[4] After ten days, the company pulled up stakes and moved to Edward Street in the city next to the Metropolitan Hotel. Bella's 'Vital Spark Company' made recurring appearances in Brisbane until the company took up more permanent residence on Racecourse Road opposite the Hamilton Hotel, Ascot in 1912.[5]

A young Edward Carroll secured the Queensland rights to the first substantial Australian dramatic photoplay, *The story of the Kelly Gang*, and made a considerable fortune touring the state in 1907.[6] Recognising that he was onto a sure winner in this new form of amusement, Carroll set up the 'Summer Nights Continentals' as a regular Friday/Saturday night event at the Brisbane Exhibition grounds during the summer of 1908. To ensure optimum success in his 'Magnificent Biograph Picture Programme', Carroll organised special trams to run direct from North Quay with 'the concert band which will furnish the instrumental music, playing on route'.[7] Carroll's venture was so successful that before the end of that summer in 1909 he had established alternate venues at the Woolloongabba and Ipswich cricket grounds.

Being the consummate business man, Carroll had his fingers in a number of pies over the following year, including buying Earl's Court, building a skating rink and going into partnership with Charles Macmahon and others to produce the early Australian film, *For the term of his natural life*. He and his brother Dan continued their interests in film production, teaming up with Snowy Baker to make a number of feature films. Although the Carrolls' participation in Australia's early film production industry ceased in the early 1920s, they did continue in the exhibition business to become directors of Birch Carroll and Coyle, controller of the largest provincial circuit of cinemas in Australia.

By 1910 a number of the larger companies such as West's, King's, and Cook's pictures had taken over leases on theatres and halls in the city, becoming a permanent feature of evening entertainment, though open-air cinemas continued to remain popular in the suburbs.

There were many practical reasons for open-air exhibition. In the days of nitrate film and limelight, cinematograph fires were common. State authorities began to insist on rigorous fire precautions including approval of buildings with adequate ventilation and egress for the crowds, as well as fire retarding bio-boxes to surround the projection equipment. Though bad weather was always a problem with open-air premises, the viewing audience did not have to deal with the stifling heat in the days before adequate air-conditioning.

Many open-air premises were known as gardens and some of these deserved the name. I suspect Tivoli Gardens located across Breakfast Creek from Newstead Park was one of these. Others were simply 'gardens' by a generous stretch of the imagination.

Brisbane had many open-air cinemas, but there were two early theatrical entrepreneurs who were notable because they were also cinematographers. Bert Ives and Syd Cook used the novelty of living pictures of local events to drum up trade and gain the edge over their larger interstate rivals. The usual format was local football or cricket matches, horse races, visiting dignitaries, the annual exhibition or major public events in the city.

Ives bought the rights to the Summer Continentals from Edward Carroll in 1909. The Gabba cricket grounds could provide seating for 6000 at 6d a seat, and the grandstands provided some protection from adverse weather. From an account in the *Daily mail* on 5 January 1911, it appears the 'Peoples' Popular Summer Nights' were well attended. The review proclaimed:

> After the heat of the long summer's day, it is not so strange that several thousand persons sought relaxation and amusements last night at the Brisbane Cricket grounds. Here fanned by a refreshing breeze, they sat under the star lit canopy and enjoyed to the full a delightful entertainment.[8]

Ives continued his open-air entertainment at the Gabba and Ipswich cricket grounds, as well as establishing other open-air venues such as the Paddington Picture Pavilion, until 1913 when he joined the commonwealth government as their chief cinematographer, a position he was to occupy for the next twenty-three years.

Cook emigrated from England as a lad and joined the Salvation Army in Mackay. He had considerable musical talent and worked in a Salvation Army showband that took him to Victoria. At that time the Limelight Department, the brainchild of Joseph Perry, was becoming not only an important propaganda tool but also an important revenue earner for the Salvation Army. Cook's musical ability made him indispensable to the company. He could play any instrument competently to accompany the films, and rapidly became adept at projection.

In 1903 Cook was put in charge of his own touring Salvation Army film company, the New Biorama Company, and wherever they toured he shot and exhibited local documentaries. In 1903 he shot the first films to be made in Tasmania.[9]

In 1905 Cook left the Salvation Army, as their wages were too meagre to support his wife and growing family, and joined up with Ebenezer Jackson, also ex-Salvation Army, to become an independent film exhibitor. After a successful term in Brisbane, he settled here in 1906, leasing the Centennial Hall

9.0 Sidney Cook of Cook's Picture Company c. 1907-1908 (JOL)

in Adelaide Street, before finally taking over the old Foresters Hall in Brunswick Street and building his own picture palace.

Cook continued his passion for actuality footage. In 1908 he was commissioned by the Queensland state government to provide living pictures of the state's main industries and beauty spots for the Franco-British exhibition. He continued to spice his exhibition programs by cinematographing such events as the eight-hour processions, election days, the tramways strike in 1911 and the Great Strike in 1912. His speciality was to shoot footage during the day and have it developed ready for that same evening's program. He had cinematograms of the polling booths during the elections on that same day of 27 April 1912 with up-to-the-minute results of the election interspersed throughout the evening's program.[10]

Cook catered for the working-class audience. Besides the theatre in the Valley, he had a chain of open-air cinemas: at the Gabba fiveways, on Logan Road opposite J. Hunter's; the Star Theatre Paddington, on Given Terrace next to the Paddington post office; the Crystal, next to Brunswick Street station; the West End Picture Gardens, Boundary Street; and also at Clayfield, Kelvin Grove and probably other suburbs. Usually they comprised rows of chairs on bare grass surrounded by a high wall, but because the capital outlay was minimal, the admission price was affordable. The *Daily mail* records the opening of the West End Picture Gardens on 7 November 1910:

COOK'S PICTURE PALACE, VALLEY.

"HOUSE FULL" AT 7.30, AND HUNDREDS TURNED AWAY LAST NIGHT.

COMPLETE CHANGE OF PROGRAMME.
TO-NIGHT, AT 8, AND EVERY EVENING.
WILL INCLUDE CINEMATOGRAMS SPECIALLY TAKEN YESTERDAY BY MR. COOK OF THE

8 HOUR PROCESSION AND SPORTS.

Every Banner and Society Represented, Cycle Races, Foot Races, Novelty Events, and Panoramas of the Thirty Thousand Spectators, making the Longest Moving Picture ever taken in Brisbane.

ESSANAY'S LATEST POWERFUL DRAMA,

A REDEEMED CRIMINAL.

Hamlet; Nobleman and Cowboys; Wreath of Orange Blossoms; Tolo and the Flag; Foolshead Commits Suicide; Taranto; Gold Mining Africa; Fitznoppe Wooing; Sydney's Great Snow; Magic Debt Collectors, &c.

PRICES, 6d., 1/, and 1/6. Doors open 7.15. Matinee, Saturday, at 2.30.

FIVEWAYS PICTURES, TO-NIGHT.

A Gigantic Success—The Popular Picture Resort of the South Side.

Notwithstanding its Great Success, the last night must be announced of our present Grand Programme, which includes the Great Australian Drama,
A RIDE FOR LIFE — or — A BUSHRANGER'S RANSOM,
And a Host of Other Star Gems.

SPECIAL ATTRACTIONS FOR WEDNESDAY NIGHT:

THE SQUATTER'S DAUGHTER. EAST LYNNE.

CINEMATOGRAMS OF 8 HOURS PROCESSION AND SPORTS.
VIVIAN THE GREAT, CONJURER, FIREFIGHTER, &c.

PRICES, 6d. and 1/; Children, 3d. and 6d. Gates open 7.15.

9.1 Advertising cinematograms of the 8 hour procession, BC 2 May 1911 (PERS)

VALLEY PICTURE PALACE. **COOK'S PICTURES. 'GABBA.** TO-NIGHT. PICTURE GARDENS.

MATINEE AT VALLEY, AT 2.30.
MATINEE AT VALLEY, AT 2.30.
MATINEE AT VALLEY, AT 2.30.
MATINEE AT VALLEY, AT 2.30.

MISS MAUD JEFFERSON
MISS MAUD JEFFERSON
Will sing at the 'Gabba
"With My Guitar" and "Love will Stay."

Mr. Sidney Cook will take a Series of

CINEMATOGRAMS OF THE POLLING BOOTHS,

IN AND AROUND BRISBANE.

These Films will be finished in time to be shown at The Valley and 'Gabba To-night.

RESULTS OF THE ELECTIONS

From the principal Metropolitan and Country Electorates will be Screened during the Evening.

Full Programme of Star Photoplays include

SAVING OF DAN. THE ANGEL. LEAGUE OF MERCY.
SAVING OF DAN. THE ANGEL. LEAGUE OF MERCY.

Western One Night Stand, Millionaire and the Squatter, and Fourteen others.
Prices as usual. Doors open at 2 and 7. 'Phones 2952 and 2130.

9.2 Up to the minute election results, BC 27 April 1912 (PERS)

> Under ordinary circumstances moving pictures are full of interest and very popular but held in the open air they are doubly so. On Saturday night despite the threatening weather, a large audience attended the opening of the West End Pictures near the West End School of Arts. A Hornsby gas engine had been installed to drive the lighting plant, and the pictures were thrown onto a large iron screen, the first of its kind in Brisbane.[11]

Cook promoted a cheap and informal viewing experience, as evidenced by this unusual and distinctive promotion for the Gabba fiveways written in the argot of the day:

> Stead's Julia heard the Blucher say to the Dook 'Let's see the Fiveway's Pictures tonight, our boots is a bit outer date, but we can easily go with nothing on, same as the Queensland Kids do on their feet'. And the Dook said, 'Let's'.[12]

Unfortunately the cultural reference is now lost.

Though Cook found a willing audience for his local footage, he continued to follow in the Salvation Army tradition of providing entertainment at impromptu sites wherever there was an audience. He was to realise a quick profit in catering for the hordes of holiday-makers in the local seaside resorts of Sandgate and Shorncliffe. He ensured the success of this venture by organising a special train for his city patrons to run from Roma Street to Shorncliffe, leaving at 6.30pm. As the advertisement explained:

> You can have a quick run to Sandgate, a high class picture show, a band recital, sea breezes, a comfortable seat on the grass. The Lot for one shilling'.[13]

And it seems from newspaper reports that the crowds were willing:

> Between 2000 and 3000 people availed themselves of the opportunity of taking their picture entertainment with full band accompaniment at Sandgate on Saturday night. The site selected – Moora Park, one end of which slopes into a natural amphitheatre elevated some 50ft or 60ft above the sea, but commanding a fine view – is an ideal one, and also possesses a carpet of buffalo grass. A metal screen has been erected, insuring a steady picture. Mr Cook presented a programme of great diversity, embracing films dealing with grave, gay, scenic, industrial and scientific subjects. One of the most popular was a series illustrating the holiday crowds at Sandgate on New Year's Day. [14]

9.3 Cook's Clayfield Pictures, 24 Jan. 1920 (JOL)

Cook lived on in Brisbane, settling into a comfortable middle age as a film exhibitor, until his death in 1937. His open-air cinemas continued to be viable in the suburbs up until the 1920s as evidenced by the flashlight photograph taken of the Clayfield Picture Palace in 1920. Nevertheless, the succeeding period from 1914 to 1928, the second half of the silent era, saw big changes nationally in the overall structure and exhibition practices of the cinema industry. 'Living Pictures' ceased to become a novelty housed in temporary accommodation. The introduction of lavish picture palaces with upholstered furniture and ice-cream parlours, and the continuous picture shows which brought exhibition times forward into the day, a much more appropriate time for women and children, became the norm in the larger city and suburban areas.[15] Open-air cinemas or the simple tin shed were simply no longer appropriate, except in the rural areas where small audiences prevailed. Only in Western Australia and Queensland, where the climate favours open-air entertainment, has open-air exhibition continued to survive.

9.4 Mowbray Picture Palace, 1914, converted to an ice skating rink during the 1960s (JOL)

Chapter 10

Brisbane on the visitors' circuit 1870s-1940s

Tim Moroney

From the late nineteenth century to the 1940s, a diversity of famous people visited Brisbane. Whether they came to entertain, lecture, preach, inspect or, in the case of aviators, end their journeys, they all helped to place Brisbane on the cultural map. They also heralded the invasion of international visitors since the Second World War. This paper gives an account of a number of these earlier visitors, their purpose in coming here, and the reception they received.

Anthony Trollope

Anthony Trollope arrived in Brisbane on 12 August 1871 as part of an extensive journey throughout Australia and New Zealand during 1871-72. According to Peter Edwards and Roger Joyce, who produced an edited version of his Australian travels, Trollope's standing among English living novelists was probably second only to that of George Eliot because of his Barsetshire novels.[1] He had originally journeyed to Australia to visit his second son, Frederick, who had taken up land near Forbes. At the same time, Trollope had convinced his publishers that a book recording his visit to the southern colonies would be commercially viable.

After briefly visiting Melbourne and Sydney, he chose Queensland as the first colony to begin his wider travels. Trollope only stayed a few days in Brisbane as the guest of the chief justice, Sir James Cockle, before travelling as far north as Rockhampton. By chance, his visit coincided with the arrival of the new governor, George Augustus Constantine, Marquis of Normanby. Trollope found Brisbane quite warm, and described it as 'a commodious town, very prettily situated on the Brisbane River with 12,000 inhabitants, with courts of justice, houses of parliament, a governor's residence, public gardens, and all the requirements of a capital for a fine and independent colony'.

The new governor's swearing-in ceremony provided Trollope with a degree of amusement since 'the governor took his oath manfully in a tight-fitting, tight-buttoned blue uniform ... no doubt prescribed by official rule but which seems to be ill adapted to the climate as any dress that could possibly be devised'. However, he did envy the governor his house 'which was spacious, well built and pretty'.[2]

After extensive travels throughout Queensland, by steamer, coach and horseback, Trollope departed Brisbane for Sydney on 29 September 1871, having been farewelled at a complimentary dinner in the Queensland Parliamentary Library. While the republican debate has provoked heated discussion in the late 1990s, it is of interest to note that in Trollope's conclusion to his book on Australia, he observed the separate, divisive interests of the various colonies, and he urged federation, which he prophesied would lead ultimately to separation from the mother country.[3]

John and William Redmond

Moving forward twelve years, it was the turn of the Irish. The brothers John and William Redmond toured Australia representing the Irish parliamentary party, while at the same time, forming branches and gaining financial support for the National Land League. Unfortunately their visit coincided with the trial of the eight Fenians accused of the murders of Lord Cavendish and J.H. Burke, the chief and under secretaries of Ireland, in Phoenix Park the previous year. Patrick O'Farrell has described the hostile reception accorded the Redmonds, as the local papers had a field day accusing them of collecting for a murder fund, fomenting civil war and even linking them with the murder of a Chinese doctor in Armidale. There were, however, supportive elements, especially among the Irish lower and middle classes who welcomed them with enthusiasm.[4]

The Redmonds visited Brisbane on 29 March 1883, and John delivered a lecture entitled 'The aims and objects of the Irish National League' at St James Roman Catholic School in the Valley. Chaired by J.M. Macrossan MP and attended by approximately 200 persons including Patrick O'Sullivan MP and a number of catholic clergy, Redmond was enthusiastically received. The chairman regretted the venue, since it could possibly give a sectarian tinge to the movement, which was incorrect, because its leaders were men of all religions, both protestant and catholic alike.

Redmond outlined the history of the original Land League, its repression, the incarceration of its leaders, the plight of the Irish landless and the need for constitutional change. He argued for the establishment of a local government system similar to the Queensland divisional boards, and stated that Ireland's franchise lagged well behind this colony's. Despite the small attendance because the organisers could not obtain a proper meeting hall, an amount exceeding £70 was collected. The Redmonds left Brisbane separately the next day to continue their campaigning in central and northern Queensland.[5]

Michael Davitt

Twelve years later, Michael Davitt, the founder of the Irish Land League, also toured Australia. O'Farrell notes that, despite the factional allegiances of Irish Australians linked to the various groups formed in the Irish parliamentary party after Parnell's death, Davitt was well respected. In the account of his Australian travels, Davitt claimed he was more interested in observing the Australian colonies' development of state socialism and prison reform than in promoting the espousal of the Irish cause.[6]

He arrived in Brisbane on 18 July 1895 by steamer, and was greeted at the wharf by an official reception committee and an enthusiastic crowd. Dr Kevin Izod O'Doherty, former Queensland MP who had just returned from Ireland after representing Westmeath in the House of Commons, was first up the gangplank to shake his hand. Later, Davitt was interviewed by a reporter at the Imperial Hotel and gave a detailed account of the recent British elections in which, despite his absence, he had been elected for the seat of Kerry West.[7]

Unlike the Redmonds' experience, Davitt's lecture in the Centennial Hall was attended by a large, overflowing crowd, and chaired by the mayor of Brisbane, Robert Fraser. Other dignitaries included Sir Charles Lilley, Justice Real, A.J. Thynne, T.J. Byrnes and other members from both houses of the Queensland parliament. Davitt analysed the recent British election in which the Liberal Party had suffered a loss of seats. He argued for Irish Home Rule, stating that the British should learn a lesson from the loss of their United States' colonies and compared that country's sovereignty with Canada, which now enjoyed dominion status within the empire. He assured the audience that Home Rule should not be seen as a catholic Ireland depriving protestants of representation, since other national leaders were protestants and, in the case of the catholic Daniel O'Connell, had fought for the toleration of all religions.

During his speech, Davitt had to endure a stream of interjections from a legislative councillor who was seated on the same platform. Despite pleas from the audience to 'put him out', Davitt rejected their entreaties, and at times engaged in vigorous exchange with the disruptive heckler. At the end of his speech, two little girls in white presented Davitt with a bouquet of flowers, to which was attached the colours symbolising England, Scotland and Ireland.[8] O'Farrell notes Davitt's expressions of confusion during his Australian visit, since a proportion of Irish Australians appeared eager to toast Queen Victoria's health and, in many homes, Victoria's and Gladstone's portraits adorned the walls along with portraits of the Irish heroes.[9] Like the Redmonds, Davitt left the next day for places north, with lectures planned for Charters Towers and Townsville.[10]

Henry Morton Stanley

On 15 December, between the visits of the Redmonds and Davitt, Brisbane audiences were entertained by a lecture from the famous African explorer and discoverer of David Livingstone, Henry Morton Stanley. Stanley's life mirrored a 'boy's own' adventure. Born John Rowlands at Denbigh in Wales of unmarried parents, he was orphaned at the age of six, raised in an English workhouse, fled to America, adopted by a rich broker named Stanley from whom he received his name, fought in the Civil War for the confederates, captured at Shiloh, drifted into journalism, hired by the *New York herald* to cover wars and special events in Europe, Asia and Africa, discovered Livingstone and spent the next twenty years exploring and opening up large areas of the African continent. Appearing at the Theatre Royal, Stanley's entrance contrasted with his adventurous lifestyle, since it 'was so modest and matter of fact, that, for an instant or two, the audience hardly appeared to realise that the hero of the Dark Continent stood before them in the flesh'. After recovering from their shock, he was greeted enthusiastically 'with loud and long applause'. The Queensland branch of the Royal Geographic Society was there in full force, and he was welcomed by Queensland's own famous explorer, Augustus Charles Gregory MLC. Unfortunately, Gregory's speech was delivered in such a low tone that not many people heard him. This was not the case with J.P. Thompson, the Society's secretary, whose address extolled the virtues of Stanley's exploration for the causes of geography, commerce and trade, since 'British trade and the influence of civilisation had been extended to the remotest parts of the earth, adding to the happiness and prosperity of millions of the race'.

Stanley then proceeded to inform the audience as to how he discovered Livingstone. However, the audience appeared more interested in the manner of the man addressing them as the *Courier* noted:

> Mr Stanley is no Colossus - in fact he is below middle height, though firmly knit and indicating in every movement and gesture the possession of a physical power beyond that which would be expected from his actual bulk. His face is more remarkable than his frame for although his figure is hard and sinewy, looking as if it could endure almost any privation, it is the fixed, determined square-cut chin and the gleam of the resolute eye which most attract attention.
>
> Stanley provided a graphic account of his adventures, which were familiar to many persons because of his published works. His tone of voice saddened when he described his parting from Livingstone: So affecting to many of the audience was this, that they were almost pleased when a few minutes later a brief peroration closed the lecture.[11]

General William Booth

Four months after Davitt's visit in 1895, religious fervour invaded Brisbane with the arrival of General William Booth, founder of the Salvation Army. Booth's wife, Catherine, had died of cancer in 1890 and, after devotedly nursing her during her illness, he now felt freer to travel abroad. The Salvation Army had been established in Adelaide in 1880, and quickly spread to other colonies.[12] Booth, aged 66, arrived in Brisbane on 2 November 1895. Meetings were held in the Brisbane Opera House, where he conducted three services: morning, afternoon and evening. His style was described as evangelical with a staccato-type delivery, being interlaced with prayer and song. A band featured prominently, while the congregation waved handkerchiefs.[13] While in Brisbane, Booth was the guest of Thomas Finney, merchant and later member of parliament. Booth also met with other Queensland MPs to discuss his 'Darkest England' scheme, based on city and country colonies, which provided homeless and unemployed persons with the opportunity to be trained as useful citizens. After leaving Brisbane, Booth travelled to Gympie, Maryborough, Bundaberg and finally Ipswich.[14]

Two other family members emulated Booth's campaigning. In 1920 his son, William Bramwell Booth, who had succeeded his father as General of the Salvation Army, visited Brisbane. Later, Bramwell's sister, Evangeline, who had spent many years in Canada and the United States and who became the first female General of the Salvation Army, paid Brisbane a visit in 1935.[15]

Dame Nellie Melba

In 1902 Nellie Melba made a triumphant tour of Australia. She was the toast of England and Europe, but because of her father's ill health, had decided to return to the country of her birth and at the same time present a series of concerts in Melbourne, Sydney, Brisbane and Adelaide. She was received like royalty. In Sydney, her third concert established a world record at that time with the net sum of £2350 being returned at the box office.[16]

She journeyed to Brisbane by train, and on crossing the Queensland border was transferred to the governor's special railway carriage. Large crowds gathered at the major railway stations en route and cheered her heartily. Similar scenes were enacted at Roma Street and Central stations, and after her arrival at the latter she was transferred to a landau and transported to the Gresham Hotel, via crowded streets.[17] Her first concert was held on 27 October 1902 at the Exhibition Hall. Prices ranged from one guinea down to five shillings. Over 2000 people lined Gregory Terrace and Bowen Bridge Road hoping to catch a glimpse of her as her carriage entered the grounds. Inside the hall, an audience of 2500 from all parts of the state, along with the governor, Sir Herbert

Chermside, was fortunate to hear her sing:

> Melba's first item, Handel's aria 'Sweet Bird' demonstrated that [her] voice is as pure and brilliant as a diamond. It carries well, the enunciation is absolutely perfect, and in the runs and shakes with which the work abounds, it is incomparably true, and of beautiful quality. In the trills there is no hardness of tone, the notes flow out with such liquid beauty, such softness and fulness [sic] that they put to shame the flute which Mr Griffith so admirably handles.

The other items included a serenade by Tosti, the 'Mad Scene' from Thomas' *Hamlet*, 'Three Green Bonnets', the 'Waltz Song' from Gounod's *Romeo and Juliet* and as an encore, 'Serenade' by Strauss. The audience did not cheer wildly but stood up and warmly applauded her for some time.[18]

Of course, Brisbane was familiar territory to Melba, having spent a year in Queensland and marrying Charles Armstrong in the capital on 22 December 1882. The following year after the birth of her son, she left her husband and returned to her father's house in Melbourne before launching into her singing career.[19] While in Brisbane in 1902, she was able to renew old acquaintances.

Noted for her generosity, Melba donated £100 to the General Hospital, £50 to the Childrens Hospital and £50 to the Lady Lamington Hospital. During her first concert, an eight-year-old boy was discovered asleep under the gallery front seats. He had sneaked in unnoticed with the intention of hearing Melba sing. Before being escorted home he remarked, 'So I didn't hear Madame Mulbay'. When Melba was told of the incident, and being assured it was true, instructions were given to the attendants who had obtained the boy's name and address. That night, 'a smiling little chap from Bowen Hills, with a severe-looking parent, sat in the half-guinea seats ... and was able to hear Melba sing without running the risk of a policeman at the hall and a whipping when he got home'.[20]

10.0 Dame Nellie Melba leaving the Gresham Hotel, Brisbane (JOL)

Melba gave two more concerts in Brisbane before taking the train back to Melbourne.

Twenty-five years later Melba returned to bid farewell to her Brisbane audiences at two concerts on 4 and 7 July 1927. Both were held at the 1902 location, the Exhibition Hall, to packed houses. The programs were a mixture of popular arias and light numbers such as 'Comin' Thro' the Rye'.[21] At the second concert, a unique event occurred, when thousands were able to hear her perform through the medium of 4QG radio. It was the first time her voice had been broadcast. The *Courier* reported that, 'Dame Melba again spoke her farewell without sadness, though obviously moved, before she led her audience in the singing of God Save the King and made her final bow'.[22]

Melba's final concert in Australia was at Geelong in 1928. After living in London for three years, she returned to Australia for health reasons in 1931 and died in Sydney at the age of 69.[23]

Lord Robert Baden-Powell

The publication of Robert Baden-Powell's *Scouting for boys* in 1908 saw the scouting movement spread like wildfire throughout the world. By the end of that year, groups of scouts with scout-masters had been established in all Australian states.[24] Baden-Powell decided that better organisation of these disparate groups could be achieved if he visited the various countries throughout the world in order to encourage, inspect and outline the scouting philosophy.

In 1912 Baden-Powell visited Australia after touring America and the East. On 11 May 1912 he arrived in Brisbane. At a lecture on the Saturday night he stated that his 'main intention is to give lads a high ideal in life, to instill into them patriotism as a sentiment, to help them to realise the sacredness of duty, and to train them to a better fitness in serving their country should its defence be necessary'.[25]

Baden-Powell's major contact with Queensland scouts, however, had occurred that afternoon. He journeyed up the Brisbane River by steamer to the old Toowong rifle range where 1000 persons had gathered. As Baden-Powell and his escort reached a group of standard bearers, a bugle was blown and approximately 860 scouts, hiding in the nearby scrub and gullies, ran towards their leader, cheering wildly. The scouts were representatives of 2800 in Queensland who had come from Mt Morgan, Rockhampton, Gympie, Ipswich, Warwick, Gladstone, Sandgate and the metropolitan districts.

After the leaders were introduced to the chief scout, an order was shouted and the various groups hurried to different parts of the ground to demonstrate their skills at bridge building, hut building, flag signalling, stretcher making and first aid. Baden-Powell inspected each group's work and praised them for their efforts. His closing remarks emphasised the universal acceptance of the movement since 'He would be able to tell their brother scouts all over the Empire what he thought of them. If ever they went to other parts of the Empire they would find brother scouts ready and willing'.[26]

Baden-Powell toured Australia twice more, in 1931 and 1934-35. In his book, *Scouting round the world*, he described the Brisbane of 1934:

> The approach to Brisbane is very peaceful, up a broad river with flat green country on either side where stand big factories and suburban bungalows till the ground rises into a district of hills covered for miles with white-roofed bungalows. In the actual town there are a few streets with fine great buildings and beyond these, in every direction, the suburbs spread far and wide.[27]

I wonder what his reaction would be to the Brisbane of today?

Charles Kingsford Smith

There were, of course, other visitors to Brisbane in the first twenty years of this century. 1909 saw the arrival of Annie Besant, former Fabian and socialist who had converted to theosophy, and after settling in India had become chairman of the Indian National Congress. In 1919 the world's favourite Scotsman, Harry Lauder, entertained Brisbane audiences at the Theatre Royal.[28]

By the 1920s, however, a new form of adventure had captured people's imaginations as the 'daring young men in their flying machines' explored the frontiers of trans-oceanic flight. Four months after Bert Hinkler had completed his solo, epic flight from London to Bundaberg, another Queenslander was set to make history. At Eagle Farm aerodrome on Saturday 9 June 1928, thousands gathered to await the Southern Cross with its four airmen, Australian pilots Charles Kingsford Smith and Charles Ulm, and the Americans, navigator Harry Lyon and radio operator James Warner, after the final leg of their Pacific crossing. The *Courier* reported:

10.1 Sir Charles Kingsford Smith (JOL)

> More than 10,000 persons shivered in the rawness of the morning at Eagle Farm aerodrome to see the big plane land. They waited for four hours, and then they saw her swoop over, her enormous wing spread of 60 feet dwarfed at a height of 2000 feet. Then she circled three times like a giant blue hawk, gradually dropping lower, until she shot over the tree tops, and alighted with graceful precision, pulling up to a standstill in a remarkably short distance.[29]

As the airmen alighted from the Southern Cross, thousands of people surged forward and surrounded the plane. Many of these risked being maimed or decapitated since the engines' propellers were still spinning.

An official party including the governor, Sir John Goodwin, the consul-general for Italy, Count G. di San Marzano, the premier, William McCormack, and the opposition representative, H.E. Sizer, welcomed the four 'Sovereigns of the Ether'. Mrs Sizer placed a garland of roses around Kingsford Smith's neck and greeted him with a kiss on the cheek. Prior to the official welcome, each airman underwent a superficial examination by Dr G.A. Murray in accordance with commonwealth quarantine regulations and then had to sign the customary form.

Members of the enthusiastic crowd hoisted the airmen on to their shoulders and, like a phalanx, slowly pushed their way forward towards the terminal. Pandemonium reigned as children were bowled over, the small cordon of police swept aside, 4QG's broadcasting equipment knocked down and the press photographers' cameras dashed to the ground. After reaching the safety of the terminal, the airmen were transferred to an official car which slowly ventured down Nudgee Road en route to a city hall reception, while a procession of private cars followed in its wake.

At the city hall, in front of a large cheering crowd, it was announced that the federal government had donated a prize of £5000 in honour of their exploits. The vice-mayor, A. Watson, welcomed them, claiming Kingsford Smith as a Queenslander and linking him to the recent success of another Queenslander, Bert Hinkler. He also visualised the day when Brisbane would be the natural airport for a Pacific service linking Australia with America. At the end of the reception, the four were driven around to the Ann Street side of the square to Lennons Hotel, where, before they could retire, Kingsford Smith and Ulm 'repaired to the lounge, armed with a paper knife and a tin of Minties [being] occupied for the greater part of half an hour opening and hastily scanning the huge batch of telegrams, cables and other messages of congratulations'.

That night the airmen were further feted at a state ministry dinner.[30] At 10.10 the next morning, the Southern Cross left Eagle Farm aerodrome cheered on by thousands of on-lookers. As a matter of interest, on their arrival at Mascot airport, Sydney, they were welcomed by 300,000 people, which amounted to one quarter of Sydney's population.[31]

Two years later on 21 October 1930, Kingsford Smith was accorded another hero's welcome in Brisbane, when, flying solo from England to Australia in an Avro Avian Sports, the Southern Cross Junior, he slashed one-third of the time off Bert Hinkler's record. History repeated itself. As in 1928 he was greeted by officials and large enthusiastic crowds at the airport, driven to city hall via streets lined with cheering well-wishers, honoured at city hall with an official reception, feted as a guest of the Davies Park Speedway that night and then left on the final leg of his journey for Sydney the next morning.[32]

Before leaving Kingsford Smith, it is worthwhile highlighting an extraordinary event reported in the *Brisbane courier* on 13 August 1932. The previous day, a Chrysler Imperial roadster was stolen from Ward Motors by a mechanic and was driven at high speed to Archerfield aerodrome. Kingsford Smith, now Sir Charles, was standing beside the Southern Cross, when he saw the roadster heading towards his plane. He immediately grabbed two rifles out of the Southern Cross and, after giving one to his mechanic, both were pointed towards the driver who, on seeing this array of armaments, swerved suddenly and smashed into the tail of the Southern Cross Midget which was standing alongside. Much to their horror, they noticed that the car's front seat was also occupied by a small girl about five years of age. After smashing into another plane, the roadster was driven at great speed towards the Aero Clubhouse. On seeing Mrs Shelley the caretaker, on the clubhouse verandah, the driver shouted out, 'Bring me some cigarettes and chocolates'.

Mrs Shelley fled inside, as the roadster was now driven up the clubhouse steps. However, because the chassis caught on the verandah, the car was reversed off and driven towards the perimeter fence, where, after three attempts, the driver managed his escape and sped down Ipswich Road towards Oxley. By this time, Kingsford Smith had managed to obtain a lift in a club member's car, which set off in pursuit. Within a mile of Oxley, they caught up to the fleeing roadster, whereupon Kingsford Smith fired two shots at the rear tyres. The driver stopped the car, was bundled out, and with Kingsford Smith's rifle in the middle of his back, marched to Oxley police station where a charge was laid against a William Rowe Elder, as a person suspected of being of unsound mind. The little girl, who was Elder's daughter, appeared unaffected by the melodramatic events, and was given into the care of Dr Fraser East.[33]

Amy Johnson

Prior to Kingsford Smith's 1930 venture, another aviation milestone was reached when the first woman to fly solo from England to Australia, Amy Johnson, landed in Brisbane on Thursday 30 May 1930. Unfortunately, her arrival was marred when her plane, a Jason, struck a barbed wire fence separating the flying field from a cornfield, and after breaking a post, overturned, badly damaging the wings. Much to everybody's relief, Johnson scrambled out unhurt, smiling and waving to the cheering crowd. She was immediately hoisted on to a dais and, clutching a garland of flowers in which the wattle predominated, was welcomed by the governor, Sir John Goodwin, the lord mayor, William Jolly and, on behalf of the commonwealth government, J.G. Bayley MHR.

Similar scenes to the welcome accorded Kingsford Smith in 1928 followed. The streets from the airport to city hall were lined with cheering crowds and during the lord mayor's official welcome, in which Johnson was granted the freedom of the city, Albert Square was 'a veritable sea of hats'.[34] While in Brisbane, Johnson was the guest of the governor and his wife. For the next six days she faced a whirlwind of engagements: a lady mayoress' reception; visits to the Australian Women's Christian Temperance Union convention and the Queensland Women Graduates Association; a government house garden party and an official dinner at night; a visit to the diggers at Rosemount Hospital; a flight over Brisbane; an afternoon river trip with members of the Science Congress; lunch with the Brisbane Rotary Club; a night at His Majestys with the Returned Soldiers League; and guest of honour at the Queensland Turf Club's Brisbane Cup meeting at Eagle Farm.

Because of health reasons, possibly exhaustion, Johnson's departure for Sydney was via an Australian National Airway's commercial flight in the Southern Sun. Her own plane, the Jason, had been repaired and flown to Sydney by L.J. Brain.[35]

Other visitors in the 1920s

Other visitors to Brisbane included: in 1921, Sir Arthur Conan Doyle lecturing on spiritualism, Lord Northcliffe, the British newspaper proprietor and founder of modern journalism, and Dame Clara Butt, the famous British contralto; in 1922, the Sistine Choir; in 1927, the pianist Jan Paderewski and violinist Jascha Heifitz; in 1929, Anna Pavlova whose season of nine performances opened the new His Majestys Theatre.[36] Two royal tours during this decade attracted tremendous interest and caused great excitement on both occasions when the Prince of Wales, later Edward VIII, visited Brisbane in 1920, and the Duke and Duchess of York, later King George VI and Queen Elizabeth II, had an extensive tour in 1927.[37]

Count Felix von Luckner

During the 1930s on the eve of the Second World War, two visitors, a German and an Austrian, appeared in Brisbane. The first, Count Felix von Luckner, was well known for his exploits as a German raider in the First World War, which had been glorified by Lowell Thomas' biography, *Count Luckner, the sea devil.* Von Luckner's life had been as exciting as Henry Morton Stanley's. Born into a noble family, he ran away to sea at the age of thirteen; sailed to Australia on his first voyage; jumped ship at Fremantle; became a kangaroo hunter, a prizefighter, a wrestler and a beachcomber; guarded the president of Mexico; rose to the rank of a naval officer through his own efforts; escaped the allied blockade of Germany in a disguised Norwegian sailing vessel; and sank half a million tons of allied shipping in the Atlantic and Pacific oceans without destroying a single human life.[38]

Von Luckner, and his wife Irma, arrived at Archerfield aerodrome on 21 June 1938. Their visit to Australia was part of a cruise throughout the South Seas in his new yacht, the Sea Devil. The von Luckners were greeted by a hundred members of the German community led by the consular representative, G.H. Witte and the president of the German Club, H. Berkemeyer. One 80-year old fan, F.G. Korsch, conspicuous by his waving hand and white beard, had travelled 600 miles to meet the count.[39]

In an interview with the *Courier-mail,* which avoided the topic of politics, von Luckner claimed that as a young teenager in Brisbane, he had stayed at the Seamen's Mission and had fought at the old Brisbane Stadium in Edward Street. He also changed his career as a billposter with a team of Hindu magicians back to that of a sailor when he boarded a four-masted schooner for America so he could meet 'Boofalo Bill'. The count prefaced all his statements with the phrase 'by Joe' which, according to his autobiography, he had adopted to overcome the natural curses that were the stock-in-trade of a seasoned seafarer.[40]

That night at the German Club, von Luckner expressed his admiration for the British, 'since admiration is the best foundation of understanding'. He claimed that 'War could not convince me that sailors, my fellow citizens of the seas, were my enemies. I had enough courage to sink ships, but not enough to deprive a good mother of her child, a child of its father, or a wife of her husband'.[41]

While in Queensland, the von Luckners were well received and, although some papers linked them with the Nazi cause, the count's humanitarian approach appeared to win admirers.

Richard Tauber

The second visitor, the Austrian Richard Tauber, appeared at the city hall in July 1938 while, by coincidence, his movie *Blossom time* was showing at the Majestic Theatre. The *Courier-mail*'s music critic waxed lyrical about Tauber's performance:

> He made voice and vocalism the vehicles of a two-way flow of liquid tone and technique. For the one, he chose lieder only; for the other, the light and popular. The one he sublimated, the other he rationalised. In relaxing strong concentration on the sublime, to urbanity for the mediocre, he never compromised with artistic principles in interpretative mode; he put 'all he had' into it.

Tauber demonstrated exemplary English diction, and he regarded the acoustics of the city hall 'as among the best of the halls in which he has sung'. Before leaving Brisbane, he performed at another three concerts.[42]

Other visitors in the 1930s

Other visitors during the 1930s included: in 1934, the British grenadier guards who marched through densely packed cheering crowds in their crimson and gold uniforms surmounted by bearskin headdress; in 1936, Lord Nuffield, the English car manufacturer; Zane Grey, American western author, who had come for the big-game fishing and to film koalas in 1936 and again in 1939;[43] and Larry Adler, also in 1939, virtuoso of the harmonica, who attracted criticism when he claimed that not many girls played this particular instrument.[44]

Noel Coward

There are two famous visitors worthy of mention in the 1940s. On 20 November 1940 Noel Coward, English actor, director, composer and dramatist, arrived in Brisbane as part of a goodwill tour to raise funds for the Australian Red Cross. From the time of his arrival at Archerfield aerodrome, he was mobbed by admiring women seeking his autograph. The *Courier-mail* was adorned with pictures of the star attending a reception held by the Queensland Authors & Artists Association at Princes Restaurant, surrounded by doting female fans.

That night Coward entertained troops at the Grovely military camp and after singing a bracket of popular songs from his shows, had the microphone removed and launched into some risque numbers, one of which contained 'the great Australian adjective'. Before leaving the camp, Coward shared a meat pie with one of the diggers. The use of the 'great Australian adjective' appeared to obsess the Brisbane press who questioned him closely about it: 'I have used it many times much to the dismay of the censor', Coward said. 'You Australians should never disown it. It is a wonderful word'.[45]

The next day, after politely turning down a trip to the Brisbane abattoir to see an example of Australia's war effort, Coward starred in a matinee concert at His Majestys Theatre which raised £456 for the Red Cross. Friday's *Courier*, however, announced that Coward 'had cancelled all the arrangements made for his tour of Northern Queensland ... because of exhaustion caused by heavy calls upon him since his arrival in Australia'. On the Monday 'after going into smoke', he flew back to Sydney.[46]

Sir Thomas Beecham

The other visitor, Sir Thomas Beecham, noted English conductor and founder of the London Philharmonic Orchestra, arrived in Brisbane in July 1940 to conduct the Brisbane Symphony Orchestra at the city hall. Much to his horror, a proscenium or sounding board, had been erected across the front of the stage in order to improve the hall's acoustics. Beecham described the proscenium as a 'giant rabbit hutch', and after one rehearsal, ordered its removal. Despite all the local scientific explanations for its presence, Beecham was obdurate and the Australian Broadcasting Commission, who was transmitting the concert, complied with his wishes. At the end of the two concerts, Beecham contributed an article to the *Courier-mail* explaining his opposition to the proscenium. Besides architectural aesthetics, since the proscenium obscured a large part of the city hall organ, Beecham noted the nature of the first rehearsal:

> There issued from the interior of the rabbit-hutch the ugliest, the vulgarest, and the most revolting mass sound yet perpetrated by any group of persons assembled together on this planet to pay ostensible homage to the combined shades of Tubal Cain, Orpheus and Saint Cecilia.
>
> The quality of the woodwind was inexpressibly coarsened by the over-resonant nature of the much lauded 'sound board', the brass section took on a deafening rowdiness reminiscent of one of our celebrated band contests in the north of England, or bagpipe competitions in the Scottish Highlands, and at one moment I distinctly felt the rostrum on which I was standing quiver as if a baby earthquake had started operations under the floor of the City Hall.
>
> To make matters worse, as there was no room for it within the hutch, the full-sized grand piano had been placed on a special platform in the hall itself, thereby dividing and shutting off nearly one half of the orchestra, including the violins, from the listeners in the auditorium.

> As soon as the pianist seriously got to work in the powerful Liszt Concerto, hardly a clearly articulated note could be heard coming from this section by those in the hall below. All coherence and clarity were annihilated, any true balance between piano and orchestra was impossible of achievement, and the whole effect was one that could have been approved only by a dancing Dervish in his sublimest moment of religious aberration.[47]

The removal of the proscenium, according to Neville Cardus, allowed the audience to hear the correct tone of the orchestra. Cardus, the renowned English cricket writer and music critic, spent the war period in Australia as a journalist for Keith Murdoch's *Herald* newspapers.[48] He had been engaged by the *Courier-mail* to cover the two Beecham concerts. In a condescending manner he wrote:

> For years Sir Thomas has been civilising the English-speaking people to the consciousness of stylish, ordered and lovely sound: he has visited the darker and remoter parts of the North of England and cajoled, persuaded and mesmerised untamed bandsmen into so many rapt (for the time being) descendants of Orpheus. He has cast his spell over the Brisbane orchestra, and, so they say, two blades of grass now grow in the place of one.[49]

Cardus, however, did praise the Brisbane choir, which performed the *Messiah* at the second concert, as the best in Australia.[50] Beecham had the final say. He was not impressed at all with Brisbane audiences and found them 'very, very cold, very chilly'. In England, the audience would have jumped to their feet at the end and shouted for ten minutes. All he received from the Brisbane audience was a polite clapping for a few seconds. When it was pointed out that perhaps the audience was waiting for the National Anthem before demonstrating enthusiasm, Beecham retorted:

> How can you give them 'God Save the King' after the 'Hallelujah Chorus' ... . We gave them three verses at the beginning. That ought to be enough.

Beecham's composure had been provoked at the beginning of the concert with people still arriving during the National Anthem and the first few bars of the *Messiah*. He stopped the performance, ordered the doors shut shouting, 'This is an auditorium, not a cabaret'.[51]

Conclusion

With America's entry into the war and Macarthur camped on our doorstep, a veritable cavalcade of famous visitors passed through Brisbane on their way to the warfront including Eleanor Roosevelt, Bob Hope, the Andrews Sisters, Gary Cooper, Charles Lindbergh along with many others. The war, and the arrival of thousands of American troops, saw Brisbane lose its innocence, and this paved the way for the constant stream of entertainers, thespians, authors and musicians who are now part of our daily lives.

Chapter 11

Popular Culture: Radio to television in the 1950s

Jennifer Harrison

John Fiske in *Reading the popular* offers the following definition of popular culture:

> Culture is the constant process of producing meanings vital to a social identity for the people involved ... it is inherently political, it is centrally involved in the distribution and possible redistribution of various forms of social power ... . Resources such as television, records, clothes, video games, and language carry the interest of the economically and ideologically dominant ... . If the cultural commodities or texts do not contain resources out of which the people can make their own meanings of their social relations and identities, they will be rejected and will fail in the marketplace.[1]

Here, two of these sources are evaluated for meanings important to social identity by assessing the relevance of radio and the emerging television industries to our everyday Brisbane lives in the 1950s. Both these forms of mass communication have survived and adapted to become dominant avenues for advertising goods, providing news items and above all, entertainment.

Radio

On 14 November 1922 the British Broadcasting Service transmitted its first program, a news bulletin and weather forecast from its London studio. Five years later more than two million receiving sets were in use in Britain and by 1929 crystal sets were widely used in Australia. Wireless came to Queensland in 1930 when technicians from Amalgamated Wireless Australia (AWA) arrived in the capital and the main regional towns and cities to establish the stations and networks. From that time, the big AWA console wireless became an essential part of every home. Over the years the size was modified or combined with streamlined record players, which eventually abandoned the big speaker funnel, the windup handle and the famous HMV dog.

This new medium had an immediacy which daily newspapers, let alone weekly and monthly magazines, could not match. Excitement was contagious, so this new form of entertainment and information was eagerly received by the public who purchased mantel radio sets, while every young lad experimented with crystal sets and memorised the dots and dashes of Morse code, especially the distress signals.

Radio, and to a large extent, television programming has developed, not because management had something impelling and vital to say to the unseen millions throughout the world, but in order to provide a market for the manufacturers of receiving sets. Hence the cart did, in a sense, come before the horse.

By the 1940s, regular programming habits had been established. The morning started with a deafening trumpet reveille ushering in rise-and-shine breakfast sessions (often with the first half hour 5.00 to 5.30am reserved for hillbilly, the forerunner of country music, for those milking at that hour). Hospital and women's programs were morning features. Lunchtime serials came after midday, while the afternoon timeslots were filled with gentle 'listening' music until the children's serials and features brought the listener to news time. A further batch of family serials started the evening's entertainment, which might feature a talk program or some dramatic representation, with broadcasting ceasing with programs such as *Songs at eventide* or music for meditation. Who can recall serials such as *Martin's Corner*; *Courtship and marriage*; *When a girl marries* (brought to you by 'When you're on a good thing, stick to it', Mortein); good old *Dr Mac*; *This man is dangerous*; *Dad and Dave*; *Dr Goddard* and, of course, the long-lasting, record-breaking *Blue Hills.* While 78rpm acetate discs were giving way to 45 doughnuts and long-playing vinyls, radio serials were on large 16 inch transcriptions (trannies), despatched daily from one station to another. Evening programs such as *Night beat* *Take it from here*; *Ray's a laugh* and *Quiz kids* blended overseas and local talent. Personalities such as Hi Ho Jack Davey, Mo McCackie, Ada and Elsie, Wilfred (Thank you for having me at your place) Thomas, Richard Murdoch and Kenneth Horne kept people glued to their sets and buying products promoted by the sponsors.

By the 1950s, seven stations were broadcasting to suburban Brisbane. Reading across the dial were: 4QR, 4KQ, 4QG, 4IP, 4BC, 4BK and 4BH. These call signs indicated an identification with locality, reflecting the origins of the stations: 4BH (Bald Hills), 4IP (Ipswich), 4GR (Gold Radio, Toowoomba), and 4QR (Queensland Radio – ABC). 4BH was the local outlet for the Macquarie Network, 4BK represented the *Courier-mail* station while 4KQ became the Labor station. A recent letter on 9 August 1993 to the editor of the *Courier* recalled that 4BH began transmission at 8am on 2 January 1932 when its call sign heralded some of the greatest music, drama, sport and top local personalities in the state's broadcasting history.[2]

This local identification was carried further with community programs. The *ABC hospital hour* under the aegis of Russ Tyson had enormous influence. 4BH had run *Smokes for sick soldiers* campaign during the 1940s, while during the war, regular *Road to victory* programs had involved the audience. *Australia's amateur hour* with Dick Fair and Terry Dear toured the country detecting new talent. These community shows were strictly programmed to contain a wide variety including favourites such as Chad Morgan starring as the Sheik from Scrubby Creek. They toured the state presenting their acts in local picture shows such as Marshall Palmer's Hollywood Theatre at Greenslopes and the Lyric and Rialto theatres at West End.

Sponsorship and advertising relied mainly on local support although several national sponsors were involved with networked shows. For example listeners heard the *Lux radio theatre* and *Palmolive half hour*, and a good sprinkling of international corporations were involved with the more expensive evening hour-long blockbusters such as the Sunbeam Corporation, Kelvinator refrigeration, and Kelloggs breakfast cereals.

Programming was prescribed by station managers. The breakfast program scheduling had to include 'songs to tap your toes to', under admonitions to 'make them leave home whistling'. Each quarter-hour bracket commenced with a bright orchestral piece, then a male singer, followed by a female vocalist, an instrumentalist and finally a vocal group before starting the whole procedure again. But the end was in sight.

During the early fifties a new phenomenon arrived, the hit parade. The opportunity to import small 45s from American companies in particular introduced new heroes – the disc jockeys, each one competing to be first on air with a new release. Local talent was recruited with some, such as the Bee Gees, becoming world stars. Record companies began actively to encourage sales by indulging in payola to ensure their artists or cover versions were heard. So while companies such as RCA occasionally bought the whole breakfast session, piano players in Woolworths and Palings, who indulged requests for the latest hits in order to sell sheet music, gradually disappeared. No longer could programs be balanced according to the variety criterion because eventually hit parades thwarted the highest intentions. Best sellers rarely featured instrumentalists; they were mainly an opportunity for vocalists, either singing solo or in groups. Several female singers scored huge hits as desperate programmers tried to offset all those male crooners. Patti Page, Doris Day, Jo Stafford, Teresa Brewer, Petula Clark and Rosemary Clooney were ensured a big coverage whilst the Ames Brothers, the Four Lads, the Platters and the constantly-revived Inkspots also received regular airplay.

News in the fifties began using investigative journalism, providing hard-hitting magazine programs such as Allan Brandt's production of *Monitor* which featured a new announcer at 4BH, Hugh Cornish, showing it was possible to make news entertaining as well as informative.

The Australian music content was laid down at five percent of total records played, so Clive Collins' 'A little boy called Smiley', 'Shiralee' and 'Life is great in the Sunshine State' were featured along with Mae Brahe's 'Bless this house'. Even a vocal rendition of the Spanish favourite 'Granada' was slotted into this session when it was found that an Australian had written some words. Horrie Dargie and his mouth organ and band were regular contributors as were Bobby Limb and Jim Gussey and their orchestras. Les Richmond on his Wurlitzer organ and Wilbur Kentwell produced records of Australian compositions to ensure the percentage was reached.

But among all the frivolity, censorship was alive and well. Songs banned from airplay during the fifties were: 'Bloody Mary', and 'There's nothing like a dame' from the new Rogers & Hammerstein production of *South Pacific*. One programmer tried to get Pat Boone's 'A wonderful time up there' and Mahalia Jackson's gospel singing banned on grounds of blasphemy. Elvis Presley records were not played on 4BH for two years because his unseen hip action was regarded as almost immoral, but ultimately his huge popularity and demanding advertisers made censoring officials reconsider the decision. Some record covers featured dusky Spanish maidens and pretty South Sea Islanders to tempt buyers, with the result that many of these were sent to the studio with brown paper glued over the torsos to ensure that announcers were not too spellbound to remember their cues.

While such high moral standards were attempted, some adulation was encouraged so that heroes were created. Leonard Teale first appeared as *Superman* and was used extensively in radio dramas; Bob Dyer gave up being the Yodelling Hillbilly from Kentucky to become the king of quiz shows; American personalities, evangelist Billy Graham and the 'Power of Positive Thinking' Norman Vincent Peale, became household names.

Women's programs were conducted by friendly, comfortable figures such as Margot at 4BK, Blanche Lather at 4BC and Dulcie Scott at 4BH. Children's shows encouraged participation, with many children learning the Olympian gods of ancient Greece by becoming an Argonaut or absorbing Aboriginal culture with the white-man created

Search for the golden boomerang. Charles Porter (Liberal politician) and Freddy Foster (pianist and dance band leader) read bedtime stories to youngsters. Community singing was conducted by George Hardman with Norma Knight at the piano, while studios were crowded with women knitting who joined in 'Bye bye blackbird', 'Lily of Laguna' and 'On the sunny side of the street'. At weekends some stations devoted the whole afternoon to commentators such as Keith Noud calling horse races in every state whilst in another season George Lovejoy would provide the rundown on rugby league. For many years radio announcer John Nash broadcast the ring events at the RNA show. One highlight was provided by Allan McGillvray who wrestled with delayed cricket broadcasts, while in the local studio advertising man Ed Lyttleton provided the sound effects required to create the authenticity of live coverage.

Radio was designed to entertain, be informative and provide a stable, secure reflection of society. In so many ways, the wireless contributed positively to what Judith Williamson has described as the 'Welfare state of 40s and 50s, which also embodies the idea of "caring from above" (though in quite a different form) than they are to contemporary capitalist ideology'.[3]

But once more change was on the way.

> The [1954 royal tour of Australia] was the last great spectacle of the pre-television era. Public and commercial radio stations combined to carry the news of Her Majesty's arrival while the ABC sent twin teams of technicians and broadcasters to leapfrog each other across the country. If the Queen blinked in Lismore, they immediately heard about it in Adelaide.[4]

Television

On 22 November 1956 two Melbourne television stations went on air to telecast the Olympic Games from that city. As the Broadcasting Control Board wanted every successful tenderer to have equal opportunity, launches were arranged so that three in each capital city, one national and two commercial stations, would open around the same time. Within six months of the first telecast, six stations were operating in Melbourne and Sydney with each screening forty hours of television a week.

This exciting new development, television, came to Brisbane in the state's centenary year with the first program telecast by QTQ Channel 9 on 16 August 1959. Once again it had been intended that the three stations would start around the same date, nominated as November 1959, but the announcement that Princess Alexandra would visit Brisbane as part of her national tour in August 1959 altered the situation. QTQ, the station whose preparations were most advanced, was given permission to commence transmission to ensure continuity in the television coverage of the royal itinerary.

From August 1959, because sets cost about £300 each, many people began viewing television on city footpaths with their faces pressed to the windows of electrical retailers where sets were showing programs. Two and a half months later on Sunday 1 November 1959 BTQ Channel 7 commenced telecasting, with ABQ Channel 2 starting the following evening. The third commercial station TVQ Channel 10 did not start until 1962.

Television could claim an audio immediacy which matched that of its predecessor radio, but with the bonus of vision. By the evening of the same day, film shot over the past twelve hours could be developed to provide dramatic video support. Important news with no pictorial content would be read in front of the station logo or a plain background or sometimes old library footage was used. Even with the immediacy of

11.0 The foundation stone of ABC television, 1958 (QN)

satellite telecasts this limitation still applies. On many occasions the availability of great pictures has ensured the inclusion of substantially minor stories, while important events are given limited exposure if no visual support has been obtained. Over the years, the industry has coped with this in various ways, and the success of CNN throughout the world has been based on having cameras and reporters in all the world's hot spots. However, even today, the usual television news bulletin scripts could fit on about half a page of the *Courier-mail* with sport and weather supplying the rest of the page. So the need for selective viewing always has been, and continues to be, advocated.

One of the slowest developments has been the exploitation of the full value of video. Despite examples by cinematographers, only in recent decades have advertising agents and television producers begun to use visual devices effectively on the small screen. In the fifties, television impact was reckoned to be in the region of 70 percent audio and 30 percent video, a characteristic which made it suitable to iron by, crochet, sort stamps or clean the silver. Hobbies were not meant to disappear nor evening chores to diminish, but slowly other activity in front of television declined markedly.

Radio could be broadcast with announcers and a few technicians, with the support of a sales department, copywriters, a record library and accounts section. On the other hand, television needed a myriad of workers. When Channel 9 commenced telecasting, the administrative staff included a general manager, a sales manager, a production manager, a chief engineer and an accountant, each with secretaries and office staff. In addition, a sales and traffic branch sold and scheduled commercials, the production department employed announcers and on-camera personnel, who were supported by studio crews to handle cameras, sets and props. The engineering department supplied studio technicians to look after the sound, maintain the cameras and provide the lighting as well as coordinating projectionists and technicians in telecine. These sections were backed by control room staff to ensure the telecast was transmitted successfully. Furthermore, a film department checked all material supplied for telecast before splicing in commercials and afterwards removed them before forwarding the programs to country stations. The news department needed cameramen, sound technicians and journalists. Publicity personnel ensured the newspapers and other media were aware of programs and specials. Artists produced station identification material and painted sets built by carpenters. On top of all these were make-up artists, wardrobe mistresses, stills photographers, who also developed film for the news department, storemen, repair and maintenance personnel, drivers, cafeteria staff and receptionists. Mount Coot-tha housed a miniature city.

Television attracted young people with new ideas who adapted and extended rapidly-developing technology. Studio cameras operated with image orthicon tubes, which recorded pictures in pinpoint pricks of light of varying density. The early black and white systems permitted a great degree of intensities through varying greys, but could not cope with bright white or close stripes without hot intense lighting. So announcers wore pale-blue shirts and compensated for shiny faces with heavy pancake makeup, a fact noted in the report on the opening night.[5]

The PAL system adopted by the Australian government was more advanced than either the British or American systems. It had a larger number of lines per screen, permitting greater definition which resulted in better pictures. The newest invention in 1959 was available to Channel 9 which had a videotape machine operating soon after its opening, but initially the tape was about 2 inches wide. This expensive machine was reserved for national programs, especially variety shows. News programs which required mobile, compact film cameras relied on 16 or 35mm film telecast by two projectors which ensured smooth changeovers as each reel finished. Keen viewers waited for the tell-tale corner cues which indicated a reel change or commercial break was imminent. Two projectors fed into a telecine chain, which also supported a slide projector. Filmed commercials could be spliced into the programs at appropriate intervals or the projectors could be stopped to use slide projectors for short commercials or station identification. Two telecine chains allowed tremendous flexibility for smooth switching and blending between slides and films. Because the film originated from different sources, the monitoring of black and white levels involved a unit which also could cope with reverse polarity film.

Networks

Just as radio stations used state identification with their call signs, so too did television broadcasters. All Queensland identifications ended in Q, with QTQ9, BTQ7 and ABQ2 followed three years later by TVQ10. Networks were again essential owing to the much higher program costs incurred by combined video and audio presentations. Initially QTQ9 was allied with ATN7 in NSW and GTV9 in Melbourne while BTQ7 linked with TCN9 and HSV7. Some years later, a radical reconstruction combined all channel 9 stations together, all channel 7, while 10 and 0 united. Therefore, when various networks recall early days and feature early footage, material is shown which originally was screened by the opposition. This re-organisation was fractured later when the limitations upon one group owning more than three stations was introduced. Over the years the Broadcasting Control Board has tried to limit monopolies, controlling newspaper, magazine, radio and television networks, but media giants now have frightening control and opportunity.

Then, as now, the lure of the new and its popularity was an incentive to tax it:

> After 1 Jan 1957 a £5 licence fee had to be paid by each family with a television set. By the middle of 1959 there were almost 600,000 licence holders.[6]

This tax was dropped later in the 1960s, one of the problems being the policing of the rule, but with the introduction of cable TV, payments have been reintroduced.

Programs

The most popular shows were *The Mickey Mouse Club, People are funny* with Art Linkletter, *Maverick* with James Garner, *Peter Gunn* with its catchy Henry Mancini theme, *The Perry Como show, Six o'clock rock, Bandstand* and all those old movies. Always, there have been fashions. In 1959 and 1960 in Brisbane, westerns were favourites: *Gunsmoke, Wagon train, Cheyenne, Kit Carson, Bat Masterson, Wyatt Earp, Have gun will travel, Rawhide, Annie Oakley, Wild Bill Hickock, Buffalo Bill, Bonanza,* and *Tombstone City.* Mount Coot-tha was littered with dead horses and men wearing black hats. At the same time, medico dramas were essential viewing. These included surly Vincent Edwards as the morose *Ben Casey* forever prescribing angiograms. He vied with heart-throb Richard Chamberlain's *Doctor Kildare* and Richard Boone's *Medic* program with its totally forgettable 'Blue Star' theme, which was warbled at every talent audition conducted by Bernard King. Australia eventually replied with the *Young doctors* and later *GP* maintained a good practice. Robert Young's *Marcus Welby MD* offered a comfortable family version, while gruff Dr Finlay and his *Casebook*, together with his wonderful housekeeper, Janet, provided a British version.

Then there were the police/detective shows like *77 Sunset Strip* with Efrem Zimbalist and comb-carrying Kookie who contrasted with Jack Webb ('Just the facts, ma'am') in *Dragnet. Richard Diamond*, private detective, worked on his own whilst Robert Stack's Eliot Ness dominated the *Untouchables. Z cars* became a cult show with Stratford Johns as Inspector Barlow and Frank Windsor as his offsider, John Watts. This cast went on to make *Softly softly.* One of the most popular programs was the New York production, *Naked City.* Over the titles each week an anonymous voice intoned, 'There are eight million stories in the naked city; this has been one of them'.

Children's programs were directed at hobbies and activities. Jim Iliffe of 4BC fame recalled his wartime flying career when he became Captain Jim making his entrance each afternoon in a helicopter. Between pushing Panda potato chips and Coca Cola, Jim and sidekick Lester Foxcroft, introduced magic segments with Churchie schoolmaster Bill Millican, post-office publicity, wild-life snippets and health hints interspersed with cartoons and serials to a school-aged audience every weekday afternoon. On Channel 7 the *Mouseketeers* had a charm all their own, which eventually was trounced in the ratings when the ABC introduced *Sesame Street. Romper room, Playschool* and *Humphrey Bear* also catered for the kindergarten set. Apart from the two American shows produced by Disney and Jim Henson, all the others were part of

11.1 George Wallace (QN)

the huge reliance placed by the stations on producing programs 'live' from the studio.

Big variety shows soon became the vogue. While the laid-back styles of Perry Como and Dean Martin lured their own fans, audiences loyally supported local productions of *In Brisbane tonight*, and George Wallace and Brian Tait in *Theatre Royal.* National extravaganzas such as Digby Wolfe's Sunday night program and Bobby Limb's variety show attempted to do what Lawrence Welk and his Bubble Machine was doing in the States. Stars of British and American theatre and television found it lucrative to visit Australia in the seasonal breaks, much the same way that Australian soap actors are now the stars of British pantomime at Christmas. Over the years it was possible to meet, among many others, Bob Crosby, Shirley Bassey, Benny Hill, Alma Cogan, Winifred Atwell, Johnny Ray, Guy Mitchell, both Frankie and Cleo Laine (unrelated), Eartha Kitt and Bob Hope as well as the ones we regarded as the real stars – all the Australian performers featured in Johnny O'Keefe's *Six O'Clock Rock* and Brian Henderson's *Bandstand.* Col Joye, Judy Stone, the de Kroo brothers, Sandy Scott, Ray Melton, Peter Allen (then part of the Allen brothers), the Bee Gees, Rob E G, Billy Thorpe and Lucky Starr were known Australia-wide.

The studios had their own orchestras, ballet corps under the indomitable Doris Whimp, costume departments and dozens of stars. Gradually the sheer costs of production reduced the numbers of these shows. Today, most shows are filmed and networked.

In June 1959 the editorial of *TV times* proclaimed, 'Sport particularly seems to be almost the program for which television was invented'.[7] Perhaps because the initial telecasts in practically every state relied heavily on outside broadcasts, Australian telecasters became world leaders in this field especially with sports programs. In a 1993 telecast from Scotland of a golf final, Australia received the program by satellite each night. Just as the series was reaching an exciting stage, the BBC went on strike. This could have proved costly to Australian stations committed to pay for satellite time. However, they recognised from the beginning that the BBC product did not compare with the usual Australian one, so they augmented the telecast with 25 additional cameras.

The golf continued to be telecast without a hitch. Using only Australian cameras, the coverage was still far more extensive than that provided by the BBC. In fact the British stations took the Australian version, so the local network made money out of the whole deal.

Another form of program, which has proved particularly adaptable to television, is the documentary. Travelogues developed from the old James Fitzgerald movies which used to feature at the Carlton theatrette – the 'as the sun sinks slowly in the west and our ship pulls out of the harbour we say goodbye to tranquil Tahiti' genre. Additionally, this expertise has been applied to wild life with good input and sponsorship by magazines such as *National geographic* and the now defunct *Life*, which pioneered magnificent photostories in the 40s and 50s.

Advertising

With the advent of television, the Americanisation of Brisbane accelerated with the presence of American soldiers, sailors and airmen during the Second World War. Most of the imported television programs on the commercial channels emanated from the US as did the commercials. Local advertisers were utilised for the 'spots': 60, 30, 20 and 10 second commercials, but major sponsorship was sought for half-hour and hour programs. In these early days, great care was taken not to schedule opposing brands anywhere near each other, and if such a situation did arise, both were given 'makegoods' to repair the damage. While local support was desperately needed, few advertising agencies produced anything very sophisticated. Perhaps the most popular commercials were the Graham Kennedy and Bert Newton ad libs on the national program, *In Melbourne tonight*. In commercials lasting up to five minutes, they lampooned products such as Glo-Weave Shirts, Raoul Merton Shoes (if they're hurtin' they're Merton) and Freedman suits, and in the process sold thousands.

Initially the systems established by radio, such as programs commencing precisely on the second, were observed by television, but now, apart from the evening news, more flexible programming is acceptable.

From the beginning, a higher percentage of air-time with Australian content was demanded than radio had enforced. Over the ensuing decades this has gradually increased. The creation of homegrown series such as *Homicide* and *Number 96* was meant to redress this balance.

With censorship nowadays, far different criteria determine acceptable conditions. Humphrey McQueen referred to the government program standards of ordinary good taste, respect for individual opinions, proper regard for needs of children and respect for law and social institutions.[8] Strict application of these has always been questioned but during live shows the director always had the opportunity to cut to another camera or cue in a commercial should the situation get out of hand.

Television heroes radiated glamour and were more closely identified with show business than their radio counterparts. The shows brought larger than life figures right into the lounge rooms of Holland Park. Newspaper columns, the television journals in 1959, *TV times* and *TV week,* were full of, not local stories, but gossip about anyone who ever set foot in a television station. The weather forecasts and women's programs were presented by Miss Australia candidates. These people received brief 'training' in meteorological patterns, but they looked good and presented prepared material as well as possible. With such encouragement, many were tempted to sing, dance and become comediennes as well. Dulcie Scott from 4BH was the first woman announcer on television to provide voice-overs for the Royal Ball in that exhausting first week of telecasts. Her journalistic style of presentation, such as an enthusiastic description of Princess Alexandra in frothy aqua ballgown like 'Aphrodite rising from the foam', limited her future appearances. Fan clubs started for many of the American heroes and Australian artists and also for cartoon characters, with *Bugs Bunny* and *Roadrunner* becoming clear favourites. In addition, fictional characters and even local producers like Bruce Grundy assumed star status.

Comedy programs were developed, in many cases harking back to the vaudevillian standup styles and sight gags unsuited to radio. Then situation comedies took over. One particular type, which attracted large audiences, was built around the perfect family; but were these a form of escapism? The happy families of *Leave it to Beaver*, *The Brady Bunch*, *Father knows best* and the *Donna Read show* ignored the crowds watching Martin Luther King, Malcolm X and the awakening of Black Power and gang culture in Los Angeles. Judith Besant in a review article of several books on newsworthy items of the 50s and 60s deduced:

> Such interpretations assume that participants all shared basic and common aspects of their identities such as their social class, and their age and that common identities automatically produced their collective actions. This determinism assumes that members of a particular 'youth culture' share the same world view, the same ways of seeing, feeling and doing.[9]

Television situation comedies have always produced shows depicting behaviour thought to be typical of, or appealing to, the masses; hence the appeal of *Coronation Street*. But how real was that Manchester enclave to viewers in West Chermside? For Brisbanites, it was sheer escapism. However, such programs have their defenders. According to Barrie Gunter, head of education research at the Independent Television Commission:

> *The Eastenders* and *Coronation Street* can be more educational than programmes expected to inform. ... Viewers can absorb certain lessons in life from dramatic portrayals, learn about situations they would not otherwise experience and select out of such programmes those ingredients which they perceive to be of personal relevance or special interest ... .

He goes on to say that:

> Studies had produced 'remarkable findings' which reveal that viewers quickly forget a great deal of the content of news programmes ... film footage can distract viewers' attention away from what the reporter or newscaster is saying, resulting in a loss of understanding of what the story is about.[10]

Impact

On this basis, can the claims of television inciting violence be sustained? Both sides can ably justify their arguments. What were some of the main effects of television on Brisbane society in the 1950s apart from the Americanisation process and the categorising already mentioned? First, the variety shows in the fifties created a demand to actually see entertainers and performers. Deals were made with large hotel chains to bring people from other cities, interstate and overseas. Brisbane people were thrust more vividly into world affairs. Audiences in Annerley, Lutwyche and Bulimba were at the Olympics, saw Kennedy assassinated and walked on the moon. They could make up their own minds about 'Tricky Dickie' Nixon and Khruschev because on the first night of television in Brisbane an hour long debate between those two men was featured. In addition there was larger involvement, especially in times of crisis such as the 1968 Townsville cyclone. With this extra identification came some responsibility. Having taken their viewers through the 1974 Darwin crisis, the stations combined to present programs to raise money for relief. Floods, fires, political events – we all were involved. As well, community benefits such as church services for 'shut-ins' developed.

In these early years while 'the box' was still a novelty, we altered the pattern of furniture in our living rooms. No longer were lounge chairs arranged around a radiator or wireless set; now they were grouped at a suitable distance from a 12 or 15 inch screen. Suitable lights were put in corners so that eyes would not be damaged, and fears of potential radiation were discussed. Hearing-aid commercials were placed on the television pages in newspapers which resulted in a great consumer response. The ubiquitous 'television dinner' was invented. Dining tables were relegated to corners and used only for guests, while children were no longer taught table manners and missed out on dinner conversation. People stayed at home, and hundreds of picture shows closed. Hobbies declined; where did all the stamp and coin collectors go? For a while, children slept less, read less and listened to radio less; many would maintain that this situation still exists. We responded to the onslaught of commercials by demanding the new inventions, everything bigger and better: refrigerators, washing machines, deep freezers and dishwashers. Well might Humphrey McQueen ask, 'Did we need colour television, and if the world's resources are limited, should colour television have come before social welfare measures, here and abroad?'[11]

For all the realism, much escapism prevailed. Television provided passive, not active entertainment, and generated armchair opinions. Selectivity ruled. If a good picture was available, the item made the news. The pictures were the ones we wanted to see. We remember King Elvis's posters at the height of his popularity. It was no accident that all those look-alikes perpetuate a time when their hero was conscripted and did his bit, not his later overweight years. For many, television had become their sole source of education; the version on television must be right.

Perhaps one of the strongest influences is that recorded by Jon Stratton, who argues that the second phase of 'bodgie and widgie' youth culture was a consumer culture.[12] This creation of a youth market was eagerly seized upon by television producers. Contemporary examples of this were the James Dean and the Marilyn Monroe cults.

While sport is covered so effectively, the huge amounts of money tendered by television companies arguably may have affected the amateur status of participants while relegating them to pawns in an even bigger game:

> Because of their huge financial contribution, TELEVISION bosses get just about everything they demand, from event starting times to the actual selection of the host city, which these days depends as much on the most profitable time-zone/prime time viewing equation for the host broadcaster as it does on the wishes of the international Olympic committee. The athletes? Oh, yair! They're out there somewhere trying for glory. But their efforts to run faster, soar higher, be stronger are not as important to the Olympic movement as they used to be since the advent of television. Today they are a very entertaining and colourful chorus line to the main attraction, the 24 carat Golden Television Spectacular.

So exploded Laurie Kavanagh in his column entitled, 'Television Gods preach their word to a zombie world'.[13]

Has the progression in electronic media been effective for spreading news? According to Neil Postman, 'If television is a continuation of anything, it is of a tradition begun by the telegraph and photograph in the mid-nineteenth century, not by the printing press in the fifteenth'.[14] On the other hand, images created by television have been readily absorbed by other current forms of media. 'In our time, the T-shirt has replaced the broadsheet as the favoured means of commenting on natural disasters, executions and other notable events', averred Larry McMurtry.[15] This idea was emphasised the same weekend by the *Australian*'s competitor when writing about Wellington in New Zealand. Under the heading, 'Windy city blows its horn', David Barber reported:

> Today half the city is wearing 'Absolutely Positively Wellington' sweatshirts and caps, or carrying bags and umbrellas with the slogan. Buildings fly 'Absolutely Positively Wellington' flags, and it's on shop window posters and bumper stickers.[16]

The reorganisation of culture extends to news and even history. As one historical writer has noted:

> To cater for the demands of TELEVISION it has been necessary for the media in general to categorise the immediate past as a series of easily recognisable 'time grabs'. Thus the division into decades or generations. The baby boomers, the hippy generation of the late 60s early 70s, the yuppies of the 80s or the 'me decade'. ... It all gives much employment for journalists and sociologists in detecting new trends in popular culture. One thing is certain – today's attitudes, today's ideas will be superceded tomorrow.[17]

By the very first new year celebrated after television arrived in Brisbane, that of 1959/60, flashback programs in sports, news and variety were featured. This grouping can be dangerous for historians because it puts the past into defined chunks, diminishing all the links that section may have with so many other aspects of our culture. False borders and sections are created which only exist for television programmers. Further, as Craig Reynolds noted, 'The video culture has assaulted narrative structures, on which so much professional history depends, even as it has perfected the 20-minute narrative (thirty minutes minus commercial breaks)'.[18]

Conclusion

What then for the future? What may be the future influence of the industry on our lifestyles? The politics of satellite technology plus that of electronic journalism now need to be considered together with recent transitions in laws. We are well down the track of losing the individuality offered in the early years by the small stations. Aggregation will make it even tougher for country television to survive because of the slicing away of local content such as news. This reduction will increase with pay-television, the spread of nationally-based programs and the imposition of government-funded multiculturalism.

Radio and television are, as was explained at the beginning, tools of our culture. To a large extent, these instruments can easily manipulate, but ultimately we still retain full control. All it takes is the flick of a switch to turn it off: 'So it's goodnight from me and goodnight from him too'.

Chapter 12

'Crazy News': Rock'n'roll in Brisbane and Bill Haley's 'Big Show', 1956-57

Raymond Evans

As an historical and a cultural phenomenon, rock'n'roll is both fugitive and unstable. Its origins, lifespan, substance and form have all proved difficult and contentious to chart and define. Jim Dawes and Steve Propes' recent volume entitled *What was the first rock'n'roll record?* provides fifty extensively argued possibilities for that crown, dating from as early as 1944; while Nick Tosches profiles approximately thirty likely predecessors to Bill Haley in the area of performance in his *Unsung heroes of rock'n'roll.*[1] Even Bill Haley in a sense predates Bill Haley in that he had recorded a string of race and hillbilly inspired numbers such as 'Rocket "88"' (1951), 'Jukebox cannonball' and 'Rock the joint' (1952) as well as 'Crazy man crazy' and 'Real rock drive' (1953) before 'Rock around the clock' received life in two breathless takes at the fag-end of an afternoon recording session on 12 April 1954.[2] 'In other words, he had played out the entire history of rock'n'roll about two years before anybody ever heard of rock'n'roll'.[3]

If rock'n'roll's beginning is well nigh impossible to pinpoint accurately, its structure and dimensions are equally baffling to delineate. It was probably first named by Cleveland disc jockey Alan Freed in the early 1950s during an undated conversation with Billy Ward, lead singer of the doo-wop group, the Dominoes. As Ward later recalled, Freed was ruminating to him on the new music – 'It's *not* authentic rhythm and blues, or jazz or pop. It has no classification really ...' – when the chorus of the Dominoes' latest hit 'Sixty minute man' – a boastful paean to male potency – boomed out:

> 'I rock'em, roll'em all night long/I'm a Sixty Minute Man!'
>
> Freed leapt to his feet.
>
> 'That's it!' he cried hoarsely. 'Rock and Roll! That's what it is ...'.[4]

Although duly labelled, however, the problem of defining what 'it' – this exhilarating noise and insistent sensual rhythm – actually was in musicological terms was another matter entirely. American cultural historian Philip Ennis has lately suggested that rock'n'roll is impossible to isolate as a single musical form, for it represents the confluence of six other major streams of American music, principally rhythm and blues and country and western, emptying like major tributaries into the river of commercial pop music, fed also by the lesser streams of jazz, folk/blues and gospel – all combining eventually in the surging torrent of rock'n'roll music. Its distinctiveness as a musical genre is therefore conflated by its hybrid nature, its 'protean ways and its fecundity'.[5] More than sixty different sub-species of early rock'n'roll may be enumerated, as one recent discography has shown.[6] Thus, like a river which is both more than the sum of its parts and ever-present whilst ever-changing, rock'n'roll remains loosely structured, 'fluid, restless and hard to chart'.[7]

In remote Australia of the early 1950s, little was known or understood of this musicological merging and complexity. Jazz, swing and hillbilly music, as segregated styles, all possessed their small, isolated minorities or adherents, somewhat apart from the white popular mainstream, crammed with tunes of largely non-danceable melodies and romantic lyrics. But black rhythm and blues, gospel and folk/blues had apparently all failed White Australia's dictation test. Thus rock'n'roll had seemingly descended, fully fledged and with its origins relatively unknown, from another country around 1955 – as mysterious as the sounds of 'Heartbreak Hotel', as incomprehensible as the lyrics of 'Long Tall Sally'. It appeared as a discrete, novel and ineffable presence, either to be absorbed viscerally or rejected utterly. It was as elating and liberating to some as it was clearly sinister and threatening to others. Though all teenagers did not endorse it, nor all adults condemn it, the lineaments of its acceptance and rejection roughly traced out a generational divide, with its most hard-core adherents and champions to be found among Australian working-class youth.

Keith Cronau recalls as a young Brisbane teenager his first public exposure to rock'n'roll in late 1955 at the Metro Theatre in Albert Street. A 'Sneak Hollywood Preview' of an unnamed movie turned out to be *Blackboard Jungle* and as the clangorous strains of 'Rock around the clock' exploded upon its opening soundtrack, the cinema erupted with a delighted roar, as couples leapt chaotically from their seats to jive in the aisles.[8] Another working-class informant, a self-proclaimed 'bodgie', remembers attending screenings of *Blackboard Jungle* in Brisbane more than a dozen times, principally to hear Haley's amplified anthem. During one session, as he bopped about in his seat to the music, he recalls being cuffed across the back of the head by an irate adult sitting behind him and ordered to sit still, be quiet and behave himself.[9]

These two incidents aptly convey the polarised mood which the new music helped to induce – especially as Haley's good-time sound was linked with Richard Brooke's stark images of juvenile delinquency in the film. On the one hand, a potential for youthful abandon and misrule was promoted, with rock'n'roll co-opted as the symbolic means of 'answering back' to regimentation and conformity; on the other, there was

12.0 Advertising for Blackboard Jungle, *1955 (PERS)*

an encouragement to increased middle class surveillance and social control – an intenser policing of 'orderly, adult-sanctioned contexts' and redoubled patrols along the border between what was seen as good, clean, respectable fun and overt delinquency.[10]

The narrow parameters of respectability in mid-fifties Brisbane are not so readily replicated from the vantage point of the present. Yet perhaps a sense of the same can be established with several random examples. On 8 September 1956 the *Courier-mail* reported under a front-page headline the unfolding of 'the city's biggest "gambling" raid' conducted by police the previous evening. The headline read: '80 ARRESTED IN TOOWONG FOR BINGO' and the report recounted how a dozen officers of the Licensing Squad had surrounded the Toowong Amateur Recreation Club Hall soon after 10pm in order to net the 80 wild-eyed 'bingo' players, who were then taken in ten patrol cars to the city-watchhouse. 'Many of those arrested were elderly people but some were teenagers', the item disclosed, as it helpfully added a description of the illegal game for the erudition of its apparently uninitiated and more law-abiding readers. Perhaps even more telling than the details of the raid and the manner of its reporting was the fact that no public outcry against over-policing occurred in its aftermath. The mass arrest was seemingly considered just retribution for straying publicly onto the suburban 'wild side'.

The mid-fifties was also a time when a local alderman would blast a practical display of women's electrical razors in an Allan & Stark store window as being 'disgusting and immodest'; and correspondents to *Truth* newspaper could liken homosexuals to 'wild beasts' requiring the lash, and West End bodgies to 'Neanderthals' – 'Simian in every respect including their apelike chattering' – without encountering appreciable public disagreement.[11] In late 1956 the Queensland Literature Board of Review was pre-occupied with banning 'romance comics' with such titles as *First kiss* and *Love secrets*, aimed principally at teenage girls.[12] 'Queensland has gone further than any other State in censoring comic books and pulp magazines', reported the *Sunday mail* with some pride; as literature board members and high court judges explained how such prohibited comics offended by emphasizing 'love at first sight' rather than obeying 'the convention that requires formal introduction' of couples.[13]

Morally, Brisbane's adolescents, in particular, were expected to walk a narrowly conformist line. Although increasingly accepted as 'teenagers' – that is, a 'separate category' of persons – they were equally regarded as dependent beings in need of constant adult supervision and a cautious monitoring which reinforced middle class norms of behaviour. Teenagers, therefore, were not 'to live in a world of their own',[14] and all sites of potential non-restraint – the street, the milk bar or hamburger shop, the railway carriage, the darkened cinema, the dance hall, party or concert were likely to be rigorously policed. Decorous, organised youth was portrayed as the essential counterpoint to troublesome, rebellious youth. Young lifesavers and nurses were presented as the obverse of the working class bodgie and widgie 'cult' and 'team spirit' promoted as the antidote to 'gang spirit'.

Periodically, the *Sunday mail* employed the device of a 'Modern Youth Panel' to convey a message of 'correct' teenage behaviour to its readers, as opposed to that of either the 'fast crowd' or 'hoodlum element'. Guided by a senior journalist, the seven young panel members declaimed upon the 'proper' behaviour for teenage parties (where parents but not alcohol were always welcome), for dating (where 'six-somes' were considered the safest proposition) and for street deportment (where it was thought 'blatant, if not immodest to walk down Queen Street hand in hand in daylight').[15] 'Letters to the Editor' fulminated against teenagers 'petting' after nightfall near the GPO. 'Our fathers would have belted us,' one writer recalled, 'No wonder the streets are infested by gangs of bodgies'. Such youths thought of nothing but 'girls, horse-races and contaminated jokes', another claimed, while the young females were almost as bad.[16] They should learn to 'sew, iron, wash and do other household chores' one *Telegraph* correspondent recommended, instead of 'painting themselves like Red Indians and gallivanting about the countryside rock'n'rolling'.[17]

In most quarters, this perceived youth crisis – which included a spate of vandalism and housebreaking, as well as a penchant for fast cars – was attributed to a breakdown in family discipline.[18] Although parents were expected to respond to the outside advice of a range of professional experts, their teenage offspring were clearly beginning to move to a different drummer. Yet, as Jon Stratton points out, it was always the ideal of the perfect bourgeois marriage – safe, stable, untroubled and life-lasting – which was held up to real working-class households to feel inadequate and inferior about.[19] Deviations from this familial 'norm' were producing young delinquents, it was maintained, because traditional parental discipline was ceding its sway to the seductive intercessions of mass culture – debasing, irrational, sensual and predominantly American. One means of combating this intrusion was to call for curbs upon the production of rock'n'roll which seemed in particular to make teenagers 'throw off their inhibitions as though at a revivalist meeting'.[20]

Yet because of rock'n'roll's protean, chameleon nature it was difficult to know where effectively to place the bans. For it was not merely appearing as a singular musical form. It was also represented by record and radio and film; it was dance and concert and performance; and it colonised a further range of non-musical registers. Around it had developed a new argot of language, a rack of spectacular fashions, a full repertoire of attitudes, an iconography of style. As David Shumway argues, more than a musical genre, whose composition was vast and obscure, rock'n'roll was most accurately 'a historically specific cultural practice' which 'took on a life to its own, not just as youth music, but as a way that youth lived, and more important, were represented as living'.[21]

Thus, small battles for and against rock'n'roll would need to be fought upon a number of fronts. For instance, teen record columns in the *Brisbane telegraph* and *Australian women's weekly* continued optimistically to promote artists like Howard Keel, Les Elgart and his Orchestra, Vera Lynn, the Dutch Swing College Band and Shirley Abicair (singing 'Smiley') for adolescent consumption. But advertisements for record stores and companies placed alongside such record columns told a different story, as Elvis Presley's 'Mystery train' or 'Hound dog', Janis Martin's 'Ooby dooby' and Bill Haley and his Comets' 'R-O-C-K' and 'Rock'n'Roll stage show' LP jockeyed with each other for sales.[22]

Rock'n'roll seems to have first surfaced as a programmed format on Brisbane radio by courtesy of a visiting American wrestler, Dr Jerry Grahame. He displayed the gems of his private record collection on Allan Lappan's 'Anything goes' program on 4BK late one evening in early October 1956, exposing Brisbane listeners to the culture shock of Little Richard and Little Willie John. These 'lovely souls rocked, rolled, jabbered, gibbered, yelled and screamed their heads off' reported an unimpressed *Sunday mail* radio critic, Joyce Stirling.[23]

Lappan and fellow disc jockey Bob Rogers continued to ban rock'n'roll records from their normal programming formats. By late November 1956, 4BH had received scores of letters from irate teenagers complaining about Rogers' 'stand against the cult of

Rock'n'Roll'. 'Is you is or is you ain't a square?' demanded one young listener: 'If you is a square, let's put you in a box, tie it with a ribbon and throw it in the deep blue sea'. Dozens of similar objections 'in the unintelligible jargon of the jive addict' were crossing Rogers' desk every day; wrote Stirling: 'Surely to goodness there must be something basically wrong with the early training of boys and girls who are capable of fastening such a strong allegiance to a subject so utterly worthless'.[24]

Yet, some six weeks later, Lappan was also forced to cede to listener pressure, introducing half an hour of rock'n'roll each Tuesday night at 9pm. 'I had to', he explained apologetically, 'the kids demanded it'.[25] Thus, rather than being duped by media manipulation, it seems clear that teenagers themselves were commanding this initial airplay by their own groundswell of popular demand.

Rock'n'roll's detractors, as well as condemning the music for its utter dissimilarity to the familiar WASP crooning and Tin Pan Alley sounds of conventional 'white pop', drew attention to its noxious racial, sexual and socially disruptive tendencies. Of this latter three-pronged attack, the racial element was the least likely to be alluded to publicly, although private complaints about 'wailing niggers' were not unknown.[26] Unlike the United States, however, Australia was not embroiled in a violent drama of racial desegregation, so campaigns against pulling the white man 'down to the level of the Negro' were muted.[27] There were oblique references to 'jungle music' as well as a degree of rage expressed about 'long-haired bodgies with their peacock-coloured, Negro dope-peddler style clothes' and 'their girls on the edge of the social gutter' screaming rock'n'roll numbers on the Ferny Grove train, but there was nothing like the fury in the American South which accompanied the prospect of racially mixed rock'n'roll concerts and dances. A year before his Australian tour in January 1957, Bill Haley and his Comets had travelled the States with such black performers as Big Joe Turner, La Vern Baker and the Platters only to be warned that the group's career might be in jeopardy if they continued to tour with 'niggers'. As Haley's son has recently recorded:

> Black artists were not even allowed to be on the stage with white artists. Bill Haley was branded a 'Communist-nigger lover'.... Small gangs of klansmen began to cause trouble at the show sites ... the newspapers called them 'Rock Riots' ... The Comets' tour bus was often vandalized ... the letters 'KKK' and 'Nigger Lovers Go Home' ... graffitied on their sides while the tires were slashed ... .[28]

Though Haley would tour Australia with this same bill of black performers (along with the white rock'n'roll cabaret act, Freddie Bell and the Bell Boys) no such negative responses were elicited here. Informants, recalling attending Haley's concerts in Brisbane, Sydney and Melbourne, had no recollection of even significantly registering that more than half of the show were African-Americans. They were *American* rock'n'rollers first and foremost, exotic and adored, though perhaps somewhat less memorable as performers because of the relative ignorance about black rhythm and blues music in Australia.

Instead, rock'n'roll was mainly targeted in Brisbane for its sexually suggestive and potentially riotous capacities. Significantly, this two-sided, integrated alarm dovetailed neatly with the major official and media concerns expressed about the questionable activities of 'widgies' and 'bodgies' respectively. As both Stratton and Lesley Johnson show, a deal of the alarm over adolescent girls becoming 'widgies' was associated first with so-called 'sexual initiation ceremonies' which incorporated them into delinquent gangs and then with promiscuous, extra-marital sexual behaviour thereafter. As the *Sunday mail* sensationally reported in December 1956:

12.1 Advertising for 'The Big Show', 1957

> Stories of gross initiation ceremonies to which widgies had to submit are common in all States. And for girls who will not submit willingly the bodgies have their techniques.[29]

Subsequently, it was argued, they became 'just joy-girls .... Anything for kicks, for a good time, for laughs'.[30] Rock'n'roll's mimetic affinities with sex were believed to encourage and legitimate such licentiousness;[31] its allegedly obscene 'leerics', 'lewd intonations' and 'repetitive ... pulsating beat', the 'suggestive' movements of its performers and the abandonment of its dancers all made for a combustible combination which ostensibly placed female adolescents seriously 'at risk'.[32]

Yet, whereas females were regarded as minors whose virginity required protection from the music, males were seen to have their 'natural ... aggressive instincts' stimulated by it.[33] Reports of rioting at rock'n'roll concerts in the United States began to appear in the local press in July 1956,[34] and this was augmented in early September by accounts of disorder at screenings of Sam Katzman's 'fad-pic', *Rock around the clock* in Great Britain. 'Frenzied mobs' of Teddy Boys – London's 'ludicrous loons in draped jackets and drainpipe trousers' – driven 'rhythm crazed' by Bill Haley's 'primitive, hotted-up jazz', it was reported, had danced and run amuck in cinemas and adjoining streets. 'A nasty feature of this rock'n'roll stuff' commented the *Sunday mail*, 'is that ordinarily normal youngsters, as well as Teddy Boy perverts get caught up in it' and, once aroused, required a 'flying squad of muscle men' to suppress them.[35] What was not reported was that much of this mayhem had been exacerbated by over-policing. Venue operators, cinema attendants and police, attempting to impose conventional audience behaviour upon animated teenagers and prevent jiving in dimly lit aisles, with force if necessary, had often provoked the very discord they were ostensibly attempting to prevent.[36]

As the initial screening of *Rock around the clock* at Brisbane's Tivoli cinema approached in mid-October 1956, some apprehension was experienced, along with reassuring noises from Joyce Stirling that if any wild reactions occurred 'in prosaic old Brisbane, I'll eat my typewriter'.[37] Nevertheless, when the film opened on 18 October for an extensive city run, 'police patrolled the aisles' to keep close watch over 'the local jive junkies [who] went along in force ... and behaved as though they had ants in their pants'.[38]

Similarly when Brisbane's first rock'n'roll dance was organised by drummer Tommy O'Connor and his group at St Francis Hall in Elizabeth Street in order to welcome *Rock around the clock* to Brisbane, the *Courier-mail* captioned a photograph of spectacularly acrobatic jitterbugging with the ominous inscription, 'NOW IT'S HERE' and accompanied the news with an Ian Gall cartoon depicting a black-jacketed youth, labelled 'VANDALISM', smashing windows, tearing down street signs and destroying young trees.[39] Early rock'n'roll events were therefore reported as though they were a challenge to civil order rather than a form of entertainment. A month later when 2000 teenagers attended a city hall concert, headlined by Johnny O'Keefe, the only accounts of the proceedings concentrated upon the police presence and the disruptive incidents which accompanied it. Although the majority were well behaved, the *Brisbane telegraph* reported that one male had been 'thrown out' for attempting to jive in the aisle, another had exploded 'a bunger' in the vestibule and there was some damage to fittings in the men's washroom.[40] Playing it safe throughout, the City Council Employees Association, who had sponsored the event, had advertised it as a 'Jazz Concert', with O'Keefe himself somewhat incongruously billed as 'the Gentleman of Jazz'.[41]

Meanwhile, towards the other end of town at the Brisbane Stadium, situated in an area historically associated with deviancy and disorder,[42] a series of rock'n'roll concerts, billed precisely as a 'Rock'n'Roll Festival' had been planned – the first occurring on 7 November. As this concert, which featured local groups headlined by Ron Gowan – a former jazz artist of the tenor saxophone – and his Rockets, had proceeded without incident, it received no subsequent press coverage. Yet a second, similar affair, again showcasing all Australian acts on Wednesday night, 21 November – the eve of the opening to the Melbourne Olympics – met with an entirely different response. Despite the major coverage devoted to the Olympic Games, the *Courier-mail* nevertheless featured a front-page leader, '"Rocker" riot in Brisbane' the next morning, and the afternoon *Telegraph* weighed in with 'Police Won't Let Youth Run City'.[43]

It would seem that this riot had been prompted by similar reactions to those occurring at such disturbances overseas. As the concert proceeded, police had had 'a very busy night' attempting to maintain tight crowd control over the 3000 strong audience within the stadium. The spirited performances had prompted 'quite a bit of commotion', and police would later claim that it had been 'unruly from the outset'.[44] Yet it was not until near the close of the performance that young couples had risen tentatively in the bleachers and attempted to dance. As they moved into the aisle, they were rapidly approached by police and 'broke up', attempting to regain their seats.[45] One of the youths, Desmond D____ , a twenty-one year old labourer, grabbed by a police sergeant, allegedly stated: 'You cops won't stop us or the manager either. This is our night!'

At his subsequent trial for violently resisting arrest, obscene language and destroying two policemen's caps, D____ would claim that he was merely returning from the toilet to his seat when he was apprehended, and had remonstrated, 'Let me go. Stop. I've done nothing!' as he was dragged struggling towards an exit by several officers.[46]

Booing became general as the struggle continued and more couples rose defiantly to dance, prompting further police intervention. Scuffles began and one of the constables was heard to exclaim, 'Let him go. The crowd is getting out of hand'.[47] In one section, youths fused the lights by tearing electrical conduit from the walls, while in another a group lit a fire.[48] Valerie K_____, an eighteen-year-old newsagency worker who was attending the concert with her employer, was surprised to see flames leaping three feet into the air, and people beginning to scatter in panic as police were diverted to extinguish the blaze. She recalls:

> The seating was wooden planks and rose up in tiers ... we were high up at the back and a group of fellows started a fire! Actually a fire blazing away a few feet from us. The next thing I remember is, we were outside near the main entrance and there was a riot. It turned into a screaming dreadful riot on the footpath and on the road and luckily for me, I was safely gotten out of the middle of it by my Boss. I remember I was excited and frightened and exhiliarated by the music and didn't want to leave![49]

As the show ended at 10.30pm and police over-extended themselves trying to handle disturbances both inside and outside the stadium, there are numerous references to punches being thrown as well as people struck across the head with handcuffs and felled to the footpath. Some teenagers were attempting to resist arrest aided by groups of others. Some tried to continue jiving in the street, bringing traffic to a halt. As police reinforcements arrived, stones and pennies were thrown at them, and soft drink bottles aimed at police vehicles. One policeman was felled by such a bottle. These disturbances continued until almost midnight. The *Courier-mail* reported:

> Several police had their caps snatched off and uniforms torn during struggles. Police stopped and dispersed a yelling crowd of several hundred teenagers who were advancing up Albert Street towards Queen Street. All traffic stopped in Albert Street between the Stadium and Queen Street ... .

Eight teenagers, six males and two females of working-class occupations, were arrested during the fracas and several later complained of furtive beatings at the Brisbane watch-house.[50]

So much for 'prosaic old Brisbane'! During the post-mortem to Australia's first serious rock'n'roll riot, there were calls for the re-introduction of the 'birch rod', the banning of rock'n'roll from radio, screen and press as well as the prosecution of firms manufacturing 'bodgie and widgie clothing'.[51] A police spokesman stated that the force would be 'readier' on the next occasion to prevent 'youth of a certain type gathering in their hundreds to control the city',[52] while a Labour alderman called for a ban on further rock'n'roll performances at the city hall. Rock'n'roll music was therefore omitted from the next 'Jazz Concert' in December and the audience warned that any 'trouble' would lead to immediate closure of the show.[53] Yet there also surfaced a strong substratum of criticism that police behaviour, more than the entertainment itself, had provoked the riot. Although the *Brisbane telegraph* fully supported police actions, the *Courier* implied that they had taken 'too serious' a view of youthful high-spiritedness. 'Letters to the

Editor' from several eye-witnesses expressed distress at the level of police violence displayed, particularly the manhandling of young women, which had further inflamed the situation. As the father of one teenager commented, 'Some sections of the audience ... needed some restraint, but certainly not the bashing that was handed out to them by the police'.[54]

At the nub of the problem lay dissonant views about proper concert behaviour – the police attempting to impose a code of conventional audience response towards a theatrical event – decorous, seated, performance-attentive and applauding on cue – and the teenagers endeavouring to behave as a *rock'n'roll* audience – aroused, animated and emotionally reactive, moving in symbiotic accord with the performer – itself, in effect, 'a part of the show'.[55] Official alarm about such concerts representing sites of disorder reflected wider concerns about disorderly working class youth and, indeed, its increased social visibility. As it was widely believed that 'all the Bodgies and Widgies in Brisbane' would be at the stadium concert, it was later charged that 'police had set out to clean up "bodgies" on the night of the ... show'.[56] Though this allegation was officially denied, it probably contains a kernel of truth.

Since at least March 1955 there had been a series of periodic police 'comb-outs' of so-called 'bodgies and widgies' in Brisbane, driving them from congregating in city and suburban streets, as well as from milk-bars and hamburger shops, and sometimes picture theatres and dance halls.[57] 'Over the last several months, systematic action has been taken to break up such elements', noted CIB Chief Inspector Bischof in June 1956. Publicising the commencement of a new drive in mid-October, he added:

> Failure to check young people has resulted in crime – even murder ... . Young men congregating around milk-bars and theatres are apt to be drawn into sex orgies and to fight among each other for the favours of young women. The more boisterous ones are given to acts of bravado and plot crime.[58]

Informants, who were teenagers dressing in recognised 'bodgie and widgie fashions' in this era, remember being constantly moved along by constables or told to stand on

12.2 A Bill Haley discography (PERS)

the edge of footpaths with their heels suspended over the gutter. They generally recall the marked aggressiveness of police officers towards them. Eddie M______, one of Brisbane's 'hard-core bodgies', reflects, 'They would beat us up – down laneways, on the street, in the watchhouse. They'd give it to you anywhere'.[59]

Following the November stadium riot, police announced the city's 'biggest round-up ever of bodgies'. The body of Arthur Lenwick, a middle-aged Scottish migrant, had been found in a Fortitude Valley laneway on the day after the disturbance and, even though the cause of his death could not be precisely determined, 'a "hit-run" bodgie gang' was suspected of his robbery and murder. CIB detectives began raiding every known 'bodgie haunt' in Brisbane, and interrogating youths at 'dance halls, milk bars, hotels, wine saloons and hamburger shops'.[60]

On 2 January 1957 it was announced that the next Lee Gordon 'Big Show' to visit Brisbane for four stadium concerts on 9th and 10th instant would contain a full complement of American rock'n'roll artists. The revelation was momentous for not only was this to be the first rock'n'roll tour to visit Australia, it was also the first time that American rock'n'rollers had travelled anywhere to perform outside the United States. By accident or by design, the performers in combination were representative of the six musical streams which had combined so fluidly to produce rock'n'roll. Bill Haley had developed his distinctive style out of country swing music and many of the six Comets had performed in the 'Big Bands' of the jazz era.[61] Together, the band's sound 'resembled a cross between western swing, Memphis rhythm and blues and Kansas City "jump bands", with perhaps the latter component predominating'.[62] The Platters, led by the glistening vocals of Tony Williams, were excellent exemplars of Black pop music from the glossier end of the doo-wop spectrum,[63] while Freddie Bell and the Bellboys represented a fine example of energetic white cabaret rock.[64] All these acts had recently featured in the film, *Rock around the clock*. La Vern Baker, an accomplished, brassy-voiced performer, had wended her way to rock'n'roll via an extensive career in gospel and jazz, and had recently appeared in the movie *Rock, rock, rock* which was about to open at Brisbane's St James Cinema.[65] 'Big' Joe Turner, the least well-known of the performers, was ironically the most accomplished – a powerful exemplar of the 'Blues Shout' from the depression years, and a boogie-woogie performer at the legendary 'From Spirituals to Swing' concerts at Carnegie Hall in 1938.[66] As Ted Fox writes, 'when the six-foot-two, 250 pounder let loose his bellowing voice, people listened'.[67] Overall, Australian audiences were about to be treated to a toothsome smorgasbord of all the popular American musical styles fusing to form rock'n'roll.

Yet the excitement generated among rock'n'roll aficionados was paralleled and publicly outweighed once more by official and media concern over the preservation of civil order. Bert Potts, the stadium manager, announced that the venue would be 'heavily guarded'.[68] Up to forty extra police would be on duty at each concert, stated Police Inspector Anthony,[69] while Potts took the added precaution of privately hiring another dozen or so off-duty officers to augment the official force.[70] 'We have decided to have extra police ... because of the riots ... both here and abroad', he stated. In most press announcements the shadow of the 'last Stadium concert riot' loomed over the proceedings. '"See you in gaol, ringtail" might be the rock'n'roll catchline in Brisbane this week' stated *Truth* newspaper, 'Police ... will be in a "see you later, alligator" mood if things get out of hand'.[71] Haley's manager, 'Lord' Jim Ferguson issued the consoling news that, if another riot erupted, the Comets would immediately play 'God Save the Queen', which would bring everyone 'quietly to attention'.[72] Significantly, however, it was also reassuringly added that 'a different class of audience' was expected from those who had attended the 'Rock'n'Roll Festival' in November.[73] The relevance of this assurance can only be appreciated if the pricings of concert seats are compared. Prices at the American concert were up to five times as expensive and even seats in the bleachers cost between twice and four times as much. Clearly, a distinction was being drawn between the audience behaviour of presumably poorer, working class 'bodgies' and 'widgies', and the more 'well-heeled' rock'n'roll 'fans'.

Another telling contrast is apparent in press accounts of the event as compared with participants' recollections. Almost a score of informants vividly recalled the concert as probably the best they ever attended, commenting effusively upon its electrically charged atmosphere, the professionalism of all the performers and the excellent singing and musicianship displayed throughout, given the rather primitive acoustics of the 'old tin barn' that was the Brisbane Stadium. The acrobatic showmanship of the Bellboys and the Comets was remembered with particular affection, as, of course, was Haley's kiss-curl 'coiled like snapped guitar strings'. Yet most of the press coverage makes little mention of either music or artistry. After sounding their dire warnings about disorder and extra policing, the *Brisbane telegraph*, *Truth* and *Sunday mail* paid the concerts themselves no further attention. The *Telegraph* featured Haley's arrival at Brisbane Airport mainly to report police action in thwarting the efforts of some 300 teenagers, chanting 'Ding Dong Bill' and 'Rock It, Man!', to obtain autographs.[74] The only mention of music *per se* in the *Sunday mail* occurred when it provocatively offered a free concert ticket to the director of the Queensland Conservatorium of Music in order to elicit the reply: 'Frankly ... I shouldn't be surprised if I went outside the Stadium three minutes after it started to be violently ill. It's a vile noise – the wretches can't play music at all'.[75]

12.3 *Bill Haley with trademark kiss curl in evidence, 1957 (PERS)*

In the only extensive press coverage of the concerts – 'Stadium shook as thousands rocked'n'rolled' – appearing in the *Courier-mail*, the accent was still upon successful crowd control, with some attention paid to the exotic appearance and novel antics of the Americans. Although 'teenagers and some older men and women clapped, fluttered their arms, gyrated their knees and jigged their heels', the *Courier* reported thankfully, '... there were no real attempts to dance or start a rush'.[76] Indeed, the relatively sedate behaviour of the Brisbanites was cause for comment in comparison with an earlier Newcastle concert where a frenzied audience had actually required 'the National Anthem to break the spell and turn [them] back into normal work-a-day

12.4 Bill Haley and his Comets from Rock around the clock, *1955 (PERS)*

people', as well as the later Sydney shows where police and 'white-coated attendants' were unable to control jiving en masse throughout the auditorium.[77] A 'few hep shrieks were just about all those well-behaved Brisbane cats cooked up when rock'n'roller Bill Haley took his Comets to the Queensland capital', commented Helen Frizell in the *Australian women's weekly*, 'Maybe it was the weather'.[78]

Yet, as we have seen, it was more likely a combination of extra-tight policing and popular memories of the recent riot which had affected this outcome. In the old stadium itself, even the seating arrangements bespoke of intense control, with the bleacher sections segregated from the dearer, ringside seats by a high, wide-meshed wire fence with strands of barbed wire strung around the top. 'Even then I used to feel ashamed and wonder what [the performers] thought of us out there [behind the wire]', one woman recalls.[79] This enclosure was ostensibly in place to prevent people in the cheaper seats from hurling bottles and other refuse into the ring during boxing and wrestling matches. The venue was, thus, at one and the same time, an environment of potential mayhem – a 'blood-house' where the smell of sweat and liniment hung in the air – and a highly regulated arena for stringent restraint. With audiences rising in tiers on four sides around a central boxing square in clear view of each other, the tension created was therefore palpable. Concerning the Haley concert, another woman recalls: 'In the sharp light thrown from the stage across the front rows of seats, you could occasionally catch the outline of a couple rising to dance; but immediately there would also appear the looming shadow of a policeman and they would quickly resume their seats'.[80]

More than 20,000 attended the Brisbane 'Haley' concerts, and during the entire month some 330,000 saw this caravan of stars in action Australia-wide. Bob Rogers considers that the tour 'wasn't surpassed in crowds, excitement and money until the Beatles came to Australia seven years later'.[81] It has been suggested that this barnstorming tour broke censorship's grip over rock'n'roll in Australia, but, upon the basis of further Queensland

12.5 Acrobatics from a Comet on stage in Brisbane, 1957 (JOL)

evidence, the outcome seems rather more complicated.[82] Following the Brisbane performances, the degree of suppression of rock'n'roll dances and concerts actually intensified, as did the frequency and ferocity of anti-bodgie drives. Johnny O'Keefe, attempting to promote a series of concerts throughout Queensland centres in March 1957, reported box office agents and theatre managers shying away, still fearing damage and disorder. 'They won't let us put on rock'n'roll concerts in Queensland', O'Keefe complained, 'Queensland is the only square state in Australia, man!'[83] Local councils at Rockhampton, Toowoomba, Ipswich and Townsville banned 'mind-deadening' rock'n'roll dancing in their public halls, and in Brisbane, Lord Mayor Reginald Groom prohibited 'this type of entertainment' at city hall.[84] Members of 'bodgie and widgie' gangs were now being dispersed whenever they congregated in public, after having their names listed in Criminal Investigation Bureau files under the Consorting Act.[85] 'The youths were warned that their behaviour was bringing them *near to conflict* with the law. They were told their names and addresses would be recorded for possible future use if they failed to reform', the *Sunday mail* explained.[86] 'We keep them on the move', police spokespersons stated: 'Let the Bodgies be warned. We will spare no effort to rid Brisbane of this menace' – as a special 'Bodgie Squad' was established in June ostensibly to eliminate the problem.[87]

Yet, simultaneously, the massive commercial potential of rock'n'roll and its many modes of cultural expression were thwarting the single-minded effectiveness of local censorship efforts. While the halls remained off-limits, the Australian recording industry was moving into high gear upon the lubrication of teenage record sales. The Australian film distribution industry, with its seriously shrinking market assailed by television's encroachment, was reaching desperately for the life-belt of regular teenage patrons at a new string of drive-in theatres.[88] The Australian record trade had become a £1,000,000 per month industry during 1956, and Queensland was named 'Australia's most record-conscious state'.[89] As Hugh Bingham, the *Sunday mail*'s record critic and a firm antagonist of rock'n'roll, was forced to admit in May 1957:

> ... the big money lies in the teenagers rushing the 'pops' – and the trade knows it. The order has gone out to record managers: 'Take care of the kid who is likely to have 10/- in his pocket'. And the additional advice 'Put your "pop" stands near the cash register'.

12.6 *Advertising for* Don't knock the rock *(PERS)*

> In the six months before his visit here, Australians bought 200,000 copies of Bill Haley's 'Rock Around the Clock' – the 'rockers classic'. That is some money. And the disc is still a big seller.
>
> Like the old wind-up gramophone, rock'n'roll is likely to take a longtime dying out. If ever. [90]

As Lesley Johnson observes, '"Bad" young people, it appeared, became juvenile delinquents; "good" young people merely became the misguided but harmless "teenage fans"'.[91] Thus, as teenagers branded 'bodgie' were continually hounded by police and clinically analysed by 'experts', and those now designated as 'fan' – an increasingly middle class appellation – were courted by admen, entrepreneurs and sales-persons, rock'n'roll was slowly moulded into a more certifiably predictable entertainment commodity, its defiant and iconoclastic potential progressively curbed – at least for the time being. No longer so universally feared and detested, this new cultural nexus was increasingly encouraged, as the economic advantage of the adolescent 'fan' was rapidly seen to outweigh the inflated social liability status of posturing and maligned 'rebellious youth'.

Pubs, publicans and the law

***A square meal sixpence ...
A perfect gorge one and sixpence'.***

Chapter 13

More than a passing trade: The social role of pubs

Maureen Lillie

It has been said that Bacchus arrived with the First Fleet and, finding the place congenial, has stayed in Australia ever since.[1] It would be impossible to consider the history of Australia fairly without acknowledging the role played by alcohol and the places in which it was dispensed. The hotel, not uncommonly one of the first buildings in a new settlement, has served as an oasis for the traveller, a social centre, a place of business and a working men's club. The pub was a key element in a male-oriented culture which for a long time reflected the way we saw ourselves and which has gathered a rich mythology about itself. What part have pubs and drinking played in Queensland's social history?

By the time European settlement began in Queensland, heavy drinking was already well established in Australia, encouraged by isolation and sexual deprivation caused by the high ratio of men to women. The fact that Moreton Bay had begun as a penal settlement had not precluded drinking there; but there was no licensed hotel in Brisbane until after the colony was thrown open for free settlement in 1842.[2] The first few years saw heavy spree drinking when squatters and pastoral workers came into town.[3] They tended to behave like sailors after a long voyage and the police magistrate urged the granting of publicans' licences so that some control could be exercised over the liquor trade.[4]

As hotels were also needed to accommodate travellers, by the end of the 1840s Brisbane had acquired several to cater for a variety of custom. There were also many hotels outside Brisbane by this time. Sometimes, as with the Royal Bull's Head Inn at Drayton, a pub that had been established to serve a pastoral run or a trade route became the nucleus of a settlement which went on to become a town. Elsewhere, as ports and trading centres were established, hotels were erected to cater to the needs of a shifting and largely male population. They were part of the European settlement process.

The role of the hotel went well beyond supplying the powerful and frequently dreadful liquor, which was enthusiastically consumed by all classes. All Queensland pubs were officially hotels, as early licensing acts required the provision of accommodation and stabling. There was, however, great variation in quality and a vast gulf existed between the rough hospitality of the bush inn, which probably offered the horse a better billet than its master, and the comforts, not to say luxuries, on offer at the main hotels in major towns. Accommodation at many smaller hotels was perfunctory and intended merely to fulfil the conditions required by the Act.[5] From the earliest years, hotels also catered to different interest groups and tended to attract customers who shared a trade or interest.

Not everyone who stayed at a hotel was a traveller and many catered for long-term guests. Single men often chose to take lodgings at a hotel such as the Metropolitan Hotel in Brisbane which advertised itself as a 'bachelor establishment'.[6] Besides providing a bed, meals and a laundry service, a hotel was undoubtedly a more lively place in which to live than a boarding house. It was also a more convenient place in which to conduct business affairs. A great many men from country districts visited Brisbane to do business and even those who had houses in Brisbane often had no place in which to entertain a visitor. For convenience, those sharing business interests might stay at the same hotel. The Bellevue Hotel, for instance, was home to many politicians during parliamentary sittings. This is reflected in its early provision of telephone and telegraph facilities.[7] Other hotels catered specially for commercial travellers by providing sample rooms for their use. Conducting business at inns was an old custom, as can be seen by the laws enacted both in England and in this country which forbade the payment of wages on the premises. This was to prevent them from finding their way too quickly into the publican's till, 'the favourite savings bank for so many'.[8] Pubs provided a useful 'neutral ground' for negotiations and so have remained an important part of Australian commercial life until very recently.

Hotels also filled an important role as social meeting places. They were centrally placed and were often the only building available which had sufficient space and catering facilities to hold auctions, weddings, church services and public dinners. Many hotels also acted as regular venues for club meetings. The Shamrock had a large upstairs clubroom,[9] as did the Prince Consort in Fortitude Valley.[10] As time went by, this use lessened as clubs acquired their own premises and the feeling grew that licensed premises were not always appropriate to the dignity of the proceedings. As early as 1865, Queensland trade unions pressed for the establishment of a trades hall in order to avoid 'having to go to public houses thereby tending to our moral degradation'.[11]

The provision of food was another important service offered by hotels and some prided themselves on keeping a good table. The type of fare offered was plain and heavy by modern standards. One French visitor in the 1880s complained that the only difference between an expensive hotel and a cheap one was the quality of the cutlery and service. He gloomily described the menus as 'invariably beef, mutton and poultry, boiled and roasted, roasted and boiled; the everlasting dish of potatoes and sometimes some soggy boiled vegetables'.[12]

Counter lunches began to be offered in the 1860s when competition between hotels was fierce.[13] Beginning with a simple sandwich and a glass of ale, by the 1880s these offerings had escalated into such substantial fare that they had become a burden to the publican.[14] Such meals were usually free, although purchase of drinks was expected. Sometimes they were just modestly priced. An 1890 advertisement for a pub counter lunch expresses the concept with a certain robust simplicity:

> A square meal sixpence. A real good feed one shilling. A perfect gorge one and sixpence.[15]

Free food was phased out after the First World War when shorter trading hours were brought in. The better hotels, then as now, also provided a venue for receptions and banquets. Catering became a less important part of the hotel trade as good quality restaurants developed in the later part of the century,[16] though this trend is reversing as more conventions are held in hotels.

13.0 Free lunch at Greaves's Australian Hotel, QF 11 Aug. 1888 (AHC)

Hotels also served as recreational centres, although the law tried to make drinking as little fun as possible by banning music, dancing, singing, gambling, skittles, cards and drinking on Sundays. Despite heavy fines, the law was not always obeyed. There are also numerous accounts of music and singing at rural hotels which suggests that policing was not always practical or was not strictly enforced. Permission for dancing and music was probably quite easily obtained for functions, as the main purpose of the ban was to reduce immoral encounters. A considerable amount of nineteenth century hotel legislation was aimed less at protecting patrons than at controlling their behaviour. While dancing might offer lascivious possibilities, it does not combine well with heavy drinking. The reporter for the Ipswich-based *North Australian*, with a certain malicious glee, described a dinner given for the governor in Toowoomba at which a party of ladies arriving in their ball gowns for a 'dear little dance' had to be sent home because 'Bacchus had eclipsed Terpsichore' and few of the diners were still capable of responding to the dancing muse.[17]

There was always billiards! The game was popular, and with skilful promotion by the makers of billiard tables, it became a pub craze in the 1890s.[18] Billiard rooms in the larger hotels were often handsomely set up and featured expensive Alcocks or Thurston tables. These were usually situated on the ground floor because of their weight, and near entrances so that casual customers as well as guests could use them. This positioning meant that many billiard rooms fell victim to the trend for enlarging bar space in the 1920s.[19]

Many more impromptu entertainments are on record ranging from skittles played with champagne bottles to boxing matches, both of which provided an opportunity for betting and both of which were illegal. Horseracing was closely associated with hotels and many early publicans put up prizes for races. Tattersalls Club was established at the Australian Hotel in Queen Street before it acquired its own premises.[20]

Hotels acted as informal clubs for the working classes although the middle class tended not to drink in pubs (at least not in public bars) and the upper classes entertained at home or drank in their own clubs. Working-class houses were often small, hot and overcrowded and most single men did not have their own home. In country areas many worked in isolated situations or were itinerant, so that pubs provided a place to meet or where a stranger in town could readily find congenial company. The fact that different pubs tended to cater for clientele of different interests underlines their role as informal clubs. The Caxton Hotel in Brisbane, for instance, advertised that its owner was an ex-seaman and interested in all aquatic sports.[21]

The main commodity that hotels supplied was, of course, alcohol and even those grand hotels which catered mainly for the better class of traveller were careful to maintain a thriving bar trade. Spirits were initially preferred because they kept better in the heat than beer or wine and were easier to transport.[22] Rum or brandy were most popular, though whisky began to gain on them in the 1860s and was easily the most popular spirit by the turn of the century.[23] Spirits dispensed in the poorer sort of hotel were cheap, rough and had often been adulterated, or 'nobbled' by a variety of frightening additives from fusel oil to tobacco.[24] While such beverages were liable to 'stop the victim's watch, snap his suspenders and crack his glass eye right across',[25] more innocuous mixtures such as rum and raspberry, known as a 'maiden's blush', were popular, though hardly refreshing in a hot climate. Beer began to gain in popularity as more was manufactured locally. It improved in quality and became cheaper, and the spread of railways made it easier to transport. The popularity of beer probably received a boost in Queensland by the high influx of immigrants in the 1880s, most of whom were from Britain where beer was by then the most popular drink.[26] It was not served chilled, though pubs tried to keep it cool by placing damp sacks or sods of earth on the barrels. By the 1870s bottled beer was readily available which helped to boost beer's popularity. By the turn of the century it was, without doubt, Queensland's preferred drink.

Hotels obviously played an important role in the community, and a 'pub culture' developed that was centred on them. It condoned heavy drinking and coarse language and behaviour, and was a male culture which centred on male interests and values. This arose from a situation where a high proportion of the population was single, male, had little or no recreation for much of the time and was paid seasonally. Women were excluded by law and by custom. At its best it offered easy companionship and release from isolation and grinding work. At its worst it was the culture of the beer belly and the technicolour yawn. It has been recalled nostalgically by some and lampooned by others as representing the ugly face of Australia. Above all, it has been considered uniquely Australian, though to a considerable extent, it was not.

Australians are not, and never have been, the heaviest drinkers in the world, although we rather like to think so. In the nineteenth century, Australians drank slightly more than Britons and less than Americans.[27] What may have been different is that heavy drinking was more widely spread thoughout the different levels of society.[28] Even in our peak consumption period, in the late 1970s, we drank less per head than America, Scotland, France or Sweden.[29]

Perhaps Australians seemed to be heavy drinkers because of the prevalence of binge drinking – a drought and then a flood, so to speak. Payment by lump sum led to the practice of 'knocking down the cheque', whereby shearers or other seasonal workers arrived at the nearest pub with a cheque for the season's work and proceeded to drink its whole value, before returning broke to work. This situation also existed on the American frontier with much the same results and tends to re-create itself where such conditions exist.

'The grand custom' of 'shouting' drinks for others is claimed to be unique to Australia; but was also practised on the California goldfields where drinking alone was considered to be mean.[30] In colonial Australia. drinking alone had no such stigma, because so many lived in isolation. However, during the gold rushes it became customary to 'shout the bar' when successful. It was a means of quickly gaining drinking companions for those newly arrived who did not know anyone, and is said to derive from the buyer 'shouting' to gain the attention of other drinkers in a crowded bar.[31] By the end of the nineteenth century the practice was common and had developed into a round in which a group of drinkers shouted each other in turn; refusal was considered offensive. It was noted in California, as here, that the custom was rigidly adhered to 'particularly among the social groups least able to afford it'.[32] It also caused people to drink more and more quickly than they had really intended. The custom seems to have faded in America along with frontier living, but lasted longer in Australia, where it was vigorously applied.

In the 1880s A.J. Boyd, a writer who signed himself as 'Old Chum', gave details of the elaborate etiquette of shouting: 'If you bought a horse you must shout, the vendor must shout, and the bystanders who have been shouted to, must shout'.[33] No wonder they drank so much; with all that shouting, they must have been hoarse!

Raffles, which have long been popular in pubs, also involved drinking. In the nineteenth century anyone could raffle anything as a means of disposing of it, and everyone who attended got a drink paid for by the owner and 'winner' of the raffle. As there might be twenty raffles in an evening, their popularity can be readily understood.[34]

There was a less attractive side to all this jollification. In 1869 the Theatre Royal in Rockhampton staged a 'thrilling drama in two acts and seven tableaus entitled *The bottle or the drunkard's doom*'.[35] It is easy now to see the funny side of such melodramas or of the more extreme sections of the temperance movement, which was first established in Moreton Bay in 1849,[36] but these reflected a very real concern about the clear connection between excessive drinking and severe poverty. There was, moreover, no social security safety net for families and female wages were pitifully low. Women who were unable to support their children often had them taken away. In this social climate, and where there was an excess of males, it is easy to see that drink and prostitution were often linked. The authorities were determined to ensure that they were kept apart, where possible. Women were discouraged from drinking with men by law, by the tenets of respectable society and to some extent by the men themselves, many of whom saw respectable female company as an unwelcome restraint.

The pub culture attitude to women was a strange one. An Australian etiquette book published in 1885 stressed that 'No gentleman is ever guilty of the offence of standing on street corners and the steps of hotels ... and boldly scrutinizing every lady who passes';[37] those who we can assume were *not* gentlemen did just that. Many Brisbane hotels with windows at ground level had a second sill inside the window on which to rest a glass. This allowed drinkers to lurk safely in the gloom of the hotel while they ogled female passers-by. Though most of the men would have considered this harmless good fun, the habit rendered whole sections of Queen Street unpleasant for an attractive woman to pass along, and persisted well into the 1970s.

Although women provided a pleasant diversion on the pavement, the only women really welcome in the bar were barmaids. Barmen had been the rule and were notably neat, dapper men with a good line in repartee, but they could not compete with 'the flaunting ribbon and pearly teeth' of a pretty barmaid.[38] These high priestesses at the temple of Bacchus were much admired by the customers and dressed well and

13.1 Treasury Hotel, c.1889 (JOL)

flamboyantly, especially at the better class of hotel, but the job carried a certain amount of social stigma.[39] Girls who took it up often had no family and were tempted by the comparatively high wages. In spite of the aura of glamour, the work was hard and the hours long. Though customers generally treated barmaids well, so little provision was made for their comfort that one barmaid supposedly died of constipation in 1883 because the pub had no toilet which she could use.[40]

Prejudice against women drinkers was possibly the most striking feature of Australian pub culture to foreign visitors and lasted well into the twentieth century. Until 1970 women in Queensland were not permitted in public bars and were barely tolerated in private ones. Even now, in some country pubs, there is a tendency for drinkers to move down wind with their beer when a woman enters the public bar. In the sixties it was not uncommon for a woman to be seen sipping her beer in a car parked outside the pub where her husband was drinking, or for a group of wives to sit in the lounge bar while all their husbands drank in the public one. There seems to have been a lingering feeling on the part of the authorities that any woman with a small port and lemon inside her was likely to turn feral. Judging by nineteenth century police reports, there may have been some grounds for this fear. In the rougher sort of pub, women tended to get just as drunk and aggressive as the men and Victorian double standards found female drunkenness unforgivable.

Changes to the pub culture began as other activities competed for recreational time and money. Following the First World War, steps were taken to cut down opening hours and the number of hotel licences. In the southern states, this led to the notorious six o'clock swill. In Queensland, longer hours continued, but the movies provided competition, as did the radio and gramophone.[41] Later, television also cut into the bar trade. People were not actually drinking less, but they were increasingly doing their drinking at home. Hotels fought back with beer gardens, television sets of their own and a more attractive environment. However, many of the circumstances which made pubs an important part of working life have changed. Few people these days live within walking distance of a pub, and drink driving is now vigilantly policed and socially unacceptable. The long and boozy lunch has all but disappeared, and most people drink at home. We have come to prefer wine to beer and this lends itself less to bar service.

Hotels have played a long and important role in the history of Queensland. As a staging post for people and horses, they helped to push European settlement forward. As a social centre for those in remote jobs or in new settlements, they provided a good deal of comfort and company. As a working man's place of recreation, they provided a welcome release from the sameness of life. An 1876 article on the possible causes of habitual drunkenness considered everything from bad teeth to air pollution, but concluded that many people drank because 'life will have action, oxygenic change and variety'.[42] There is probably something in that, and as people move back into the city and have less social contact, the local pub may well experience a revival. However, pubs will never be quite the same again. Barry Mackenzie is no doubt dead of renal failure, and my local is serving up calamari, chardonnay and karaoke!

Chapter 14

Brisbane's Irish brewers and cordial manufacturers

David Larkin

This may appear to be a rather strange topic for someone who does not drink beer, but even to the non-imbibing it is obvious that the most popular brew in Brisbane is XXXX. It has been said that it was named because the manufacturers could not spell the word beer, but I like to think of it as a reminder of the four Irish families from the Castlemaine goldfields who started it all in the 1850s.[1]

Synonymous with this brand is the Mr Fourex mascot who some believe represents Paddy Fitzgerald, icon of the Castlemaine Brewery in times past. 'Aha!' you say, 'there's the Irish connection'. In fact Castlemaine was founded by two Fitzgerald brothers – but more of them later.

Patrick Charles Fitzgerald belonged to a different family. He was the grandson of Thomas Henry Fitzgerald, native of County Monaghan, who founded the Queensland sugar industry. This family's connection with Castlemaine stems from T.H. Fitzgerald's business investments with George Wilkie Gray, and through the marriage of Thomas Fitzgerald's daughter Annie to John Devoy, successor to Gray as managing director of Castlemaine.

Castlemaine Brewery

James Newman, born in 1836 in Galway, left Dublin in 1854 and travelled to Victoria. He arrived at Castlemaine and was employed by Moore & Reid, storekeepers of Fryerstown and Tarilta. In 1860 he established James Newman & Co., storekeepers and merchants at Guildford near Castlemaine. The business was sold in 1875.

On 1 January 1876 Newman formed a partnership with Edward and Nicholas Fitzgerald which became the Castlemaine Brewery. A wine and spirits branch was also established at Elizabeth Street, Castlemaine, trading as J. Newman & Co. Newman became manager of the Castlemaine Brewery in 1886 and purchased the Victorian operations by 1891. He remained manager and traded until 1905 when he moved to Melbourne. Castlemaine's Victorian operations merged with Carlton & United in 1906.

Newman was chairman of Castlemaine Agricultural Society, president of the school of mines, president of Castlemaine Cricket Club and a foundation member of the Pioneers & Old Residents Association of Castlemaine. He died at his residence, Lismore, 406 Albert Street, East Melbourne on 12 July 1910, leaving his wife Jane, two sons and three daughters.

Nicholas Fitzgerald was born in 1829 at Galway, son of Francis Fitzgerald, brewer, and his wife Eleanor Joyce. He graduated from Trinity College, Dublin, in 1845 and took up a scholarship at Queens College, Galway, where he became a lawyer. Before arriving in Melbourne in 1859, he went to Ceylon and India. Fitzgerald married Marianne, daughter of Sir John O'Shannessey, premier of Victoria, and remained in Victoria where he died in 1908.

Edward, brother of Nicholas, was also a barrister and solicitor in Ireland before emigrating to Victoria in 1856. He established Fitzgerald & Co., distillers, at Winters Flat, Castlemaine in 1857, and in 1860 entered a partnership with his brother Nicholas, who in 1863 became a director of the South Australian Brewery. In 1876 they merged with Newman and established Castlemaine Brewery in Brisbane, which was acquired by Quinlan Gray & Co. two years later.

Perkins & Co.

By 1857, two more Irish families from Tipperary had arrived in Victoria. Patrick Perkins emigrated from Cashel with his family in 1855. Born in October 1838, he was the son of Thomas Perkins, farmer, and his wife Ellen Gooley. The family was successful on the goldfields. Paddy and his brother Thomas (1841-76) acquired an £8000 share in Reedy Creek Mine and later established a store and brewery at Castlemaine.

Perkins visited Queensland in 1866 and established the Toowoomba Maltings in 1867. He opened the Perkins & Co. Downs Brewery at Toowoomba two years later. Due to his many investments, he installed his brother-in-law, William Grene Power, as manager of the Downs Brewery in 1873. Perkins settled at Brisbane in 1876 where he took over David Lyons brewery at Mary Street and established Perkins & Co. Toowoomba Ale Brewery.

Perkins was a member of the Legislative Assembly for Aubigny on the Downs from 1877-83 and served as minister for lands in the McIlwraith government from 1879-83.

14.0 City Brewery (JOL)

By 1887 he had disposed of much of the Toowoomba Brewery to Castlemaine Fitzgerald Quinlan Gray & Co. With Thomas McIlwraith he then floated Perkins & Co., a large brewing and hotel enterprise which was managed by the Gooleys. Perkins invested and lost heavily in the Mount Morgan mine and was elected to the Legislative Council in 1893. He died at Hawthorn, Melbourne, on 17 May 1901, almost destitute.

William Gooley was born at Cashel, Tipperary, in 1854, son of William Gooley, brewer, and his wife Norah Dwyre. The family arrived in Castlemaine in 1857 with William Grene Power. The Gooleys moved to Queensland with their Perkins cousins, and William Gooley became manager of Perkins & Co. City Brewery at Mary Street 1886. Two years later he built the Jubilee Hotel at Leichhardt Street, Fortitude Valley, which he owned until 1897. Gooley is remembered in the Perkins & Co. 'Pasteurised Lager Bier', bottled by Gooley's patent, and in the 1930s Castlemaine Perkins 'Gooley's XXX Boar Stout'. He died on 30 September 1916 and was buried at Nudgee with his wife Margaret (1857-1947), a son and daughter.

William Grene Power, the son of Edward Power and Mary Ann Grene, was born at Clonmel, Tipperary, in 1835. He was educated at Carlow College and emigrated to Victoria in 1857. Power was a miner and brewer at Castlemaine, Bendigo and Ballarat. He became the mayor of Jamieson, Victoria, in 1866 before moving to Queensland in 1873 as manager of Perkins & Co. Downs Brewery at Toowoomba. He married Mary Teresa (1845-79) the sister of Paddy Perkins. Power was elected a member of the Legislative Council in 1883 and was a director of the Queensland Deposit Bank from 1886-92. He died at Nundah on 14 August 1903 and was buried with his wife at Toowong.

These were the Castlemaine Victoria origins of the famous XXXX brewery, but Brisbane families also contributed to the brewery culture.

Michael Quinlan had no personal involvement in the brewing business, having died before his firm took over Castlemaine. He was born about 1830 in Tipperary, the son of Michael Quinlan and Elizabeth Campbell. Quinlan arrived in Brisbane with his sister Anne aboard the Emigrant in 1850. He set up a business at Bowen Terrace in 1860 and by 1871 had established Quinlan Donnelly & Co., merchants, importers and mercantile shipping agents. By 1876 they had large premises on the corner of Queen and Eagle streets. Quinlan married Kate Keane whose niece married George Wilkie Gray. Quinlan died in July 1878 and was buried in the Gray family plot at Nudgee Cemetery.

George Wilkie Gray was born in Sydney in 1844, the son of Alexander Gray, brewer from Antrim, and his wife Margaret Hall. The family arrived in Sydney from Ireland in 1839. Gray was an accountant in Sydney before moving to Queensland in 1863 where he worked for Clark Hodgson & Co. at Ipswich. He became manager of that firm in 1867. Gray joined Quinlan Donnelly & Co. in 1868 and married Quinlan's niece Maria Emma Boulderson. He became a partner in the firm, establishing Quinlan Gray & Co. which merged with the Castlemaine Brewery in 1878 as Castlemaine Fitzgerald, Quinlan Gray & Co.

Castlemaine Perkins

In 1878 Gray established the Milton Brewery, and a decade later the company amalgamated with Perkins & Co. to form Castlemaine Perkins Quinlan Gray & Co. Gray was managing director of the brewery until his death in 1924. Gray's second wife was Lillian Eleanor, daughter of Paddy Perkins.

The XXXX brew was introduced as the mainstream lager in 1916. XXX and XXXX brands had been used for many years by both Perkins and Castlemaine breweries.

Gray had many diversified business interests in timber, shipping and real estate in Brisbane and Melbourne, and a keen interest in hotels, mining, cotton and sugar in particular. He helped establish the sugarcane industry with Thomas Henry Fitzgerald and many notable catholic businessmen of Brisbane. He was adviser to the Sisters of Mercy on their Geraldton sugar plantations and Brisbane properties. Gray was managing director of Queensland Sugar Co. in 1880 and in that year installed the first telephone in Brisbane. He was chairman of directors of a number of companies and a member of the Legislative Council from 1894-1921. Gray was also an active sportsman in cycling and rowing and played in the first inter-colonial cricket match between Queensland and New South Wales in 1864-65.

He bought Eldernell at Hamilton from Judge Mein's estate in 1890 for £11,000 and died there on 24 September 1924, leaving the house to his wife Lillian and his life assurances to the Sisters of Mercy. This enabled them to build the Mater hospital. That home is now Bishopsbourne, the residence of the anglican archbishop of Brisbane.

Gray's successor at Castlemaine was John N. Devoy. Born in 1858 at Athy, Kildare, he was the son of Patrick Devoy of Kildare and Ann Reilly of Cavan. He was also the nephew of his namesake, the American patriot John Devoy of Boston. The family arrived in Brisbane aboard the Landsborough in 1865.

Devoy was first employed by George Raff & Co. from 1871–73 before working at Quinlan Donnelly & Co. He became assistant manager of Quinlan Gray & Co. in 1888, then managing director, succeeding Gray in 1908. Devoy was appointed to the board of directors at Castlemaine in 1915 and again succeeded Gray as managing director of Castlemaine in 1924. Devoy was a corporal in the Queensland Volunteer Rifles from 1870-83 and captain of the Irish Rifles from 1890-93.

Devoy married Annie, daughter of Thomas Henry Fitzgerald of Geraldton in 1908. They had no children of their own, and Annie was very generous to her Fitzgerald nieces and nephews. Devoy was a prominent member of many clubs including Tattersalls and the Queensland Irish Association. He died at his home at Bardon in 1942, leaving his estate to his sister Maggie O'Carroll who had pre-deceased him. After a legal battle by the O'Carrolls, a considerable amount of Castlemaine shares was lost to the Fitzgerald family who consolidated their interests from Annie Devoy's previous generosity.

Another Irishman who had an involvement with Castlemaine and Perkins was Peter Murphy. Born in 1853 at Mohill, Leitrim, he was the son of James Murphy, storekeeper, and his wife Ann King. Murphy worked for his uncle at a wine and spirits store at Mohill before emigrating to Brisbane on the Indus in July 1871.

Murphy worked as a labourer, bullock team driver and police constable in north Queensland before returning to Brisbane. He established a grocer's shop at Red Hill and obtained a spirits dealer's licence in 1879. Murphy owned the Railway Co-op store and spirits agency in partnership with William Helion from Offaly. He married Helion's niece, Ellen Imelda Bulcock, in 1885. The Helion family were mostly publicans. Murphy became the wealthiest publican in Brisbane, acquiring the Burgundy Hotel at Roma Street in 1883 and the Transcontinental the following year. He was president of the Queensland United Victuallers Association for several terms, and in 1893 he became the chairman of Perkins & Co. City Brewery, and later a director of Castlemaine Perkins at Milton. Murphy was the main spokesman for the liquor trade in Brisbane.

Murphy invested mostly in the businesses of catholic friends, in particular McDonnell

& East, of which he was a third partner and initial chairman. He held directorships in many Brisbane companies and was a member of the Legislative Council from 1904-25. He died at his home in Hamilton in 1925 and was buried at Nudgee Cemetery.

Other Brisbane breweries

Another Brisbane brewery was that of Bulimba Brewery operated by the Queensland Brewing Co. Irishman Henry Bolton was manager of this company from 1887-93. Born in Galway in 1842, the son of C.E. Bolton, he arrived in Victoria in 1861 and became a brewer at Heathcote and Seymour by 1869. Bolton was president of Seymour Shire Council from 1869-76, a member of the Victorian parliament from 1880-84 and postmaster-general from 1881-83.

In 1884 Bolton and his wife, Annie (nee Eagan), moved to Brisbane to reside at Elizabeth Street. Queensland Brewing had its brewery at Bulimba and central office in Charlotte Street. They were manufacturers of 'Bulimba XXX sparkling ale and extra stout – available in bulk and bottle'. From 1890, Queensland Brewing was registered at Florence Street, Teneriffe. In 1896 Bolton moved to Mackay as agent for Queensland Brewing at the City Brewery, Cemetery Street, Mackay, where he died in 1900.

Laurence Cusack, a wholesale family grocer, established his store in 1869 at Leichhardt Street, Spring Hill, five years after his marriage to Mary Early. They sold tea, wine and spirits at his establishment in 1883. He was also a commission agent and had a public weighbridge at Stanley Street, South Brisbane. Cusack was listed in 1887 as a brewer at Chester Street, Fortitude Valley, while the Phoenix Brewery appears at the same address from 1890-93. Cusack, the son of Lawrence Cusack and Bridget Malone, died on 1 June 1915.

Eclipse Brewery was located at Wickham Street, Fortitude Valley, from 1893-96 and then at Stanley Street, South Brisbane, from 1896-99 with R.D. Early as manager. There

14.1 Queensland Brewery (JOL)

were two other breweries in Brisbane, but it is not known if there is any Irish connection. Victoria Brewery was listed at Kangaroo Point from 1883-84 with J.H. Hocker as proprietor. West End Brewery at Montague Road, South Brisbane, appeared from 1890 with George B. Nichol and Albert Lanfear as managers in 1896. It was listed at Boundary Street in 1899.

Cordial manufacturers

The Queensland liquor industry provided more than the beverages brewed by beer manufacturers. Ale, porter, bitters and stout were complemented by other 'aerated waters' such as ginger beer, ginger ale, lemonade, soda water, horehound and hop beer. Indeed, cordial manufacturers were prevalent in Queensland before the establishment of the beer industry by Paddy Perkins.

Frederick Smith and his Irish born wife, Emma Victoria Allen from Tuam, Galway, established a cordial and soda water manufacturing business at Drayton in 1857. They moved to Toowoomba in 1867 and to Ipswich in 1869, eventually settling at Gladstone in 1873. Interestingly, there is a Ginger Beer Creek at Calliope near Gladstone. Some of the early publicans also made, or attempted to make, their own cordials and beers. By the 1880s, a number of publicans were also listed as cordial manufacturers.

The earliest and most successful cordial manufacturer in Brisbane was Michael Ryan. Born in Tipperary about 1833, Ryan arrived in Brisbane aboard the Argyle on 28 July 1852 with his parents and family. Michael married Anastasia Mooney, whose family was well-connected in Brisbane business enterprises. Her father, Patrick Mooney, an early selector and timbergetter, was killed by a falling tree at Pine Rivers in September 1851. Her sister Ellen was the wife of John Arthur Manus O'Keeffe who built many heritage buildings in the city. Another sister, Mary, was the wife of Jeremiah Scanlan, a leading Brisbane publican. Her brother James Mooney was another successful Brisbane publican.

Michael and Anna had a large family and established a cordial manufacturing business at Boundary and McConnell streets, Spring Hill by 1867. He was listed as manufacturing ginger beer in 1876 and lemonade in 1886 Ryan's business included his sons by 1883 (there were seven, two of whom became priests), and was listed at McConnell Street as M. Ryan & Sons. In 1893 Michael and James Ryan established the Artesian Aerated Water Co. at Prospect Terrace and Stephens Road, South Brisbane (Highgate Hill). Ryan died in 1900 and was buried at Nudgee Cemetery. The family grave, with sculpted portraits of Michael and Anastasia, is a magnificent memorial to a large, diverse and very successful family. They also owned the Gresham Hotel. Michael's brother, William, started a similar business about 1874, and by 1883 operated an establishment with his wife Jane (Orr) at Susan Street. William died in 1886 and Mrs William Ryan is listed as a ginger beer and hop beer manufacturer at Susan Street from 1887-96 when she moved to Agnes Street in Fortitude Valley. She continued the business into the next century.

Another Irishman had a cordial manufacturing business listed at Ann Street in 1874. Michael O'Leary was known to be in business in 1883, although the nature of his trade was not disclosed. In that year his son Michael O'Leary borrowed money from him to build the tramline from Johnstone River to the harbour for Fitzgerald's sugar mill. Michael Jr was a timbergetter in north Queensland before settling at Innisfail. Apart from these two snippets of information, nothing is known of Michael O'Leary Sr or his cordial manufacturing business.

Owen Gardner & Sons operated a cordial manufacturing plant at William Street, Brisbane, from 1874 into the next century, but it is not clear whether he was Irish. It is claimed that Gardner later took over Michael Ryan's established cordial business.

These are but a few of the many drink manufacturers of early Brisbane.

Chapter 15

Legislation and hotels

Judy Rechner

Adults could eat, drink, sleep and make merry in a hotel, but from the early days there were restrictions. Legislation governed the size of the drinking vessel, the hours of drinking and the number of bars and sitting rooms in a hotel. Adulterated grog was banned, but not until the 1930s were there legislative provisions regarding the preparation and consumption of food or requirements for kitchens and dining rooms. From 1884, hotel guests could expect bathrooms and toilets, but publicans did not have to cleanse and disinfect premises thoroughly until 1912. Women, children, Aborigines and aliens were all protected from the evils of alcohol by benevolent legislators. It was not until 1961 that women were permitted to drink and buy alcohol in the lounge bar.

Knowledge of legislation is a prerequisite to any research on the subject. This paper provides an overview of the legislation applicable to hotels in the colony and state of Queensland until the early 1960s, especially relating to accommodation requirements, licensing hours and prohibited activities. When researching hotels or the people involved, it is necessary to know the responsible agencies, the information required by them and what was published in the *Government gazette* and newspapers. The legislation is discussed chronologically to show when changes occurred and when clauses were first introduced. Where a clause or statute was not cancelled or amended, it is not repeated with each survey of new or amended legislation. For example, gambling and prostitution on premises remained prohibited activities from inception of legislation. It is only since deregulation that hotels have not had to supply accommodation and ensure that publicans live on the premises.

Publicans Act 1848

When Queensland separated from New South Wales in 1859, public houses operated under the Licensed (Publicans) Act of 1848: An Act to consolidate and amend the laws relative to the licensing of public houses and to regulate the sale of fermented and spirituous liquors in New South Wales.[1]

An innkeeper or publican required a publican's general licence to sell liquor from a house.[2] Annual licence meetings were held at the petty sessions of each police district on the third Tuesday of April with the court comprising three justices.[3]

Licence requirements

- Licensee to display his name and a lamp from sunset to sunrise.[4]
- Licensee or publican could be a man or woman.[5]

- Licences could be transferred from person to person, or house to house within the police district.
- Applications to transfer a licence were made at a special session.[6]

Accommodation, minimum requirements[7]

- 2 moderate sized sitting rooms.
- 2 sleeping rooms ready for use.
- Stables large enough to house 6 horses.
- Publican required to offer travellers and their horse(s) accommodation and food, even if they were not guests.
- Accommodation for guests and horse(s) independent of the publican and his family's needs.

From early days until recently, the publican's private accommodation had to be separate from that provided to the public.

Hours of opening[8]

- 4am to 10pm October to March.
- 6am to 10pm April to September.
- 1pm - 3pm Sundays, Good Friday and Christmas Day.
- Bona-fide lodgers and travellers were excused from these closed periods.

Prohibited under the act

- Skittle ground or ball court, dice, bowls, billiards or quoits or any gambling games on the premises.
- Facilities or equipment for any such games on their premises.
- Drunken behaviour, disorderly conduct, unlawful games or gaming, prostitution, or persons of notoriously bad character meeting together or remaining in their premises.[9] These prohibitions remain on the books.
- Engaging in barter; money accepted only for services, accommodation and alcohol sales.
- Selling alcohol to Aboriginal natives.[10]
- Billiards on any Sunday, Good Friday or Christmas Day.

Licensing fees[11]

- £50 for annual licence fee.
- £10 annual licence for each billiard table; publicans had to apply for billiards' licence.

Publicans Act 1863

The colony of Queensland introduced its own legislation, the Publicans Act, in 1863.[12] This repealed the NSW acts, replacing them with this Queensland version, which was very similar. Previously licensed inns and public houses (hotels) were henceforth deemed to be licensed by this act.[13]

Publicans were required to have a licence, which allowed for the sale and supply of liquor by the innkeeper or publican in the house or premises described in the licence. Schedule A, the application for a publican's licence, showed that the licence was for a house known by a specific sign, for the licensee to keep a common inn, ale-house or victualling-house, and to sell alcohol.[14] The act was concerned with the sale and supply of liquor. Morally, legislators frowned on drunkenness, disorderly conduct, prostitution and gambling but they had little concern for cleanliness and hygiene. There was scant reference to food for customers, except that publicans had to supply accommodation, food and stabling to all travellers. There was no mention of food for those drinking on the premises. Yet food could not be sold to prostitutes or morally degenerate people or those who became drunk or misbehaved.

Licensing requirements

- Annual licence meeting on 3rd Tuesday in April with monthly meetings as necessary.
- Licence meetings the responsibility of each district's court of petty sessions, and advertised in *Government gazette*.
- Monthly meetings on 2nd Tuesday of the month (except April) for new applications and transfer of licences, with appropriate fees lodged within 30 days of meeting.
- Clerks of petty sessions to seek police approval for new applicants or transfer of licences.[15]
- Brewers, distillers and retailers of liquor ineligible to sit on petty sessions dealing with publicans' licences.[16]
- Brewers, distillers, retailers of liquor, public servants, bailiffs, licensed auctioneers and criminals not permitted to hold publican's licence.[17]
- New applicants required to advertise 3 times in 2 public newspapers relevant to the town or place.[18]

Newspaper advertisements for hotel licences often included brief descriptions of the hotel, its facilities and information about the publican. In April 1884 an advertisement for a provisional publican's licence by Edward McQuade for the Royal Exchange Hotel, Toowong, declared that he was living in Kangaroo Point and intended to build a brick and stone house to replace the Railway Hotel. The new hotel would have 1 bar, 3 sitting rooms, 8 bedrooms and McQuade's private quarters. It was also noted that he owned the land.[19]

15.0 St Patricks Tavern, Kangaroo Point, c. 1870 (JOL)

15.1 Shamrock Hotel, c. 1876 (JOL)

Requirements concerning the display of a sign and burning of a lamp[20]

- A sign to display the publican's name in legible letters at least 2 inches long and the words licensed to retail fermented and spirituous liquors.
- Sign to be prominently displayed and kept in good order.
- Sign to be displayed outside the premises or house.
- Lamp to burn from sunset to sunrise.[21]
- Lamp to be positioned over the door or within 20 feet of the premises. It had to consist of 2 oil burners or 1 gas burner.

Accommodation minimums and requirements[22]

- 3 sitting rooms of moderate size and 6 bedrooms of moderate size in corporate towns.
- 2 sitting rooms of moderate size and 4 sleeping rooms of moderate size in country districts.
- Rooms always to be prepared for guests.
- Decent privies and urinals to be provided on or near the premises for the use of customers to prevent nuisances and offences against decency.
- Stables large enough for 4 horses and sufficient wholesome horse feed.
- Publicans to supply accommodation, food and stabling to all travellers if room(s) available.
- In corporate towns the publican could apply for exemption from providing stables.

Hours of opening[23]

- 4am to 12pm Monday to Saturday.
- 6am to 9am and 1pm to 3pm Good Friday and Christmas Day for take away sales.
- 1pm to 3pm on Sundays for take away sales.
- Lodgers and travellers had the right to buy refreshments at any time.

Licence fees

- £30 annual licence fee due by 30 June of each year.[24]
- £30 fine for selling alcohol if unlicensed.[25]
- £10 fee for each billiard or £5 for each bagatelle table.[26]

Prohibited under the act[27]

- Billiards and bagatelle on a Sunday, Good Friday and Christmas Day.
- Cards, dice and other forms of gambling.
- Music or dancing without permission.
- Drunkenness, disorderly conduct and prostitution in any place that food or liquor sold or consumed.
- Selling alcohol to Aborigines.
- Paying of wages or salaries by employers other than the publican to his employees.
- Seizing a person's goods if they failed to pay a debt.

Other obligations[28]

- Minimum size for selling alcohol was ½ a pint (8 ounces).
- Money and/or cheques for all payments, no bartering allowed.

Contemporary advertisements and hotel auction notices show that publicans enticed customers to visit and stay in their hotels. The Cremorne Hotel at Breakfast Creek advertised access by water or by road. Recreations included quoits and rowing. Moreover it was promoted as an ideal venue for weddings and picnic parties, and had an abundant supply of ice.[29] Brisbane publicans of the 1860s obviously thought the dining room and other facilities attracted customers. The Hotel & Cafe de Paris advertised not just its excellent cuisine but also its plunge and shower baths. It was an excellent place to rest and relax, and supplied stabling.[30] Although the cleanliness of hotels, food preparation standards and dining room service were not controlled by legislation, service offered and quality of food relied on management and consumer demand. Many ordinary hotels only offered billiard tables and bagatelles to attract clients.

The benevolent, moralistic Queensland government was intent on preventing drunkenness. Anyone who became drunk in a hotel could be prohibited from buying or consuming alcohol for one year and could be declared a drunkard for 'excessive use of spirituous or fermented liquors so misspend waste or lessen his estate' so that he or his family was penalised or his health damaged.[31]

From 1863-85 several pieces of legislation were introduced. These made minor amendments to the 1863 act and had some impact on hotel legislation. Liability was limited by the Innkeepers Protection Act of 1864. If the publican supplied a lockable box or receptacle for the safe custody of a patron's valuables and displayed the appropriate notice near the principal entrance, then liability for loss was reduced to just £20. Liability was also limited to £2 for injury to guests, and injury or loss of their larger property, goods or animals.[32]

The Municipal Institutions Act was amended in 1867 with parts of a municipality allowed to be declared as 'first-class'. In those areas no new timber buildings could be erected. External walls had to be constructed of brick, stone, iron or other non-flammable fabric. Similarly, roofs could not be made of flammable material such as wooden shingles. Further, walls and roofs of any extant structure could not be repaired or added to using timber; only fire resistant materials could be used.[33] These requirements explain the dearth of timber hotels in urban centres.

There were flaws in the Publicans Act of 1863. The government, still concerned about drunkenness and publicans allowing drinkers to put too much on the tab, brought in amending legislation in September 1864.

1864 amendments

- Drunks could be imprisoned for up to 48 hours.
- Publicans could not sue for debts of £2 or more, unless the debt was owed by a bona-fide lodger or traveller.[34]
- Alcohol in quantities of 2 gallons or more could not be sold except in towns gazetted in the *Government gazette*.

The act of 1870 to regulate the licence money payable by country publicans sought to assist rural publicans.[35]

Rural hotels

- A country publican's licence cost £15, half the cost of a city or town licence.
- Country house, inn or hotel was defined as a distance of 5 miles from a town boundary.

The need to advertise a renewal of a publican's licence was rescinded with the amendment to the Publicans Act of 1872.[36] While licences were published in the *Government gazette* from 1860 to 1914, advertisements in newspapers only appeared until 1872.

The Publicans Act was further amended in 1879 with the introduction of district licensing boards comprising five members: the police magistrate as chairman; the mayor, president or chairman of the local authority, if applicable; and justices of the peace appointed by the governor-in-council.[37] Responsibilities included issuing licences and provisional certificates confirming that the house was a fit and proper place for the sale of fermented and spirituous liquors. If the house was not completed, the applicant had to provide the dimensions and a description. Moreover, the board could insist on changes and stipulate the use of certain materials and type of construction.[38] The act was amended the following year.

While licensing boards could dictate the type of fabric and construction, they did not specify the dimensions or types of rooms. Applications for a publican's licence for an inn or hotel did not include the words victualling house, but did require a description of bedrooms and sitting rooms, excluding those required by the publican and family.

Some aspects relating to hotels were covered under other legislation. The Health Act of 1884 introduced sanitary provisions and regulations for the municipalities of Brisbane, Bundaberg, Charters Towers, Cooktown, Gympie, Ipswich, Mackay, Maryborough, Rockhampton, Roma, Sandgate, Toowong, Toowoomba, Townsville and Warwick, and the divisions of Booroodabin, Toombul and Woolloongabba. Henceforth, they applied to any future declared municipalities or divisions.[39]

Section 37 of the Health Act governed all new or rebuilt homes, houses, schools, factories or other buildings in which persons were employed. From 1884 these structures were required to have sufficient water closets, earth closets, or privies. Furthermore, toilets had to have secure privacy. In work or accommodation places the local authority was responsible for ensuring that sufficient toilets were provided for each sex. Therefore, from 1884, any hotel built or rebuilt required suitable gender differentiated lavatories if they were in a declared local government area.[40]

Under the act, a local authority health officer inspected buildings. If a building was filthy or dilapidated, the officer could enforce its purification or repair, and the local authority had the right to force owners to whitewash, cleanse or purify the whole or part of a building.[41]

Licensing Act 1885

The economic upswing and urban expansion of the 1880s saw Brisbane's entrepreneurial developers boom and bust. Many hotels were built and remodelled in this period.

The 1885 act defined liquor as wines, spirits, beer, porter, stout, ale, cider, perry, or any other spirituous or fermented fluid 5 percent or more of proof spirit.[42] The name of the licensee was changed from publican to licensed victualler and a publican's licence became a licensed victualler's licence. A licence district was the police district, or a district constituted by this act, such as a remote mining district.[43]

The licensing authority in each district comprised the police magistrate, local government chairman and justices of the peace appointed as licensing justices for a district. Restrictions were imposed on those who could be appointed. Brewers, distillers, spirit merchants, retail sellers of liquor, hotel owners, landlords and/or mortgagees of any licensed house within the district, members of temperance groups, and anyone with an interest in brewing, distilling or selling of liquor were among those banned from sitting on the board.[44] It is interesting that representatives of temperance groups and those involved in the trade were ineligible to sit on the boards.

Each January a list of all licences, names and places was published in the *Government gazette*.[45] Also, clerks of petty sessions were required to keep a register listing all licences and certificates issued:[46]

15.2 Newmarket Hotel, c.1901 (JOL)

Registration requirements

- Alphabetical listing of licensees.
- Type of licence or certificate, and if new, transferred, temporary or removed.
- Locality and name of each licensed premises.
- Accommodation provided.
- Name and residence of each applicant.

An application for a licensed victualler's licence was required to show the number of sitting rooms and bedrooms exclusive of the applicant's personal needs, stabling facilities (if any) and the number of bars (1 or 2).

To enforce the power of the licensing authority, the act provided for inspectors. These could be a licensing inspector or sub-inspector, and if the district did not have one appointed to it, then the police inspector or highest-ranking police officer would do the job:

Inspectors' duties[47]

- Inspect all licensed premises when applications for new, transfer or removal of a licence were made.
- Inspect premises noting all alterations.
- Inspect, examine and report to the licensing authority.
- Attend quarterly sessions and any other required meetings.
- Inspect for adulterated grog.

Licensing requirements

- A licence could be refused on the grounds of 'incompleteness or unfitness of premises'.[48]
- Licensees could add more rooms or refurbish premises without losing their licence.
- Licensees could not diminish the amount of accommodation or reduce the cubic capacity of rooms below the specifications.[49]
- Licensees were required to live on premises and not take 7 or more days absence without permission. They had to apply for such leave and give their reason. They could be refused.[50]
- Licensees were required to open hotel, house or inn 'for public convenience during lawful hours'.[51]
- If a female licensee married, her licence conferred on her husband the same privileges, duties, obligations and liabilities.[52]
- Premises licensed prior to this act were deemed to be legal even if the accommodation was less than this act.[53]

Accommodation requirements for urban and country hotels still included the same number of rooms, but minimum requirements for town hotels were prescribed. The government was determined that town hotels would offer visitors reasonably clean, comfortable rooms, but no requirements were given for either town or rural hotels for dining rooms, food preparation areas, kitchens or servants' rooms:

Accommodation minimums and requirements - common requirements for both town and rural hotels[54]

- Rooms always ready for use, that is 'fit for public accommodation'.

- Privies and urinals in accordance with Health Act of 1884 and local by-laws or suitable for guests' needs, that is all new or replacement buildings must have sufficient facilities with privacy for each sex.

Accommodation requirements for hotels within 5 miles of a municipality boundary[55]

- 3 moderate size sitting rooms and 6 sleeping rooms for town.
- Rooms a minimum of 800 cubic feet with a minimum of 9 foot high ceilings.

Accommodation requirements for rural hotels beyond the 5-mile limit[56]

- 2 moderate sized sitting rooms and 4 moderate sleeping rooms.
- Stabling for 4 horses with forage provided.

Opening hours[57]

- 6am to 11pm Monday to Saturday, closed on Sundays for liquor sales.
- 6 to 9am, 1 to 3pm and 8 to 10pm on Good Friday, Christmas Day for door sales only.
- Publican could choose to close from 10pm till 7am, all day Good Friday and Christmas Day.
- Urban publicans could refuse to serve liquor to travellers on a Sunday.
- Lodgers, bona-fide travellers, accident or sickness victims were exempt from normal hours.
- They could both buy and consume alcohol.
- A bona-fide traveller was someone 5 miles away from their previous night's lodgings.
- No stated requirement for providing food.

Other obligations and requirements

- One bar or counter was legal, an application needed if more than one bar or counter was desired.[58]
- Applications for a second bar had to specify the situation of each bar.[59]
- Both bars had to be accessible to the passing street trade.[60]
- Supply accommodation for all bona-fide travellers unless they were drunk or of disreputable character.[61]
- Sell liquor only in vessels of imperial measure.[62]
- Billiards and bagatelle tables still required a licence but the hours of opening were restricted to:
- 8am to midnight, then the area had to be closed until 8 the next morning.[63]
- Closed Sundays, Good Friday and Christmas Day.[64]

To help fill the colony's coffers the publican had to pay fees:

Licensing fees[65]

- £30 victuallers licence for hotels in town, municipality or within 5 miles of a municipality.
- £15 for a country licensed victuallers licence.
- £10 fee for a second bar or counter.
- £10 annual fee for each billiard table.
- £5 fee for bagatelle table licence. Obviously this game was losing popularity.

Prohibited under the act

- Selling liquor to boys or girls below the legal age limit, 18 years or younger, for consumption on the premises or door sales.[66]
- Selling alcohol to insane people, either those temporarily or permanently insane.[67]
- Selling liquor to Aboriginals, Pacific Islanders, Polynesians or any half caste.[68]
- Making or selling adulterated liquor or having in the hotel liquor they were not authorised to sell.[69]

To satisfy temperance groups, the government introduced local option. Communities had the right to become dry areas. Part 6 of the act dealt with the way in which ratepayers of a district could elect to be a dry area.

The act was amended in 1885, but the changes related to spirit merchants and higher charges for offences by licensed victuallers.[70]

Although a new local government act was introduced in 1902, many of its statutes had been on the books for years. Since 1864 in any locality declared a first-class area, timber buildings were forbidden and external walls had to be built of fire resistant fabrics. From 1878, local government bodies were given the right to make their own by-laws whereby they could regulate building materials, construction and form.[71] Section 258 stipulated that non-flammable materials were to be used in first-class areas for external walls, framework and roofs, and repairs and alterations.[72] In 1887 divisional boards were given many of the same duties and rights as councils. The preliminaries of the Local Authorities Act of 1902 stated that fire-resistant materials included bricks, stone, iron, steel, slate, tile, flagstone and concrete. It reiterated the requirement to use fire-resistant materials for all buildings in first-class areas. The act also permitted the local authority to order the repair or destruction of a structure in a dangerous state and the council could order the repair, removal or rebuilding of any building in a neglected, ruinous or dilapidated condition. Furthermore, all buildings used by the public had to be substantially constructed with sufficient safe entrances and all such entrances kept free of obstructions.[73]

Liquor Act 1912

It was not until 1912 that hotel legislation was redrafted to consolidate and modernise the 1885 act and subsequent amendments.[74] Important aspects of this act related to health, accommodation and the upkeep of the buildings. Although the Health Act of 1900 affected hotels, the sanitary requirements largely reinforced and expanded upon previous legislation. One remarkable innovation of the 1912 act was the provision of bathrooms. In many parts of Queensland this must have presented a few problems, and there was no stipulation of an adequate water supply for these baths. Brisbane suburban hotels not on water reticulation would also have faced difficulties.

An important element of the act was the requirement for hotels licensed from earlier days to bring accommodation and facilities up to 'modern' standards. The licensing inspector was given the power to act on ineffectual upkeep, unhygienic facilities and to enforce the standards of accommodation. The act not only set minimum room sizes but required decent sleeping facilities for hotel staff, with the same room sizes and ventilation requirements for all.[75]

The licensing board was replaced with a licensing court. This consisted of a 'Police Magistrate sitting alone' or if no police magistrate was in the locality, a fit and proper person appointed by the governor-in-council. The licensing district remained the police district and a listing of licences was still published in the *Government gazette*.

Inspectors and their duties[76]

- Under the act inspectors could be an inspector or sub-inspector of police, or the person in charge of a police district.
- Special inspectors and sub-inspectors could be appointed.
- Inspectors had the right to enter licensed premises at any time to inspect for cleanliness, disrepair, hygienic sanitary conditions, and answer that the hotel contained the prescribed accommodation. If not satisfied, the inspector could serve an order upon the owner or post a duplicate order on the front or principal door.
- To report on the condition of premises and furniture.
- To report on the manner in which the house has been conducted during the past 12 months,
- To note the character of the persons frequenting the house.
- To record the number, locality, and distance of other licensed premises in the neighbourhood.
- To report on sleeping rooms, sanitary conveniences and provision for fire escapes.

Accommodation requirements and minimums common to all hotels[77]

- All rooms always ready for guests.
- All rooms to have walls a minimum of 9 feet high.
- All rooms to have a window or other ventilating opening with a minimum of a 2 square foot opening to the fresh air and not more than 5 feet from the floor.
- Sleeping rooms of at least 1000 cubic feet, with a minimum of 600 cubic feet sleeping space per person.
- Servant's sleeping accommodation of similar dimensions and ventilation.
- Separate male and female privies, urinals and baths in a room or rooms set apart for the purpose.
- Fire escapes required, that is sufficient doors and facilities to allow escape in cases of fire.

Sanitary conveniences[78]

- Minimum of 2 toilets for bar patrons, kept according to public health requirements.
- One of these public conveniences reserved for females.
- Sufficient other privies and sanitary conveniences for lodgers and staff.
- When not in use, conveniences must be locked, with the keys accessible to guests and lodgers.
- All sanitary conveniences to be kept clean and hygienic in accordance with public health requirements.

Like earlier acts, the 1912 act continued the differentiation between urban and rural hotels:

Accommodation requirements and minimums for town or city hotels – within 5 miles of a city or town[79]

- 3 moderate-sized sitting rooms, 6 sleeping rooms.
- New licences required 12 sleeping rooms.

- Premises must have front or principal door apart from bar entrance, providing access that does not pass through a bar room.
- Where necessary, stabling for a minimum of 3 horses.

Requirements for rural hotels, those beyond a city, town or 5 mile boundary:[80]

- 2 moderate-sized sitting rooms, 4 sleeping rooms.
- New licences required 8 sleeping rooms.
- New hotels to have principal entrance or door separate from the bar, and a bar entrance.
- Where necessary, stabling and forage for a minimum of 4 horses.

If an application for a new licence was for an established hotel, then accommodation and facilities had to comply with the 1912 legislation. If the application was for a new hotel or for alterations to a hotel, the plans and specifications had to fulfil these 1912 requirements and be approved.[81] As licences could change hands fairly frequently, the extra sleeping rooms would be added and a new front door or principal door which allowed guests, especially women and children, to enter the hotel without passing among the grog-swilling people at the bar.

Opening hours in 1912[82]

- 6am to 11pm Monday to Saturday.
- Hotels closed on Sundays, Good Friday, Christmas Day.
- Publicans could choose to close from 9pm to 7am.
- Hotels closed during polling hours for both state and federal elections.
- During prohibited days and hours all doors and entrances to bar area to be locked.
- Lodgers had the right to consume alcohol with a meal between 12.30pm and 2.30pm during closed days.

Parliament had long debates about opening hours and Sunday closing. Rural politicians argued that Sunday travellers needed a cool drink in a comfortable place after long hours on hot dusty roads, and that hotels were often the only suitable places. The 1912 legislation did not allow such travellers a refreshing Sunday drink, as pubs were closed on Sundays. However, a bona-fide lodger could be allowed a drink with a meal on Sundays. To cater for the needs of commercial travellers, guests were allowed a drink with their meal, but only between the set hours of 12.30pm and 2.30pm.

Publicans' lives were not easy. They still could not take a holiday of more than 7 days without permission.[83] Rather than opening for 17 hours, from 6am until 11pm, publicans could restrict their bar trade to 13 hours, 7am until 9pm. They had Sundays off, except for feeding bona-fide lodgers. When they were closed, all bar entrances were to be locked. Although the bars were closed and no alcohol was sold, sitting rooms were still available for activities such as church services and meetings.

The prohibited days were more onerous for country publicans than urban licensees. Sunday closing was not very fair, as this was often the day when people came to town. Closing on election days must also have reduced profit margins. This was to prevent unscrupulous political types buying drinks for electors. Furthermore, under the criminal code of 1899, licensed premises could not be used for electioneering purposes.[84]

Other obligations and requirements[85]

- Publicans to keep premises, both bar and accommodation, in an hygienic condition and good repair.
- Licensees responsible for thoroughly cleansing and disinfecting all rooms, passages, stairs, floors, windows, doors, walls, ceilings, sanitary conveniences and drains of the licensed premises.
- Fire escapes to be provided.

Annual licence costs[86]

- £15 if annual value assessed at less than £50.
- £20 if the hotel's assessed value was more than £50.
- Assessment was based on rent, premiums payable and other annual costs.
- £20 annual fee for the second bar.
- £10 was the fee for each billiard and £5 for a bagatelle licence.

A woman could not hold a victualler's licence unless she was a widow, separated or divorced, or if she already held a licence. Others restricted from holding a licence included police, criminals, brewers, distillers, retailers of liquor, public servants, licensed auctioneers, or a wife of one of the aforementioned.[87] Women and children were still protected from the contamination of the evil of grog by male legislators.

Prohibited under the act[88]

- Games, dancing, public singing, theatricals and musical performances without permission.
- Room(s) or spaces could not be hired by private groups without permission.
- Serving females in any bar or room next to a bar. Ladies could have a drink in the dining or sitting room if it was across a passage from the bar(s).
- Serving or selling alcohol to anyone under 21.
- Selling of alcohol for take away or drinking on the premises to Aboriginals or Pacific Islanders.
- Refusing accommodation and/or stabling and feeding of horses unless the person was drunk or an undesirable.
- More than the maximum of 2 bars, counters or places where alcohol was served or sold and only where approved and specified. However, the licensee could close one of the bars.
- New or reconstructed bars divided by a glass, wood or other fabric screen or partition, except for one immediately in front of the door to the street. The law required an uninterrupted view of the bar or counter.[89] The quiet snug, or nook or a place by a fire was forbidden as neither of the bars could be screened. (No wonder some drank in clubs.)

The moralistic legislators of 1912 were obviously trying to restrict the public using hotels and enjoying unrestricted dancing, singing or other entertainment.

Section 69 of the act attempted to overcome the problem of tied-houses and thus break the breweries' monopoly. Breweries could provide a mortgage for a licensee and hold the lease as a security, but the licensee had the right to purchase alcohol and supplies from any distributor. This caused much debate in parliament, as several politicians had connections with breweries or the liquor trade.[90]

The 1912 act reflected contemporary concepts of cleanliness and hygiene. Henceforth, publicans really had to ensure that hotels were clean. A licence could be forfeited if premises were not clean, kept in good repair, lacked accommodation, furnishings or had insufficient sanitary conveniences. Furthermore, the publican could not consume too much of his own grog or allow clients to get drunk, because if the licensee was a drunkard or allowed drunkenness or the hotel was conducted in an improper manner, the licence could be rescinded.[91] The licensing court could also order the removal of a licence if a hotel's condition deteriorated so that the premises became dilapidated or 'ruinous' and the owner refused to remedy the situation, or when the premises were no longer suitable as a hotel.[92]

Often, hotels were physically moved. Licensees could apply for permission to move a hotel to a new site. If permission was granted, the need to provide accommodation was waived for the duration of the removal and re-erection of the hotel.[93] However, licensees could only hold one pub licence and they were still required to live on the property.[94]

Liquor Act amendments and regulations 1914-34

Various amending acts were introduced between 1914 and 1934. Restrictive Sunday trading hours led to agitation and lobbying until the act was amended in 1914. Bona-fide travellers, anyone who had travelled 20 or more miles from where they had slept the previous night, were allowed to drink at prohibited times.[95] Arguments about travellers and drinking were resolved in 1926 by an amendment, which defined guests as persons in the company of a lodger. Bona-fide lodgers and their guests could drink at any time but not at a bar.[96] In 1923 publicans' lives were made less stressful when opening hours were reduced to 12 hours, from 8am to 8pm.[97]

Requirements for toilets and bathrooms[98]

- Sexually segregated bathrooms and toilets with separate approaches.
- A minimum of at least 1 toilet for every 12 bedrooms.
- Bathroom to include a white vitreous enamelled cast iron plunge bath that included a shower.
- Bathrooms to include a lavatory basin and sufficient water supply.
- All bathrooms, baths, basins and fittings in good repair, clean and sanitary.
- Every bathroom door lockable on the inside.
- All sanitary conveniences, fittings and equipment to be examined and certified by the local authority.

Regulations for sleeping accommodation[99]

- Ensure cleanliness and maintenance of floor coverings, walls, ceilings, fanlights and toilet utensils.
- Unoccupied bedrooms must have windows, doors and fanlights left open for cross ventilation.
- All doors to be fitted with a lock and guests provided with a key.
- Fresh bed linen to be provided to each new guest and changed weekly.
- Mosquito nets, if provided, to be kept clean and maintained.
- Clean and fresh towels to be supplied to each room.
- Hotels required to have sufficient galvanised iron rubbish bins.

Although these 1931 regulations were innovative at the time, such requirements are now taken for granted.

Liquor Acts Amendment Act 1935

Amendments to liquor legislation were produced in 1935.[100] The major impact of this 1935 amending act was the introduction of a three-member licensing commission, one to be a judge of the supreme court or the chairman of the industrial court. All members were appointed by the governor-in-council. This new agency responsible for issuing licences, the licensing commission, had incredible powers. It could dictate prices for board and meals and order publicans to add rooms and upgrade facilities such as water supply.

Definitions[101]

- Licensing district was a petty sessions district rather than a police district.
- Licensed victualler meant the person, body corporate or firm holding the licensed victualler's licence.
- Premise referred to the 'house or place, and the curtilage thereof, and extends to every room, billiard-room, closet, sanitary convenience, cellar, yard, stable, outhouse, shed or any other' structures belonging to or appertaining to such house or place.

Accommodation and licence changes

- Accommodation and/or essential services not described as sections 23-5 of 1912 act but replaced by regulations.[102]
- Accommodation still to be provided to travellers, and if stables on site then forage and accommodation for horse(s) to be supplied.[103]
- Commission could order licensee to provide additional accommodation and/or sanitary conveniences.[104]
- When cancelling a licence, commission was required to consider local people's needs, supply of accommodation in the area and distances between licensed premises.[105]

Hours of opening[106]

- 8am to 8pm Monday to Saturday.
- Prohibited days: Sundays, Good Friday, Anzac Day, Christmas Day and during polling hours for state and federal elections.
- During prohibited days and hours all external doors and entrances to be closed and locked.
- Exceptions applied to bona-fide lodgers and travellers.
- Consumption of alcohol by bona-fide lodger(s) and their guest(s) at any time but not at a bar.
- Bona-fide travellers could drink (other than at the bar) with a meal between 12.30 and 2.30pm.
- Bona-fide travellers must arrive from a place 20 miles distant and intend to stay that night.

A bar was defined as a place perceived to be for the purpose of obtaining liquor, stocked with various liquors for sale and consumption, and fitted for the convenience of the drinking client.[107] Section 62, 'bars and adjoining rooms', included a new item. Licensees were not allowed to let or sublet any bar or allow others the right to sell liquor.[108]

Liquor regulations 1936

New regulations for hotels were published in 1936. Rather than the act detailing accommodation and facilities for services these matters were put into regulations.[109] For the first time requirements for hotel dining rooms and kitchens were prescribed.

Kitchen and dining room regulations[110]

- Where required, all doors to be fitted with a self-closing and flyproof door and doors kept closed when not in use.
- Where required, all windows and other openings to be fitted with a close fitting flyproof gauze screen.
- Dining rooms of an adequate size and well appointed, with sufficient appliances for serving guests their daily meals.
- A kitchen and/or servery to be properly equipped.
- If required, sufficient stabling for a minimum of 2 horses and/or accommodation for 2 motor vehicles.

Fire escapes and fire prevention [111]

- In places with adequate water supply the licensee to ensure water outlets with approved taps and hoses attached to walls at places directed by the commission.
- If inadequate water supply, the licensee to ensure hand fire-buckets, filled with clean water and ready for immediate use, or hand chemical fire-extinguishers or other approved alternatives, to be located at positions directed by the commission. Some rural Queensland hotels still have red fire buckets filled with sand outside bedroom doors.
- Hotels of 2 or more stories with no alternate escape stairs to install approved fixed or portable fire-escapes.

Most of the 1936 sanitation regulations were the same as those of 1931. However, regulation 33 was new:[112]

Sanitation

- Bedrooms to be separated from, and not to be in direct communication with, the dining room, kitchen or any food related room.
- Adequate supply of water and soap to be supplied to each room.
- All basins and baths to be provided with clean towels.

Liquor Acts Amendment Act 1941

This amendment changed the definition of lodger to a person who slept the night and was still in residence at 10 the next morning.[113] During prohibited hours all doors, windows and entrances to any bar or any place where liquor was stored or sold were still required to be locked, but the licensee and staff were allowed access for cleaning and deliveries.[114]

Hours of opening were also modified under this 1941 amendment, and regulations relating to bona-fide lodgers and their guests:

Opening hours and variations

- 10am to 10pm, Monday to Saturday.
- Bona-fide lodgers and their guests could buy or drink alcohol at any time, but not at a bar.
- Bona-fide travellers could consume drinks between noon and 2pm, and 5pm to 7pm.
- Bona-fide travellers could not drink at a bar or buy liquor to take away.
- Bona-fide traveller was someone who had travelled 40 or more miles.
- Bona-fide travellers must sign visitors' book.

During the Second World War, the governor-in-council's emergency powers included closing a hotel down, stopping the sale of alcohol for drinking on the premises or take away, and preventing bona-fide lodgers and travellers from drinking.[115]

Liquor Acts Amendment Act 1945

A few changes were introduced in 1945. Licensees not only had to keep the place clean, hygienic and in good repair but ensure that they provided the prescribed accommodation, necessary furniture, furnishings, fittings and other equipment and that they were kept in good order and condition. Licensees were required to store and sell 'all classes, kinds, and descriptions of liquor' that locals could reasonably expect to purchase, unless the hotel owner was a brewer. The government had obviously given up their attempts to reduce the control of breweries over tied-houses.[116]

Officialdom still frowned upon women drinking in hotels. Amendment 18 stated that no female could be served in any part of a hotel where liquor was sold, or in any room with direct access to any bar or place where liquor was sold over the counter.[117]

Section 62 amended regulations concerning bars and adjoining rooms. A licensee was not only prohibited from letting or subletting a bar but could not allow any other business within the hotel, except with the commission's approval.[118] Hotel shops, like tobacconists, barbers and hair dressing salons, could entice customers to city hotels but even the sub-letting of dining rooms required permission from that powerful authority, the licensing commission.

One innovation was the provision of meals for the public. Legislation regarding accommodation to travellers was amended so that licensees could be ordered to provide board and/or food for the public whether they were bona-fide travellers or not. The commission could order licensees to supply victuals or meals for more than the number of resident guests and specify the types of meals and serving times, and prices of such board and meals.[119]

Liquor Act amendments 1950s

In 1952 the government allowed licensees to apply to physically move the pub or licence to a new property if the publican felt that the hotel was no longer economically viable due to changed traffic conditions. However, if the commission believed that the convenience of the public, particularly the travelling public, and the requirements of that locality were affected, it could approve moving the licence to other premises in the locality. Moreover, the commission could approve moving the building, or just parts of the hotel.[120]

In 1954 the restriction on a maximum of only two bars was lifted. A new legal point of sale, bottle departments as places for the purchase of alcohol, was legalised.[121] Places for drinking were extended to include tables in gardens and under awnings. Although this legislative amendment allowed outdoor drinking areas or beer gardens, which would encourage tourists, the screening of areas to create nooks and secluded drinking areas still needed permission.[122]

The commission was given more power in 1954 especially with regard to accommodation, services and safety.[123] It could demand:

- More sitting rooms, sleeping rooms if needed.
- Installation of ventilation, cooling, heating, lighting, cooking equipment etc.
- Bath facilities, closets, privies, and other sanitary necessities.
- Installation of water storage system.
- Installation of fire alarms and fire fighting equipment.[124]

The Liquor Acts Amendment Act of 1958 redefined a bar as any room or place with a counter used for the sale of, and stocked with, liquor. A bar did not include a servery used to supply liquor to customers when in a beer garden, lounge, dining room or some other area.[125] Furthermore, every hotel was required to have at least one public bar with a sign displaying 'Public Bar' on or near every entrance to such a bar. The commission retained the right to decide which bar was the public bar.[126]

Liquor Act amendments 1960s

1961 amendments show a more modern approach to hotel legislation.[127]

- A bar could be termed a lounge bar. Females could only be served and sold alcohol in a lounge bar, provided the bar was in or next to the lounge or dining room. Lounge bars were required to have tables and chairs and the words 'Lounge Bar' prominently displayed on, over or near every entrance to it. The commission could withhold permission to call a bar a lounge bar.
- Beer gardens having become a way of life in sunny Queensland, legislation dealing with them was introduced.
- Publicans required to stock and sell biscuits and one other prescribed food type, for immediate consumption, at all places where alcohol sold or supplied.

In 1965 the already wide-ranging powers of the commissioners were increased with an amendment to section 51 which allowed old buildings or those in 'ruinous, damaged or dilapidated condition' to be declared unfit or inadequate. If the situation was not acted upon, the commission could withdraw the licence.[128] The rights of lodgers, boarders and travellers to drink during prohibited hours were still causing debate; 'board' was defined in 1965 in terms of someone at a hotel enjoying three full daily meals.[129]

We take for granted many of the aspects which legislators introduced. When going to a pub for a drink we expect the pub to have several bars, and food available. If staying in a hotel, we take for granted clean rooms, soap and fresh linen and an entrance separate from the public and lounge bar. When buying alcohol, we go to the bottle shop or liquor barn. Yet, many of these things are recent innovations.

Brisbane hotels now offer alcohol, food, and entertainment, and some even provide accommodation. However, some of the old legislation is still in place. Licensees still display a sign stating their name and, thankfully, are prohibited from selling adulterated grog. Permission is still required to use the premises for dancing, entertainment and gambling machines, although opening hours are now very flexible. Some hotels are licensed to open from 10am until 2am, others from 8am until midnight. Clearly pubs today can have the hours to suit their needs – just as long as the licensing body approves!

Measures

See manuals for more exact conversion tables, especially for larger multiples.

Area

perch (p): 30.25 square yards = 25.3 square metres (m^2)
rod (rd): 40 perches = 1012 square metres
acre (ac): 4 roods = 0.405 hectare (ha)
square mile: 640 acres = 259 hectares

Distance

inch (") = 25.4 millimetres (mm)
foot ('): 12 inches (ins) = 30.5 centimetres (cm)
yard: 3 feet (ft) = 0.914 metres (m)
chain: 22 yards = 20.1 metres
furlong: 10 chains = 201 metres
mile (m): 1760 yards = 1.61 kilometres (km)
fathom: 6 feet depth = 1.83 metres

Liquid

pint (pt) = 568 millilitres (ml)
gallon (gal): 8 pints = 4.55 litres (L)

Money

penny (d): 4 farthings (3) or 2 halfpennies (2)
1d in 1890s = 31c in 1920s-30s, 42c in 1999
shilling (/-) = 12 pence
1/- in 1890s = $3.76 in 1920s-30s, $5 in 1999
pound (£): 20 shillings
£1 in 1890s = $75 in 1920s-30s, $100 in 1999
florin: 2 shillings
sovereign: 20 shillings
guinea (gn): 21 shillings

Temperature

degrees (E): 32 fahrenheit = 0 celsius
$c = (f - 32) \times 5 \div 9$

Weight

ounce (oz) = 28.3 grams (g)
pound (llb): 16 ounces = 0.454 kilograms (kg)
stone (st): 14 pounds = 6.35 kilograms
ton = 1.02 tonnes (t)

Abbreviations

Note the following abbreviations in notes, references and captions

ADB	Australian Dictionary of Biography
AHA	Australian Historical Association
AHS	Australian Historical Studies
AMJ	Australian Municipal Journal
ARHS	Australian Railway Historical Society
BC	Brisbane Courier
BCC	Brisbane City Council
BGGS	Brisbane Girls Grammar School
BGS	Brisbane Grammar School archives
BHG	Brisbane History Group
CCR	Commonwealth Census Reports
CM	Courier-Mail
CPD	Commonwealth Parliamentary Debates
CSIL	Colonial Secretary In-Letters
CSOL	Colonial Secretary Out-Letters
DM	Daily Mail
DS	Daily Standard
EO	Evening Observer
JAS	Journal of Australian Studies
JOL	John Oxley Library, State Library of Queensland, Brisbane
MB	Morning Bulletin, Rockhampton
MBCC	Minutes of the Brisbane City Council
MBC	Moreton Bay Courier
MBMC	Minutes of the Brisbane Municipal Council
MWTC	Minutes of the Windsor Town Council
NM	Northern Miner, Charters Towers
NTQ	National Trust of Queensland
PA	Pughs Almanac
PERS	Personal communication
Q	Queenslander
QAG	Queensland Art Gallery
QCA	Queensland Cricket Association
QDG	Queensland Daily Guardian
QF	Queensland Figaro
QGG	Queensland Government Gazette
QN	Queensland Newspapers
QPD	Queensland Parliamentary Debates
QPOD	Queensland Post Office Directories
QPP	Queensland Parliamentary Papers
QSA	Queensland State Archives
QVP	Queensland Votes and Proceedings
RHSQ	Royal Historical Society of Queensland, Brisbane
RPBMC	Report of the proceedings of the Brisbane Municipal Council
SM	Sunday Mail
SMH	Sydney Morning Herald
T	Telegraph; Brisbane Telegraph
TS	Typescript
UP	University Press
UQ	University of Queensland
UQP	University of Queensland Press

Notes

Note the format below for volume or series number/issue number: page number.

Chapter 1: *Patricia Joynes,* The Brisbane River: A source of recreation

1 CM 12 Feb. 1938,12.
2 MBC 18 Apr. 1857, 2.
3 QPOD 1890, 466.
4 QPOD 1890, 466; 1892, 761; 1891, 502.
5 Q 11 Feb. 1893, 277.
6 QPOD 1900,1200.
7 BC 19 Sep. 1896, 5.
8 BC 31 Jan. 1889, 5; EO 31 Jan. 1889, 4.
9 BC 26 Jan. 1889, 2; 31 Jan. 1889, 5.
10 EO 23 Jan. 1889, 5.
11 Booroodabin Divisional Board minutes OM 65-64, JOL.
12 *Australasian builders & contractors news* 22 Jun. 1889, 598.
13 BC 5 Oct.1889, 4.
14 QPOD 1891, 431.
15 QPOD 1892, 761.
16 QSA BRI/U4 1924-39.
17 Wilson Cooper, 'Bathing in the Brisbane River', 31 Dec. 1988.
18 Constable J. Noller to Snr Sergeant E. Stephenson, 4 May 1928, QSA BRI/U4.
19 BC 19 Sep. 1896, 5.
20 BC 13 Dec. 1894, 7.
21 BC 7 Sep. 1895, 2.
22 EO 17 Sep. 1895, 7.
23 BC 19 Sep. 1896, 5.
24 BC 13 Dec. 1894, 7.
25 SM 28 Feb. 1926, 5.
26 QF 10 Aug. 1889, 219.
27 EO 8 Aug. 1889, 1, 6.
28 Wright 1959, 28.
29 BC 18 Sep. 1895, 7.
30 BC 21 Dec. 1895,2.
31 Wright 1959, 28.
32 Q 19 Nov. 1892, 967.
33 BC 13 Sep. 1897, 2.
34 CM 12 Feb. 1938, 12.

Chapter 2: *Ian Jobling,* Cricket and cycling in the 1890s

1 Jobling 1988.
2 The author acknowledges the research assistance of two former students, Colleen Reeves and David White.
3 Morrison 1888.
4 Q 4 Dec. 1897.
5 QCA minutes, AGM, 1891.
6 QCA minutes, Sep. 1893.
7 Brewer & Dunn 1925; BC 8 Jan. 1895.
8 QCA annual report, 6 Aug. 1895.
9 BC 14 Mar. 1895.
10 BC 21 Dec. 1896.
11 BC 7 Sep. 1897.
12 Wright 1989.
13 BC 26 Nov. 1897.
14 Q 4 Dec. 1897.
15 Woodforde 1970.
16 Drummond 1978.
17 Lynam n.d.; Carmichael 1900.
18 Fitzpatrick 1979.
19 BC 28 Oct. 1892.
20 Q 6 Apr. 1893.

21 Fitzpatrick 1978.
22 Lawson 1973.
23 Fitzpatrick 1979.
24 Q 1 Jun. 1895.
25 Lawson 1973.
26 BC 29 Aug. 1887.
27 BC 8 Sep. 1900.
28 BC 16 Jan; 16 Jun. 1893.
29 BC 7 May 1895.
30 Brunsdon 1896.
31 BC 1 Apr. 1895.
32 Lawson 1973.
33 BC 21 Oct; 4 Nov. 1895.
34 Q 27 Apr. 1895.

Chapter 3: *John Kerr,* Train excursions for the masses in the 1890s

1 QSA LWO/A23 1726/65.
2 QSA WOR/A1 216/66.
3 BC 1 Nov. 1865, 3.
4 MBC 14 Nov. 1874 ex BC.
5 Public timetables were published in QGG until 1889.
6 T 19 Oct.1880, 3.
7 Q 21 Apr. 1883, 6256. See also, enquiry into collision, QVP 1883, 699.
8 Report on Oxley/Darra accident, QVP 1884, 3: 639.
9 Timetable for 25 Jan. 1889, QGG.
10 Kerr & Armstrong 1985.
11 Q 13 Jan. 1883, 45.
12 T 28 Jun. 1884.
13 T 21 Jun. 1884, 3; 28 Jun. 1884.
14 Kerr 1988.
15 QGG 1882, 31: 1200.
16 E.g. BC 18 Oct. 1904, 4.
17 E.g. BC 5 Jul. 1875, 3; Commissioner's report, QVP 1876, 26. For regular use of goods trucks at holiday times, see QVP 1886, 17. Special convertible wagons constructed for goods and passengers, see commissioner's report QVP 1887, 117.

Chapter 4: *Robert Longhurst,* Southport in the 1890s: Decline and temporary fall from favour

1 Q 7 Oct. 1905, 17.
2 *Southern Queensland bulletin*, 22 Jun. 1889, 2.
3 *Week*, 16 Feb. 1889, 12.
4 *Logan witness*, 27 Apr. 1889, 3.
5 Whitfield 1969, 20-3.
6 *Southern Queensland bulletin*, 31 Oct. 1891, 2.
7 Q 8 Aug. 1891, 271
8 Q 22 August 1891, 341
9 BC 14 Feb. 1893, 5.
10 *Southern Queensland bulletin*, 12 Dec. 1891, 2.
11 Q 3 Mar. 1894, 389.
12 *Southern Queensland bulletin*, 3 Apr. 1893, 2.
13 Q 27 Apr. 1895, 782.
14 Q 16 May 1896, 924.
15 BC 6 Apr. 1896, 5.
16 BC 14 Apr. 1897, 7.
17 BC 28 Jul. 1897, 4.
18 BC 17 Apr. 1895, 6.
19 BC 18 May 1898, 3.
20 BC 17 Mar. 1897, 6.
21 Reports in BC 26 May 1897; 9 Jun. 1897; 24 Jun. 1897; 29 Sep. 1897; 13 Oct. 1897; 16 Feb. 1898.
22 BC 6 Jul. 1898, 4.
23 Q 7 Oct. 1905, 17.

Chapter 5: *Barry Shaw,* Sandgate in the 1890s: Attractions and minor irritations

1 BC 24 Dec. 1873. For Sandgate's early development, see Mackenzie-Smith 1995.

2 Lawson 1973, 230.
3 As early as 1854 an advertisement offered for sale two marquees 'for the use of any spirited individuals who desire to commence the settlement of Sandgate, the future Brighton of Moreton Bay'. MBC 9 Sep. 1854. However it was Thomas Dowse, the Brisbane auctioneer, who, through the pages of MBC, was most persistent in promoting Sandgate in these terms. E.g., MBC 29 Jan. 1859 & 27 Apr. 1859.
4 *Cassell's picturesque Australasia* in BHG 1988, 145.
5 McConnel 1897, 20.
6 BC 11 Mar. 1890.
7 BHG 1990, item 7.
8 T 17 Dec. 1894
9 Lawson 1973, 230.
10 BC 30 Jan. 1905.
11 BC 10 Jul. 1905.
12 BC 20 Nov. 1909.
13 BC 2 Jan. 1895.
14 BC 5 Nov. 1897.
15 BC 28 Dec. 1896.
16 Howrah or Howgah, as it sometimes appears in QPOD, was the home of George Bond, ironmonger and managing director of Perry Brothers in Brisbane. Today the house is called Blue Waters. See BHG 1990, item 25; Watson & Mackay 1994, 88, 191.
17 BC 28 Dec. 1900.
18 BC 9 Jul. 1890.
19 BC 16 Sep. 1893.
20 The original building with its double-gabled-roof still survives. BHG 1990, item 18.
21 Cited in *Northside chronicle*, 18 May 1988.
22 BC 23 Jan. 1893.
23 Millais Culpin to a friend, 20 May 1891, BHG 1989, 87.

Chapter 6: *Pam Barnett,* Painters and patrons: Art in Brisbane 1890-1906
1 Jenner, hand written memoir, QAG files.
2 Jenner, notes, QAG files.
3 Jenner, handwritten account of art in Queensland, QAG files.
4 Lawson 1973, 176.
5 Minutes of trustees' meeting, BGS archives.
6 Thomas MacLeod, 1841-86, trained at the Glasgow Industrial School of Design. He worked for *Queensland punch* and as an illuminator of parliamentary records before commencing teaching, first at Ipswich Grammar School, then at Brisbane Grammar School in 1870.
7. Kerr 1992, 157. Joseph Augustus Clarke, 1840-90, taught drawing at Brisbane School of Arts from 1881, and gave a ladies' water-colour class.
8 Annual report of the headmistress 1889, BGGS archives.
9 Annual report of the headmistress 1891, BGGS archives. The headmistress stated that art 'under the able tuition of Mr McFadyen ... had progressed beyond my expectations'.
10 Maynard 1983, 448.
16 Holyoake 1975, 382-84.
12 Catalogue for art union drawing, QAG files.
13 Q 1 Feb. 1890.
14. Maynard 1983, 448.
15 Copy of letter by Jenner, QAG. The addressee is not noted on the letter, but 'Honoured Sir' at the beginning suggests the chairman of trustees, rather than Rivers.
16 Q 13 Apr. 1895, 699.
17 Jenner, notes, QAG file.
18 Maas 1984, 141.
19 MacAulay 1985, 116.

Chapter 7: *Shirley McCorkindale,* Books and reading in the 1890s
1 Melville 1896, 46.
2 PA 1890.
3 Lawson 1973, 176.
4 *The constant source* 1982, 2-3, 6.
5 BC 16 Jun. 1866, 4-5.
6 Lawson 1973, 176.
7 Brisbane School of Arts, library sub-committee, 25 Apr. 1892, OM71-25, JOL.
8 Brisbane School of Arts, general committee, 9 Mar. 1892, OM71-25, JOL. Non-members could purchase reading room tickets at 1s a week or 2s 6d a month.

9 Brisbane School of Arts, general committee, 17 Aug. 1892, OM71-25, JOL.
10 Brisbane School of Arts, general committee, 16 Oct. 1895, OM71-25, JOL.
11 Brisbane School of Arts, general committee, 8 Oct. 1890, OM71-25, JOL.
12 Brisbane School of Arts, library sub-committee, 6 Aug. 1890, OM71-25, JOL.
13 Brisbane School of Arts, library sub-committee, 12 Feb. 1896, OM71-25, JOL.
14 Brisbane School of Arts, general committee, 15 Feb. 1899, OM71-25, JOL.
15 Brisbane School of Arts, library sub-committee, 18 Dec. 1895, OM71-25, JOL.
16 Brisbane School of Arts, general committee, 15 Apr. 1896, OM71-25, JOL.
17 Day 1999, 89.
18 AHR 1892, 211.
19 AHR 1892, 9.
20 AHR Aug. 1894, 131, 133.
21 AHR May 1894, 53.
22 AHR Feb. 1895, 7.
23 AHR Jun. 1895, 46.
24 AHR Jun. 1895, 46.
25 Guyatt 1970, 248. For further details on the emergence of a labour press, see Kirkpatrick 1997, 116-24.
26 Guyatt 1970, 250.
27 *Boomerang* 19 Nov. 1887, 6.
28 *Worker* 1 Mar. 1890, 1.
29 Guyatt 1970, 250.
30 *American national biography* 1999, 520-21.
31 *Worker* 13 Dec. 1890, 2.
32 *Worker* 4 Jun. 1890, 9.
33 *Worker* 7Aug. 1890, 14.
34 *Brisbane School of Arts centenary*, 1849-1949, 24.
35 BC 3 Oct.1895, 7.
36 BC 26 Apr. 1902, 12.

Chapter 8: *Margaret Maynard,* Proliferating habits: Leisure and clothing in the 1890s
1 Lawson 1973, 194. See also Maynard 1988, 141-50.
2 Baudrillard 1981, 76-7.
3 Wilson 1985, 35.
4 *Australian etiquette, or, The rules and usages of the best society in the Australasian colonies,* 1885.
5 Russel 1988.
6 Priestley 1984, 115.
7 Inglis 1880, 236.
8 Q 18 Aug 1900, 413.
9 See illustrations of picnicking and boating dress in Christmas supplement, *Sydney mail* 1895.
10 Wilson 1985, 160.
11 Fletcher 1984, 163.
12 'Dress reform', *Court* 3, 1895, 48; 'In fashion's path', *Woman* 1, 1892, 6; 'The coming woman', *Dawn*, Jan 1890, 12.
13 McCrone 1988, 233.
14 Q 1 Oct. 1898, 652.
15 Howell 1992, 143, 149.
16 Ibid, 148.
17 'Wheels' supplement to *Flashes of society and sport,* 30 Apr. 1896, iv.
18 'Cycling for women', BC 1 Jul. 1893, 7.
19 'Ladies bicycling club', BC 17 Jul. 1897, 4.
20 Winkworth 1989-90, 8: 97.
21 'Wheels', 10.
22 Fletcher 1984, 182.
23 'The rational dress question', *Australian storekeeper's journal* Nov. 1895, 198.
24 'Wheels', iv.
25 'Ladies' classes at the Brisbane gymnasium', BC 26 Jun. 1893, 6.
26 *Australian etiquette, 535.*
27 See comments of Henry Slocum, 'Lawn tennis as a game for women', *Outing*, 1889 in *Men and women dressing the part* ed. Claudia Brush Kidwell and Valerie Steele, 1989, 114.
28 McCrone 1988, 232.
29 QF 14 Jan. 1888, 68; 13 Oct.1888, 604.
30 'Dress and fashion', Q 6 Aug 1887, 211; Q 6 Sept 1890, 460. My thanks to Judith McKay for these references.
31 Advertisement for Chapman & Chapman's New Summer Corsets, Q 5 Jan 1895, 29.

32 Lawson 1973, 206.
33 Howell 1992, 160.
34 *Australian etiquette, 357.*
35 Knight 1897, 66.
36 Q 1 Oct 1898, 646.
37 Patrick 1987, 359.
38 *North Queensland register* 13 May 1896, 28.
314 *Queensland punch* 1 Nov. 1881, 14.

Chapter 9: *Sue Ward,* Brisbane by night: Al fresco 1900-1914

1 DM 13 Aug. 1904. no. 18, 'Public Amusements', was one of a series of feature articles entitled, 'Brisbane by night', published in the *Daily mail.*
2 DM 9 Oct. 1906.
3 DM 21 Dec. 1904.
4 DM 28 Mar. 1907.
5 DM 26 Dec. 1912.
6 Pike & Cooper 1980.
7 DM 9 Nov. 1908.
8 DM 5 Jan. 1911.
9 I am indebted to Chris Long for early information on Sidney Cook given in his seminar, 'The history of Queensland cinema', at the Queensland State Library, 15 Sep. 1993.
10 BC 7 Apr. 1912.
11 DM 7 Nov. 1910.
12 BC 5 Jan. 1911.
13 BC 5 Jan. 1911.
14 BC 7 Jan. 1911.
15 Bertrand 1989 is a useful reference for the development of the cinema industry from its beginnings in 1896 to the late 1980s. UQ postgraduate Sylvia Yates is compiling a Queensland database.

Chapter 10: *Tim Moroney,* Brisbane on the visitors' circuit 1870s-1940s

1 Trollope 1873, 15.
2 Trollope 1873, 82.
3 Trollope 1873, 743-44.
4 O'Farrell 1987, 225-29.
5 BC 30 Mar. 1883.
6 O'Farrell 1987, 236.
7 BC 19 Jul. 1895.
8 BC 20 Jul. 1895.
9 O'Farrell 1987, 236.
10 BC 22 Jul. 1895.
11 BC 15 Dec. 1891.
12 Collier 1965, 87-88.
13 BC 5 Nov. 1895.
14 BC 4-6 Nov. 1895.
15 Lack [1959], 19, 100.
16 Murphy 1909, 180-205.
17 BC 27 Oct. 1902.
18 BC 28 Oct. 1902.
19 *Australian encyclopedia* 1965, 6:28.
20 BC 29; 31 Oct. 1902.
21 BC 5 Jul. 1927.
22 BC 8 Jul. 1927.
23 *Australian encyclopedia* 1965, 6:29.
24 Ibid 2:88.
25 BC 13 May 1912.
26 BC 13 Dec. 1912.
27 Baden-Powell 1935, 90.
28 Lack [1959], 10, 16.
29 BC 11 Jun. 1928.
30 BC 11 Jun. 1928.
31 Carroll 1980, 62.
32 BC 22 Oct. 1930.
33 BC 13 Aug. 1932.
34 BC 30 May 1930

35 BC 30 May-5 Jun. 1930.
36 Lack [1959], 22, 23, 25, 47, 61.
37 Lack [1959], 20, 47.
38 See Lowell 1962.
39 CM 22 Jun. 1938.
40 Von Luckner 1958,19.
41 CM 23 Jun. 1938.
42 CM 25 Jul. 1938.
43 Lack [1959], 97, 107, 111, 123.
44 CM 17-20 Feb. 1939.
45 CM 21 Nov. 1940.
46 CM 22 Nov. 1940.
47 CM 27 Jul. 1940.
48 Cardus 1980, 223
49 CM 22 Jul. 1940.
50 CM 22 Jul. 1940.
51 CM 26 Jul. 1940.

Chapter 11: *Jennifer Harrison*, Popular culture: Radio to television in the 1950s

1 Fiske 1989.
2 CM 9 Aug. 1993.
3 Williamson 1985, 88.
4 Connors 1993, 374.
5 CM 17 Aug. 1959.
6 McQueen 1978, 214.
7 *TV times* Jun. 1959.
8 McQueen 1978, 214.
9 Besant 1993, 82.
10 Gunter 1992.
11 McQueen 1978, 215.
12 Stratton 1992; see also chapter 12.
13 CM 4 Jan. 1993.
14 Postman 1987, 86.
15 McMurty 1993, 45.
16 Barber 1993, 32.
17 Bessant 1992, 17.
18 Reynolds 1992, 31.

Chapter 12: *Raymond Evans*, 'Crazy News': Rock'n'roll in Brisbane and Bill Haley's 'Big Show', 1956-57

1 Dawes & Propes 1992; Tosches 1991.
2 Haley & von Hoelle 1990, 69-95.
3 Tosches 1991, 106.
4 Ennis 1992, 18.
5 Ennis 1992, 17-21.
6 Kocandrle 1988.
7 Ennis 1992, 22.
8 Cronau interview 1 Oct. 1993.
9 Anon. 1986, 'Interview with a Bodgie'.
10 Gilbert 1985, 16.
11 CM 27 Mar. 1957; *Truth* 3 Jun. & 7 Oct. 1956.
12 CM 10 Oct. 1956.
13 SM 11 & 18 Nov. 1956.
14 Johnson 1993, 104.
15 SM 12 Aug. & 3 Oct. 1956, 10 Feb. 1957.
16 *Truth* 13 May 1956.
17 T 10 Jan.1957.
18 Watson 1983.
19 Stratton 1992, 159-68.
20 Hill 1991, 682.
21 Shumway 1991, 755.
22 T 1 Nov., 6 & 16 Jan. 1957.
23 SM 14 October 1956.
24 SM 25 November 1956.
25 SM 13 January 1957.
26 Evans 1978, 11.

27 Martin & Segrave 1993, 41.
28 Haley & von Hoelle 1990, 119.
29 SM 2 Dec. 1956.
30 SM 8 Jul. 1956.
31 Hill 1991, 683.
32 Martin & Segrave 1993, 15-26.
33 Johnson 1993, 102.
34 SM 22 Jul. 1956.
35 CM 4 Sep., 3 Sep. 1956; SM 9 Sep. 1956; *Truth*, 16 Sep. 1956.
36 Denisoff & Romanowski 1990, 65-77; Martin & Seagrave 1993, 27-39; Hill 1991, 687-90.
37 SM 23 Sep. 1956; *Truth* 7 Oct. 1956.
38 CM 20 Oct. 1956, 5 Jan. 1957.
39 CM 16 Oct. 1956.
40 T 7 & 14 Nov. 1956.
41 CM 13 Nov. 1956.
42 Evans 1989, 47-60; Fisher 1989, 17-46.
43 CM 22 Nov. 1956; T 22 Nov. 1956.
44 CM 11 Dec. 1956.
45 T 7 Dec. 1956.
46 T 13 Dec. 1956.
47 T 13 Dec. 1956.
48 T 22 Nov. 1956; CM 23 Nov. 1956.
49 Valerie K____ communication, 5; 13 Oct. 1993.
50 CM 22, 30 Nov., 11 Dec. 1956; T 22 Nov., 11 & 13 Dec. 1956.
51 CM 27 Nov. 1956.
52 T 22 Nov. 1956; CM 23 Nov. 1956.
53 CM 23 Nov. 1956; T 17 Jan. 1957.
54 CM 27 Nov. 1956.
55 Shumway 1991, 763.
56 Valerie K____ communication, 5 Oct. 1993; CM 30 Nov. 1956.
57 SM 28 Jul. 1957.
58 SM 14 Oct. 1956.
59 Eddie M____ interview, 1 Oct. 1993 .
60 *Truth* 25 Nov. 1956; SM 25 Nov. 1956.
61 Swensen 1983; Haley & von Hoelle, 1990.
62 Hatch & Millward 1987, 76-77.
63 Shaw 1975, 143-44.
64 Gillett 1970, 24, 52.
65 Wood 1971, 12-14.
66 Silvester 1988, 139-44.
67 Fox 1993, 172.
68 T 2 Jan. 1957.
69 *Truth* 6 Jan. 1957.
70 CM 5 Jan. 1957.
71 *Truth* 6 Jan. 1957.
72 CM 8 Jan. 1957.
73 CM 5 Jan. 1957.
74 T 9 Jan. 1957.
75 SM 6 Jan. 1957.
76 CM 10 Jan. 1957.
77 SMH 15 Jan.; 18 Jan. 1957.
78 *Australian women's weekly* 23 Jan. 1957.
79 Valerie K____ communication, 6 Oct. 1993.
80 Interview with June. L____ 4 Oct. 1993.
81 Rogers & O'Brien 1975, 27.
82 Haley & von Hoelle 1990, 141.
83 CM 20 Mar. 1957.
84 T 17 Jan. 1957.
85 *Truth* 27 Jan. 1957; SM 6 Jan. 1957.
86 SM 27 Jan. 1957.
87 SM 7 Apr. & 9 Jun., 1957; Braithwaite & Barker 1978, 40-42.
88 SM 23 Nov. 1956.
89 SM 19 May 1957; CM 22 Apr. 1957.
90 SM 19 May 1957.

91 Johnson 1993, 108.

Chapter 13: ***Maureen Lillie,*** **More than a passing trade: The social role of pubs**

1 E.G. Saint cited in Powell 1988, 2.
2 Johnston 1988, 90.
3 Connors 1995, 497.
4 Johnston 1988, 90.
5 Marin La Meslee 1883, 111-12.
6 Morrison 1888, 201.
7 QF 7 Jan. 1888, 13.
8 BC 30 Nov. 1865
9 Morrison 1888, 205.
10 QF 28 Aug. 1888, 315.
11 Minutes of 4 Sep. 1865 QSA LWO/A23 1865/1668.
12 Marin La Meslee 1883, 46.
13 See, for example, the counter lunch offered by the City Buffet Hotel, BC 10 Oct. 1865, 5.
14 Freeland 1966, 134.
15 Fahey 1992, 83.
16 Girouard 1975, 12.
17 *North Australian* 10 Apr. 1860.
18 Girouard 1975, 14.
19 Freeland 1966, 175.
20 Morrison 1888, 202.
21 Morrison 1888, 207.
22 Gibson-Wilde 1988, 152.
23 Girouard 1975, 12.
24 Drink Inquiry findings cited in Powell 1988, 36.
25 Muir 1976, 302.
26 Powell 1988, 27.
27 Powell 1988, 50.
28 Summers 1975, 356.
29 Powell 1988, 12.
30 Powell 1988, 43.
31 Kelly 1994, 6.
32 Powell 1988, 44.
33 Cited in Kelly 1994, 10.
34 Kelly 1994, 10.
35 *Bulletin* 26 Oct. 1869, 3.
36 Johnston 1988, 250.
37 *Australian etiquette* 1885, 158.
38 *Cooktown courier* 25 Sep. 1875, 3.
39 Kelly 1994, 41.
40 Summers 1975, 356.
41 Freeland 1966, 178.
42 *Cooktown courier* 22 Jan. 1876

Chapter 14: ***David Larkin,*** **Brisbane Irish brewers and cordial manufacturers**

1 See also O'Lorcain (Larkin) 1994, 112-20.

Chapter 15: ***Judy Rechner,*** **Legislation and hotels**

1 Licensed (Publicans) 1848 in Pring 1862.
2 Ibid., 946.
3 Ibid., 948.
4 Ibid., 953-54.
5 Ibid., 953.
6 Ibid., 951-52, s.10 & 11.
7 Ibid., 954.
8 Ibid., 955-56.
9 Ibid., 953.
10 Ibid., 955.
11 Ibid., 949.
12 Publicans Act of 1863 in *Queensland statutes* 1874.
13 Ibid., s.61
14 Ibid., s.5.

15 Ibid., s.23.
16 Ibid., s.16.
17 Ibid., s.7.
18 Ibid., s.9.
19 BC 10 Oct. 1865, 8.
20 Publicans Act of 1863, s.32.
21 Ibid., s. 33.
22 Ibid., ss. 34, 35.
23 Ibid., ss. 41, 55.
24 Ibid., s. 18.
25 Ibid., s.3.
26 Ibid., s. 30.
27 Ibid., ss.29, 31, 36-37, 51-52.
28 Ibid., ss.39-40.
29 BC 10 Oct. 1865, 8.
30 BC 16 Dec. 1865, 2.
31 Publicans Act of 1863, s.50.
32 Publicans (Innkeepers) Protection Act of 1864, s.93.
33 Municipal Institutions Act Amendments 1867.
34 Publicans Act of 1864 Amendment, ss.5-6.
35 The Country Publicans Licensing Act of 1870, ss.1, 3.
36 Amendment to the Publicans Act 1872.
37 Licensing Boards Act Amendment Act of 1880, ss.1-2.
38 Licensing Board Act of 1879, s.11.
39 Health Act 1884, s.5.
40 Ibid., ss.37, 38, 40.
41 Ibid., ss.48, 49.
42 Licensing Act of 1885 in *Queensland statutes* 1911.
43 Ibid., s.4.
44 Ibid., ss.4, 6, 7.
45 Ibid., s.59.
46 Ibid., s.19.
47 Ibid., ss.4, 20, 87.
48 Ibid., ss.33, 50.
49 Ibid., s.31(4).
50 Ibid., s.86.
51 Ibid., s.101.
52 Ibid., s.57.
53 Ibid., ss.27, 50.
54 Ibid., ss.25-26.
55 Ibid., s.25
56 Ibid., s.26
57 Ibid., ss.75-78.
58 Ibid., s.68.
59 Ibid., s.76.
60 Ibid., s.68.
61 Ibid., s.74.
62 Ibid., s.65.
63 Ibid., s.38
64 Ibid., s.62
65 Ibid., s.53.
66 Ibid., s.67.
67 Ibid., s.67.
68 Ibid., s.67.
69 Ibid., s.87
70 Amendments to the Licensing Act of 1885.
71 Local Government Act of 1878, s.167.
72 Ibid., s.258.
73 Local Authorities Act 1902, part 8 – Buildings, ss.165, 167-68, 170, 176.
74 Liquor Act of 1912, An Act to consolidate and amend the laws relating to the sale of intoxicating liquor, and for other purposes connected therewith, in *Acts of the Parliament of Queensland* 1912.
75 Ibid., ss.23-25.
76 Ibid., ss.19, 23, 25, 63.
77 Ibid., ss.23-25.

78 Ibid., s.24.
79 Ibid., s.23.
80 Ibid., s.25.
81 Ibid., s29.
82 Ibid., ss.81, 86.
83 Ibid., s.94.
84 Criminal code, s.106(3).
85 Liquor Act of 1912, ss.63, 64.
86 Ibid., s.58.
87 Ibid., s.22.
88 Ibid., ss.71, 74, 80, 88.
89 Ibid., s.74.
90 Ibid., s.69.
91 Ibid., s.48.
92 Ibid., s.38.
93 Ibid., s.38(6).
94 Ibid., s.22(4).
95 Liquor Act Amendment of 1914, Two amendment acts in 1920 related to the Local Option. Anzac Day was added to the prohibited days in 1921.
96 Liquor Act Amendment of 1926, s.2, s.6 amended s.81.
97 Liquor Act Amendment of 1923.
98 Sanitary conveniences regulations 1931, Regs.8, 17-19, 20-23, 30-31.
99 Sanitary regulations of 1931, Regs.3, 6.
100 Liquor Acts Amendment Act of 1935, An Act to provide a measure of Liquor Reform and to amend The Liquor Acts, 1912 to 1932, in certain particulars; and for other purposes in *Public acts of Queensland 1828-1936.*
101 Ibid., s.3.
102 Ibid., s.19
103 Ibid., s.68
104 Ibid., s.19
105 Ibid., s.38
106 Ibid., s.69.
107 Annotation in Liquor Acts Amendment Act of 1935 in *The public acts of Queensland 1828-1936*, vol.5: Land to Local Bodies' Loans Guarantee. Sydney, Butterworth, 1936, s.62.
108 Liquor Acts Amendment Act of 1935, s.62.
109 Regulation 10 dealt with city, town and areas within the 5 mile boundary while regulation 11 concerned country hotels. Regulations in regard to dining rooms, kitchens, stables and garages were the same for both. The number of sitting rooms, sleeping rooms remained the same. Liquor Regulations of 1936, QGG 29 Oct. 1936.
110 Liquor Regulations of 1936, regs 10 & 11.
111 Ibid., reg.32.
112 Ibid., reg.33.
113 Liquor Acts Amendment Act 1941.
114 Ibid., s.62(7 & 8).
115 Liquor Acts Amendment Act 1941, s.78a.
116 Liquor Acts Amendment Act 1945, s.47.
117 Ibid., s.58(d).
118 Ibid., s.62(5A).
119 Ibid., s.68.
120 Liquor Acts Amendment Act 1952, s.49.
121 Liquor Acts Amendment Act 1954, amendment 18 of s.19.
122 Ibid., s.18(2).
123 Ibid., amendment 18 of s.19.
124 Ibid., s.38(v).
125 Liquor Acts Amendment Act 1958, amendment 3.
126 Ibid., s.68D.
127 Liquor Acts Amendment Act 1961, ss.61, 66A, s.67.
128 Liquor Acts Amendment Act 1965.
129 Ibid., s.68(3).

References

Note the format below for volume or series number/issue number: page number.

General

Australian encyclopaedia 1965, Grolier Society, Sydney.

Bohle, Bruce ed. 1975, *The international cyclopedia of music and musicians*, 10th ed. Dent & Sons, London.

Brisbane History Group 1985, *Brisbane: Housing, health, the river and the arts,* ed. Rod Fisher, BHG papers no. 3, Brisbane.

Brisbane History Group 1992, *Brisbane: The Aboriginal presence, 1842-60,* ed. Rod Fisher, BHG papers no. 11, Brisbane.

Brisbane History Group 1994, *Brisbane: Cemeteries as sources*, ed. Rod Fisher & Barry Shaw, BHG papers no. 13, Brisbane.

Brisbane History Group 1995, *Brisbane: People, places and progress*, ed. Rod Fisher & Barry Shaw, BHG papers no. 14, Brisbane.

Brisbane History Group 1997, *Brisbane: Corridors of power*, ed. Barry Shaw, BHG papers no. 15, Brisbane.

Chambers encyclopaedia 1969, International Learning Systems Corp., London.

Evans, Raymond 1989, 'Night of broken glass: The anatomy of an anti-Chinese riot' in BHG 1988a, ch.3.

Fisher, Rod 1989, 'Old Frog's Hollow: Devoid of interest, or a den of iniquity?' in BHG 1988a, ch.2.

Hartnell, Phyllis 1979, *The concise Oxford companion to the theatre*, UP, Oxford.

Johnston, W. Ross 1988, *Brisbane: The first 30 years*, Boolarong, Brisbane.

Joyce, Roger B. 1984, *Samuel Walker Griffith*, UQP, St Lucia.

Kerr, John 1988, *Brunswick Street, Bowen Hills and beyond*, ARHS, Brisbane.

Kerr, John & John Armstrong 1978, *Destination South Brisbane*, ARHS, Brisbane.

Knight, John James 1897, *Brisbane: A historical sketch of the capital of Queensland*, Biggs & Morcom, Brisbane.

Lack, Clem [1959], The chronological table of chief events in Queensland history, TS

Marin La Meslee, Edmond 1883, *The new Australia*, trans. Russel Ward 1975, Heineman Educational, Melbourne.

McConnel, Mary 1897, *Our children's hospital 1876-1901*, Thomson Bros, Brisbane.

Morrison, W. Frederick 1888, *Aldine history of Queensland*, Aldine Publishing Company, Sydney.

O'Lorcain [Larkin], David A. 1994, 'Irish graves at Nudgee Cemetery', BHG in BI & G 1994, Ch. 13.

Summers, Anne 1975, *Damned whores and god's police: The colonization of women in Australia*, Allen Lane, Melbourne.

Trollope, Anthony 1873, *Australia*, ed. Peter Edwards & Roger B. Joyce 1976, UQP, St Lucia.

Whitfield, Georgina 1969, 'Industrial conditions in early Brisbane', *Queensland heritage*, 1/10: 20-3.

Nineteenth century culture

Aldenhoven, W. 1910, 'An Australian watercolour painter: Henry Tebbitt', *Studio*, 51, no. 212: 139-42.

Anon. 1890, 'The coming woman', *Dawn*, Jan: 12.

Anon. 1892, 'In fashion's path', *Woman* 1: 6.

Anon. 1893, 'Cycling for women', BC 1 July.

Anon. 1893, 'Ladies' classes at the Brisbane Gymnasium', BC 26 June.

Anon. 1895, 'Dress reform', *Court* 3: 48.

Anon. 1895, 'The rational dress question', *Australian storekeeper's journal*, Nov.

Anon. 1896, 'Wheels' supplement in *Flashes of society and sport,* 30 April: iv.

Anon. 1897, 'Ladies bicycling club', BC 17 July.

Anon. 1887; 1890, 'Dress and fashion', Q 6 Aug; 6 Sept.

Australian etiquette, or, The rules and usages of the best society in the Australasian colonies 1885, Peoples Publishing Company, Melbourne.,

Baudrillard, Jean 1981, *For a critique of the political economy of the sign*, Telos Press, St Louis.

Bradbury, Keith. & Glen Cooke 1987, *Thorns and petals', 100 years of the Royal Queensland Art Society*, RQAS,. Brisbane

Brewer, F.J. & R. Dunn, 1925, *Municipal history of South Brisbane*, Pole, Brisbane.

Brown, Julie & Margaret Maynard 1980, *Fine art exhibitions in Brisbane 1884-1916*, Fryer Memorial Library Occasional Publication no.1, UQ., St Lucia.

Brown, Julie & Margaret Maynard 1978, 'Painter and photographer: Brisbane in the 1880s and 1890s', *History of photography*, 2, no. 4, Oct: 315-33.

Brisbane History Group 1988, *Brisbane by 1888: The public image*, comp. Rod Fisher, BHG sources no. 1, Brisbane.

Brisbane History Group 1988a, *Brisbane in 1888: The historical perspective*, ed. Rod Fisher, BHG papers no. 8, Brisbane.

Brisbane History Group 1989, *Brisbane: Butterflies and beetles*, ed. Ray Sumner, BHG sources no.4, Brisbane.

Brisbane History Group 1990, *Sandgate/Shorncliffe heritage tour*, comp. Barry Shaw, BHG tours no.8, Brisbane.

Brisbane School of Arts centenary, 1849-1949, 1949, comp. Percy E. Hunter, The School, Brisbane..

Brunsdon, F.C. 1896, 'The reign of the wheel in Australia, III Queensland', *Review of reviews*, Aug. 20, in Colleen Reeves 1983, 'Cycling clubs and racing in Queensland society, 1875-1900', TS, Dept of Human Movement Studies, UQ.

Day, Leanne 1999, 'Brisbane Literary Circle: The quest for universal culture', JAS 63: 87-93.

Drummond, J. 1978, 'Centenary celebration - a nostalgic experience', *National cycling* (Aug.-Sept.) 7, no.12.

Evans, Susanna 1982, *Historic Brisbane and its early artists*, Boolarong, Brisbane.

Fitzpatrick, J. 1978, 'On two wheels around Australia', *Canberra times* 22 Feb.

Fitzpatrick, J. 1979, 'The spectrum of Australian bicycle racing', in R. Cashman & M. McKernan, *Sport in history: The making of modern sporting traditions*. UQP, St Lucia.

Fletcher, Marion 1984, *Costume in Australia 1788-1901*, Oxford UP, Melbourne.

Guyatt, B. Joy 1970, 'The publicists – the labour press 1880 to 1915', in Denis Murphy, Roger B. Joyce & Colin A. Hughes eds 1970, *Prelude to power: The rise of the Labor Party in Queensland 1885-1915*, Jacaranda Press, Milton.

Holyoake, Mary 1975, 'Art unions – catalysts of Australian art', *Art and Australia*, 12/4, 382-84.

Howell, Reet & Maxwell Howell 1992, *The genesis of sport in Queensland*, UQP, St Lucia.

Inglis, James 1880, *Our Australian cousins*, Macmillan & Co, London.

Jenner, Irene 1978, 'Isaac Walter Jenner pioneer artist of Brisbane, Queensland', *Art and Australia* 15, June: 393-4.

Jobling, I. 1988, 'Sport in 1888: An historical perspective', in BHG 1988a, ch. 11.

Kerr, Joan 1992, *Dictionary of artists working in Australia to 1870,* A.P..

Kirkpatrick, Rod 1997, 'The 1890s constitutional debates through the eyes of the Queensland press', in BHG 1997, ch. 12.

Lahey, Vida 1959, *Art in Queensland*, Jacaranda Press, Brisbane.

Lawson, Ronald 1973, *Brisbane in the 1890s: A study of an urban Australian society*. UQP, St Lucia.

Lynam, Frank n.d., 'History of Queensland amateur cycling', TS, JOL, Brisbane.

Maas, Jeremy 1984, *Holman Hunt and the Light of the World*, Berkeley, London.

MacAulay, Bettina 1985, '"A humble beginning" for Queensland's National Art Gallery', in BHG 1985, ch. 14.

MacAulay, Bettina 1987, 'L.K.W. Wirth (1858-1950), artist and linguist', in Manfred Jurgensen & Alan Corkhill eds. 1987, *The German presence in Queensland over the last 150 years,* Proceedings of an International Symposium, Aug. 24, 25, 26, UQP, St Lucia.

Mackenzie-Smith, John 1995, 'Sandgate before the railway', in BHG 1995, ch.1.

McCrone, Kathleen 1988, *Playing the game: Sport and the physical emancipation of English women 1870-1914*, University of Kentucky, Lexington.

Maynard, Margaret 1980, 'Aspects of taste: Exhibitions of art in Brisbane 1876-87', *John Oxley journal*, 1, no.6: 16-29.

Maynard, Margaret 1983, 'Queensland's National Gallery: The opening collection, 1895', *Art and Australia*, 20, no.4 (winter): 488-91.

Maynard, Margaret 1988, 'Cheerily doth he push northward, the black coat and shining topper of civilization': Dress and the urban experience', in BHG 1988a, ch. 12.

Melville, Adam G. 1896, 'The book trade in Australia', Library Association of Australasia, *Conference proceedings 1896*, Occasional papers in librarianship 7: 41-46.

Nissen, Judith comp. 1999, *Queensland architects of the 19th century: Index to the biographical dictionary*, BHG sources no. 7, Brisbane.

Priestley, Susan 1984, *Making their mark*, Fairfax, Syme & Weldon Associates, McMahons Point.

Queensland Parliamentary Library 1982, *The constant source: A brief account of the Queensland Parliamentary Library*, Brisbane.

Reeves, Colleen 1983, 'Cycling clubs and racing in Queensland society, 1875-1900'. TS, Dept of Human Movement Studies, UQ.

Russel, Penny 1988, 'The relationship between family life and class formation in nineteenth century Melbourne', *Lilith* 5.

Slocum, Henry 1889, 'Lawn tennis as a game for women', *Outing*, in Claudia Brush Kidwell & Valerie Steele, eds. 1989, *Men and women dressing the part*, Smithsonian Institution Press, Washington.

Tardent, Henry A. 1916, *The life and works of Richard John Randall (Australia's greatest artist) and other essays on art*, Cumming, Brisbane.

Watson, Donald & Judith McKay 1994, *Queensland architects of the 19th century*, Queensland Museum, Brisbane.

Wilson, Elizabeth 1985, *Adorned in dreams: Fashion and modernity*, Virago Press, London.

Winkworth, Kylie 1989/90, 'Women and the bicycle: Fast, loose and liberated', *Australian journal of art* 8: 97.

Woodforde, J. 1970, *The story of the bicycle*, Universe Books, New York.

Wright, A.H. comp. 1959, *The history of the Bulimba electorate 1859-1959*, The Centenary Committee, Brisbane.

Wright, David 1989, 'The evolution of the Brisbane Cricket Ground', Master of Human Movement Studies qualifying thesis, UQ.

Twentieth century culture

Baden Powell, Robert 1935, *Scouting round the world*, Herbert Jenkins, London.

Barber, David 1993, 'Windy city blows its horn', *Good weekend magazine, Sydney morning herald*, 26-7 June 1993, 32.

Bertrand, Ina 1989, *Cinema in Australia: A documentary history*, NSWUP, Kensington..

Besant, Judith 1993, 'Sex Pistols, be-bop, boogie and youth cultures of the 1950s and 1960s', JAS 36, March 1993, 82.

Bessant, Bob 1992, 'History and the humanities under attack', *AHA Bulletin*, 72, Dec.

Braithwaite, J. & M. Barker 1978, 'Bodgies and widgies: Folk devils of the fifties' in *Two faces of deviance: Crimes of the powerless and the powerful,* eds. P.R. Wilson & J. Braithwaite, UQP, St Lucia.

Cardus, Neville 1950, *Second innings*, Collins, London.

Carroll, Brian 1980, *Australian aviators: An illustrated history*, Cassell, Sydney.

Collier, Richard 1965, *The general next to God*, Collins, London.

Connors, Jane 1993, 'The 1954 royal tour of Australia', AHS, April.

Dawson, J. & S. Propes 1992, *What was the first rock'n'roll record?* Faber & Faber, Boston.

Denisoff, R.S. & W. Romanowski 1990, 'Katzman's "Rock around the clock": A pseudo event?', *Journal of popular culture,* 2/1: 65-78.

Ennis, P.H. 1992, *The seventh stream: The emergence of rock'n'roll in American popular music,* Wesleyan UP, Hanover.

Evans, R. 1978, 'Johnny O'Keefe: A personal memory', *Klatschblatt*, 2 (5 Oct.) 10-12.

Fiske, John 1989, *Reading the popular*, Unwin Hyman, London.

Fox, T. 1993, *Showtime at the Apollo*, Da Capo Press, New York.

Gilbert, J. 1986, *A cycle of outrage: America's reaction to the juvenile delinquent in the 1950s*, Oxford UP, New York.

Gillett, C. 1970, *The sound of the city: The rise of rock and roll,* Souvenir Press, New York.

Gunter, Barrie 1992, *The weekly telegraph*, no.60, Sept. 1992.

Haley, J.W. & J. von Hoelle 1990, *Sound and glory: The incredible story of Bill Haley, the father of rock'n' roll and the music that shook the world*, Dyne American, Wilmington, Delaware.

Hatch, D. & S. Millward 1987, *From blues to rock: An analytical history of pop music*, Manchester UP,Manchester.

Hill, T. 1991, 'The enemy within: Censorship in rock music in the 1950s', *South Atlantic quarterly,* 90/4: 675-708.

Johnson, L. 1993, *The modern girl: Girlhood and growing up*, Allen & Unwin, Sydney.

Kocandrie, M. 1988, *The history of rock and roll: A selective discography*, G.K. Hall, Boston.

Martin, L. & K. Segrave 1993, *Anti-rock: The opposition to rock'n'roll*, Da Capo Press, New York.

McMurty, Larry 1993, 'Back to Waco', *Australian magazine*, 26-27 June, 45.

McQueen, Humphrey 1978, *Social sketches of Australia 1888-1975*, Penguin, Sydney.

Murphy, Agnes G. 1909, *Melba: A biography*, Chatto & Windus, London.

O'Farrell, Patrick 1987, *The Irish in Australia*, NSW UP, Kensington.

Pike, Andrew & Ross Cooper 1980, *Australian film 1900-1977: A guide to feature film production*, Oxford UP/ Australian Film Institute, Melbourne.

Postman, Neil 1987, *Amusing ourselves to death: Public discourse in the age of show business*, Methuen, London.

Reynolds, Craig 1992, 'Post structuralism in a department of history', *AHA Bulletin*, 72, Dec.

Rogers, B. & D. O'Brien 1975, *Rock'n'roll Australia: The Australian pop scene, 1954-1964*, Cassell, Stanmore.

Shaw, A. 1974, *The rockin' 50s*, Hawthorn Books, New York.

Shumway, D.R 1991, 'Rock and roll as a cultural practice', *South Atlantic quarterly,* 90/4: 753-73.

Silvester, P.J. 1988, *A left hand like god: A history of boogie-woogie piano*, Da Capo Press, New York.

Stratton, Jon 1992, *The young ones: Working class culture, consumption and the category of youth*, Black Swan Press, Curtin University of Technology.

Swenson, J. 1983, *Bill Haley*, Star Books, Aylesbury.

Thomas, Lowell 1962, *Count Luckner, the sea devil*, Popular Library, New York..

Tosches, N. 1991, *Unsung heroes of rock'n'roll: The birth of rock in the wild years before Elvis*, Secker & Warburg, London.

Von Luckner, Felix 1958, *Out of an old sea chest*, trans. E. Fitzgerald, Methuen, London.

Watson, J. 1983, 'Juvenile delinquency in 1950's Australia', History Hons thesis, UQ.

Williamson, Judith 1985, *Consuming passions: The dynamics of popular culture*, Marion Boyars, London.

Wood, G. 1971, *An A-Z of rock and roll*, Studio Vista, London.

Hotels

Brisbane History Group 1993, *Brisbane hotels and publicans index 1842-1900*, comp. Merle Norris, BHG sources no. 6, Brisbane.

Fahey, Warren 1992, *When Mabel laid the table: The folklore of eating and drinking in Australia*, State Library of New South Wales, Sydney.

Freeland, J. Maxwell 1966, *The Australian pub,* Melbourne University Press, Melbourne.

Gibson-Wilde, Dorothy & Bruce Gibson-Wilde 1988, *A pattern of pubs: Hotels of Townsville 1864-1914*, James Cook UP, Townsville.
Girouard, Mark 1975, *Victorian pubs*, Yale UP, London.
Kelly, W. 1994, *Booze built Australia*, Classic Books, Brisbane.
Marin La Meslee, Edmond 1883, *The new Australia*, trans. Russel Ward 1975, Heineman Educational, Melbourne.
Powell, Keith 1988, *Drinking and alcohol in colonial Australia 1788 - 1901 for the eastern colonies*, Monograph series 3, Australian Government Publishing Service, Canberra.

Hotel legislation

Licensed (Publicans) Act of 1848, *Statutes in force in the colony of Queensland to the present time*, ed. Ratcliffe Pring, Government Printer 1862-1864, Brisbane.
The Publicans Act of 1863, *The Queensland statutes in four volumes*, Government Printer 1874, Brisbane.
Amendments to the Publicans Act of 1864, *The Queensland statutes in four volumes*, Government Printer 1874, Brisbane.
Amendments to Municipal Institutions Act of 1867, *The Queensland statutes in four volumes*, Government Printer 1874, Brisbane:
An Act to regulate the license money payable by country publicans of 1870, *The Queensland statutes in four volumes*, Government Printer 1874, Brisbane.
Amendment to the Publicans Act of 1872, *The Queensland statutes in four volumes*, Government Printer 1874, Brisbane.
The Local Government Act of 1878, *Statutes in force in the colony of Queensland*, Government Printer 1881, Brisbane.
Licensing Board Act of 1879, *Statutes in force in the colony of Queensland*, Government Printer 1881, Brisbane.
The Health Act of 1884, *Queensland statutes in five volumes*, Government Printer 1889, Brisbane.
Amendments to the Licensing Act of 1885, *The Queensland statutes in six volumes*, Government Printer 1911. Brisbane.
The Licensing Act of 1885, *The Queensland statutes in six volumes*, Government Printer 1911, Brisbane.
Criminal code, *The public acts of Queensland 1828-1936*, Land to Local Bodies' Loans Guarantee, vol. 5, Butterworth 1936, Sydney.
The Local Authorities Act of 1902, *Acts of the parliament of Queensland: The Queensland statutes*, pt 8 – buildings, Government Printer 1902, Brisbane.
The Liquor Act of 1912, *Acts of the parliament of Queensland: The Queensland statutes: sessions of 1911, 1912 and 1913*, Government Printer 1913, Brisbane.
The Liquor Act Amendment of 1914, *Acts of the parliament of Queensland: The Queensland statutes*, Government Printer 1914, Brisbane.
The Liquor Act Amendment of 1923, *Acts of the parliament of Queensland*, Government Printer 1927, Brisbane.
The Liquor Act Amendment of 1926, *Acts of the parliament of Queensland*, Government Printer 1927, Brisbane.
The sanitary conveniences regulations for Licensed Victuallers' premises of 1931, QGG.
The Liquor Acts Amendment Act of 1935. *The public acts of Queensland 1828-1936*, Land to Local Bodies' Loans Guarantee, vol. 5, Butterworth 1936, Sydney.
The Liquor Regulations of 1936, QGG.
The Liquor Acts Amendment Act of 1945, *Acts of the parliament of Queensland 1945-1946*, Government Printer 1946, Brisbane.
The Liquor Acts Amendment Act of 1952. *Acts of the parliament of Queensland 1952*, Government Printer 1953, Brisbane.
The Liquor Acts Amendment Act of 1954, *Acts of the parliament of Queensland 1954-1955*, Government Printer 1955, Brisbane.
The Liquor Acts Amendment Act of 1958, *Acts of the parliament of Queensland 1957-1958* Government Printer 1958, Brisbane.
Liquor Acts Amendment Act of 1961, *Acts of the parliament of Queensland*, Government Printer 1962, Brisbane.
The Liquor Acts, 1912 to 1965, Liquor Acts Amendment Act of 1965. *The statutes of Queensland*, Government Printer 1965, Brisbane.

Index

Note italics used for illustrations

Brisbane History Group Papers
Stylesheet for contributors

This serial, which focuses on the history and heritage of the Brisbane region, commenced in 1981. Each volume comprises papers given orally at BHG sessions and additional articles related in subject matter.

Contributors may be invited to submit papers for publication or inquire themselves whether a particular article would be acceptable in a forthcoming volume. Drafts should be forwarded to the publication coordinator for consideration by the editorial committee and referees. Inclusion does not preclude publication elsewhere for a different audience; but contributors are asked to discuss this with the coordinator and to acknowledge publication in the BHG Papers. Contributors receive one free copy of the whole volume.

The new series of papers from Number 11 onwards is typeset on personal computer, desktop designed, offset or docutech printed and produced as a custom-sized paperback in perfect binding. The print run of several hundred copies is marketed widely to members, libraries, schools, societies, professionals and the general public.

Contributors are asked to forward drafts shortly after the related BHG session. If a paper is given orally, it may be amended or reshaped as necessary. There is no strict word limit, as long as everything is pertinent to the subject and succinctly expressed. Notes and references are kept to an essential minimum. The onus is on authors, not the editors, to provide a complete, accurate and presentable manuscript for publication.

Drafts should be submitted in crisp single-spaced typing on A4 sized paper and if possible on 3 1/2 inch computer diskette in recent IBM compatible format (e.g. WordPerfect, Word or ASCII text file). They need to be set out in accordance with the BHG style of publication in the latest volume. Otherwise they may be returned to contributors for amendment.

The required publication style is exemplified by the BHG Papers from Number 11 onwards. The basic format for the end-notes and reference list is set out in the *Style manual* of the Australian Government Publishing Service.

Notes are indicated in the text by superscript running numbers placed after and above the nearest appropriate punctuation mark, and not by author and date in brackets. The notes themselves and the accompanying list of references are set out at the end using the author-date format, but omitting the abbreviations 'vol.', 'no.' and 'pp.' (e.g. 4/1:147-8 or 4:147-8).

The alphabetically arranged list of references includes all cited and other useful works, except newspapers, lesser manuscripts and obvious printed sources already in the notes (with authors' family and given names (not initials), year plus small alpha-letter if more than one title by that author, titles of books with place and publisher, or titles of articles and serials with volume and page numbers).

Relevant illustrations of various kinds should be included with captions and sources stated, but these should be kept to an essential minimum. Good contrast, black and white prints are best, up to A4 in size (which may be reduced later). Letters of permission from the owners or repositories concerned are also needed for the BHG to reproduce (as a non-profit, community and educational association).

A cover sheet should be added with the contributor's preferred title, given and family names (not initials), and a sentence or two of self-description (e.g. occupation, status, positions, research activity, publications) for the contributors' page.

Please contact the publication coordinator regarding these matters, including particular requirements and queries. The BHG looks forward to publishing papers by amateur, public and academic historians as professionally and beneficially as possible.

Dr Barry Shaw
Publication Coordinator
(07) 3353 2210 (after hours)

Brisbane History Group
PO Box 12
Kelvin Grove DC, Q4059

Brisbane History Group Publications

Papers

1 *Brisbane: Public, practical, personal*, 1981
2 *Brisbane: Archives and approaches*, 1983
3 *Brisbane: Housing, health, the river and the arts*, 1985
4 *Brisbane at war*, 1986
5 *Brisbane: Aboriginal, alien, ethnic*, 1987
6 *Brisbane: People, places and pageantry*, 1987
7 *Brisbane: Archives and approaches II*, 1988
8 *Brisbane in 1888: The historical perspective*, 1988
9 *Brisbane: Local, oral and placename history*, 1990
10 *Brisbane: Mining, Building, Story Bridge, the Windmill*, 1991
11 *Brisbane: The Aboriginal presence 1824-60*, 1992
12 *Brisbane: The ethnic presence since the 1850s*, 1993
13 *Brisbane: Cemeteries as sources*, 1994
14 *Brisbane: People, places and progress*, 1994
15 *Brisbane: Corridors of power*, 1997
16 *Brisbane: Squatters, surveyors and settlers,* 2000
17 *Brisbane: Relaxation, recreation and rock 'n' roll, 2001*

Sources

1 *Brisbane by 1888: The public image*, 1987
2 *The Brisbane Courier in 1888: A select subject index*, 1987
3 *Brisbane Town news from the Sydney Morning Herald 1842-46*, 1989
4 *Brisbane butterflies and beetles*, 1989
5 *Brisbane River Valley 1841-50*, 1991
6 *Brisbane hotels and publicans index 1842-1900*, 1994
7 *Qld architects of the 19th century: Index to the biographical dictionary*, 1999
8 *Brisbane timeline: From Captain Cook to CityCat*, 1999
9 *Moreton Bay in the news 1841-60: A select subject index,* 2000

Tours

1 *Petrie-Terrace walk/drive*, 1981 rev. 1989
2 *South Brisbane civic precinct walk*, 1985, 1986
3 *South Brisbane: Southbank suburbs drive*, 1986
4 *Caboolture to Kilcoy drive*, 1986
5 *Town to Toowong riverpath walk*, 1986
6 *Brisbane 1888 drive*, 1988
7 *Eastern suburbs placenames drive*, 1990
8 *Sandgate and Shorncliffe walks*, 1990
9 *Old Coorparoo Shire drive*, 1991
10 *Brisbane River Valley drive*, 1991
11 *Colonial George and William Street walk*, 1991
12 *Spring Hill walk: St Pauls to Gregory Terrace*, 1993
13 *Bald Hills drive*, 1993
14 *Northern suburbs Windsor to Kedron drive*, 1993
15 *Brisbane city churches walk/drive*, 1994
16 *Stafford and Wilston-Grange drive*, 1995
17 *Brisbane historical pub drive*, 1995
18 *Yeronga heritage walk/drive*, 1996
19 *Spring Hill walk: Wickham Terrace*, 1997
20 *St Lucia Campus walk*, 1998
21 *Stombuco heritage drive/walk,* 1999
22 *Our federation 1901: Brisbane heritage trail*, 2001

Studies

1 *Brisbane's forgotten founder: Sir Evan Mackenzie of Kilcoy*, 1992
2 *Brisbane house styles 1880-1940: A guide to the affordable house*, 1998

Information about the BHG and its publications may be obtained by letter or phone or by visiting the BHG web page http://www.powerup.com.au/~bhginc.